Minnesota Orchestra at One Hundred

A COLLECTION OF ESSAYS AND IMAGES

Minnesota
Orchestra

Published by the Minnesota Orchestral Association
1111 Nicollet Mall, Minneapolis, Minnesota 55403
www.minnesotaorchestra.com

Printed by Bolger Concept to Print
Minneapolis, Minnesota

Designed by Kathy Timmerman
Minneapolis, Minnesota

ISBN 1-893274-06-3

Library of Congress Control Number 2002111532

Contents

∾

The Minnesota Orchestra, November 5, 2001

Preface

WHAT A DIFFERENT WORLD IT WAS when the Minnesota Orchestra played its first concert in November 1903. Theodore Roosevelt was president. The Wright Brothers were poised on the brink of the world's first airplane flight, Henry Ford had just organized the Ford Motor Company, and the phonograph was still considered a recent technology. Although the State of Minnesota was not yet 50 years old, its determined citizens yearned for classical music of the highest quality for their community. They wanted a professional orchestra—and proceeded to build one.

That fledgling organization, which performed just ten concerts in its first season, now enters its 100th anniversary season, having grown into the state's largest performing arts organization and one of the world's renowned orchestras.

The Minnesota Orchestra at 100. Such a simple turn of phrase—and yet one that imports so much. Of course, it marks a passage of time that encompasses dramatic changes in our society. But a century of concert seasons also represents the very personal stories of thousands of masterful musicians, nine music directors, legions of board members, supporters, volunteers and staffers and generations of music-loving audiences, who contributed to the lineage of a great symphony orchestra, always striving to bring it to new heights.

As we contemplated this anniversary season, we pondered how best to share the story of the Minnesota Orchestra, an Orchestra that was one of the trail-breaking pioneers of the early radio and recording days. How best to convey the generous artistic legacy of the Orchestra, which, through its early and frequent cross-country tours, was instrumental in spreading the symphonic tradition across turn-of-the-century America?

We chose to illuminate this history through a collection of essays and images that would be both intimate and grand. We did not seek to pen the definitive account of the Minnesota Orchestra—that task is most appropriately undertaken by an author in an independently published volume. Rather, we gathered nine distinguished writers and asked them to explore the elements that have defined greatness in this Orchestra, that have contributed to its considerable reputation. In the celebratory spirit of a *Festschrift*, we gave our writers free reign to compose their essays as best fit the topic and their own connection to the Orchestra. Tone, style, and length vary widely in our eclectic collection; what unifies are the accolades that each writer ultimately offers for a musical institution that has served its community for a century.

Although we aspired to acknowledge as many individuals as possible, the demands of space and the scores of people to recognize made this an impossible feat. At the outset, then, we offer gratitude to the board and donors who sustain the Orchestra, to the corporations that set a philanthropic example, to the staff members who contribute mightily behind the scenes, to the volunteers who give generously, to the audiences who love music—and to the musicians who bring it to us.

We offer profound thanks to those who came before us, shaping the way and launching the Minnesota Orchestra legacy. We hope that this collection shares a bit of that extraordinary legacy—and we hope it may long continue.

David J. Hyslop
President, Minnesota Orchestral Association
September 2002

Introduction

BEFORE SHE DIED ON MY EIGHTEENTH BIRTHDAY, my mother wished me nothing so banal as a happy life. She wished for me a full and passionate one. And so when I arrived in Minnesota 31 years ago, the newest member of the Minnesota Orchestra, fresh from the world's finest conservatories with all my arrogance intact, I wondered how life as an initiate in this great Orchestra would measure up to her plans for me.

∾

My musical odyssey had begun one Friday afternoon when my father brought home a cello and announced that I was to take my first lesson the next morning.

I was five.

I proved not to be one of those rare children with a natural inclination to practice. I was blessed instead with parents—both pianists—who somehow had the fortitude to make me. But I learned that there was freedom on the other side of that grueling hour, and so, practice I did.

My reward every year was to accompany my father that vast distance from Newark, New Jersey, to Carnegie Hall, where I was permitted to sit (quietly!) in the empty hall while my father rehearsed in the chorus with the New York Philharmonic. Those mornings with Leonard Bernstein were my introduction to a breathtaking new world: the world of symphonic music. I was transfixed. There was a purpose after all to those lonely hours I spent struggling with technique and bow control while my friends jumped rope in the street outside.

Fortunately I never paused to consider how few first-rate orchestras there were and consequently how few spots for eager young cellists. The year I finished my studies, two orchestras had openings. One of them was the Minnesota Orchestra, whose reputation and recordings were venerated throughout the music world. I decided this ensemble might be equal to my talent and ambition.

I auditioned.

MARCIA PECK

Marcia Peck studied at the Curtis Institute in Philadelphia and the Schumann Konservatorium in Düsseldorf. Her teachers include Orlando Cole, Antonio Janigro, Bernard Greenhouse, Zara Nelsova, and Mstislav Rostropovich. A finalist in international competitions in Prague and Florence, she took first place in Mainz, Germany. She has been a member of the Argentine chamber group La Camarata di Bariloche, the Bakken Quartet, Symphony Chamber Players, Musical Offering, and the Grand Teton Music Festival. Peck received a 2001 Minnesota State Arts Board Artist Fellowship for her novel-in-progress, Water Music.

In the early days of this century, while our country was developing a serious tradition of string playing, orchestra ranks were often fleshed out with European players. In the 1960s heightened sensitivity toward civil rights dictated that auditions be held behind a screen. One inadvertent result: Women began to win the coveted positions. Superbly trained Soviet instrumentalists followed in the 1970s, and sometime after that, highly accomplished Asians, many of whom had studied here in the United States.

When I was hired, eleven of the 97 musicians were women. I soon met the handsome horn player who later became my husband. At four months old, our daughter was the first child ever to accompany the mostly male Orchestra on tour.

My colleagues were from all over the map. Most had earned their way here with stints in lesser orchestras. A number had played with the Seventh Army Symphony, the army of occupation in Germany after World War II. I had found a spot in a truly international profession.

I loved to listen to the veteran musicians recount their experiences with every new score we tackled: This work they had played with Heifetz, that one with Rubinstein, another with Rachmaninoff himself. They told tales of the old Pullman tours across the country and how many times they had repeated a given program. I used to wonder if I would tire of playing those mainstays of the repertoire I knew I would face again and again. How many times could I practice, rehearse, and perform Beethoven's Fifth and still feel a sense of discovery?

Now I have played fourth chair cello (the best seat in the house, I would argue) with this Orchestra nearly one third of its life. It is my turn to embody the treasured performances of our collective history. A Bruckner Eighth with Klaus Tennstedt, Mahler Second at Kennedy Center, the visiting artists I have cherished: Menuhin, Szeryng, Horowitz. The list is long.

Marcia Peck

And so I have come to realize that I am part of a lineage.

One of my teachers studied with Felix Salmond, who premiered the Elgar Cello Concerto. Another was a pupil of Diran Alexanian, who played chamber music with Brahms.

My own cello is 250 years old. I have coaxed out its tone for nearly 40 of those years. I wonder whose hands before me shaped its sound and whose care delivered it safely to the nineteenth and twentieth centuries so that I could see it into the 21st. How many times did those other cellists play Beethoven's Fifth before I ever came along to worry about overdoing it? How did they shape those phrases? How softly did they succeed in playing that passage in the third movement without sacrificing color? What did they decide to do to articulate the arpeggios? Did they match the rest of their section? (My daughter doesn't identify Beethoven's Fifth, like any normal person, by those famous first four notes, perhaps the most recognized motif in all music. All the time she was growing up, she heard me practice the middle movements—found on every audition—which my astonishing colleagues appear to execute so effortlessly.)

Being part and parcel of a grand tradition was to be, I learned, a humbling experience. I grew to revere our community, which has loved great music enough to establish and maintain an Orchestra of the highest stature. No orchestra worth its mettle can spring up overnight, no matter how illustrious its players. It takes years of learning to anticipate one another, of devotion to a concept of sound, of interpreting the musical ideas so many different ways that we can adjust to a conductor and to each other instantaneously.

I have been awed by our guest artists, who bring their grace and expertise and generosity of mind, who lift us and inspire us with their musicianship and depth of thought. And who bless us with their friendship. Thanks to Sommerfest and its remarkable opportunities for collaboration, I want it on my tombstone: She played Tchaikovsky Sextet with Josh Bell and Pam Frank!

I have learned constantly from my colleagues, an extraordinary blend of musicians who, nourished by each other, have taught me to go beyond myself. We have this in common: We sit in service to great music. We know what it is to work on scales, etudes, tone production over and over and over, struggling to understand where the difficulty lies, listening and correcting. We know what it is to try to build a phrase, working with the tools of our trade: breath, balance, timing, direction. With every performance one hundred people put their disparate personalities aside to respond as one organism. We know that every performance depends on every one of us. A solo in one part of the Orchestra, no matter how beautiful, cannot succeed if somewhere else a balance is off or a rhythm muddy. My colleagues have taught me that we play for each other, for no one listens as critically as we do. Or as supportively.

Finally, I have been humbled by the music itself. When my father brought home that pint-sized instrument all those years ago, I fell in love with the cello. But in the Orchestra I fell in love with music. I had not the least idea that I was embarking upon, not merely a career, but a life so profoundly gratifying that I know it more than fulfilled my mother's wish for me. And I think she would not mind that it has been a happy one in the bargain.

Now, of course, I feel foolish that I ever worried about the Beethoven Fifth. The question was never, Will the Orchestra measure up, or Will the repertoire measure up, but. . . . Would I? What I didn't realize was this: that I had been granted a life with great music as my constant companion and that the masterpieces of our repertoire would have more to say to me after all these years. Not less. That year after year I would reach into the scores, go deeper and find more to open my heart and enlarge my spirit. And how hard it will be one day to relinquish my beloved chair.

This book is dedicated to the Hamm twins,
Mrs. DeWalt Ankeny, Sr., and Mrs. Theodora Lang,
who were born on the day the Orchestra played its
first concert—November 5, 1903.

∾

These music lovers represent a century of concertgoers
whose lives have been enriched by great orchestral performances.

One Hundred by Nine
The Music Directors

ROY CLOSE

Roy Close grew up attending Minnesota Orchestra concerts at Northrop Auditorium in the 1950s and 1960s and covered the Orchestra as a music critic for the Minneapolis Star *and* Saint Paul Pioneer Press *during the 1970s and 1980s. He is now associate director of resource development for Artspace Projects, a Minneapolis-based national nonprofit real estate developer for the arts.*

IT'S EIGHT O'CLOCK on a concert night at Orchestra Hall. An hour ago the Hall was nearly empty, but now vacant seats are few. The Minnesota Orchestra is onstage—including the concertmaster, as always the last to enter, who has just led the musicians in their familiar pre-concert ritual: oboe, strings, winds, *tutti*, silence. The house lights dim, the audience grows quiet, the players are ready. It's time.

A door opens, and here he comes: the music director himself, striding purposefully to the podium, bathed in applause that he acknowledges with a bow before turning to face the players. Opening the score in front of him, he lifts his baton. The musicians raise their instruments. For a breath-taking moment, time stands still. And now the downbeat, and another Minnesota Orchestra concert is underway.

This scene has been repeated myriad times over the last hundred years. Generations of audiences have come and gone. More than a thousand musicians have experienced the joys and challenges of Orchestra membership. And who can count all the guest conductors, soloists, and choristers?

But in the Orchestra's first 100 seasons there have been only nine music directors.

Nine, count 'em: Emil Oberhoffer, Henri Verbrugghen, Eugene Ormandy, Dimitri Mitropoulos, Antal Dorati, Stanislaw Skrowaczewski, Neville Marriner, Edo de Waart, and Eiji Oue.

{ Emil **Oberhoffer**
1903–1922 } { Henri **Verbrugghen**
1923–1931 } { Eugene **Ormandy**
1931–1936 } { Dimitri **Mitropoulos**
1937–1949

1903   1913   1923   1933   1943

Why these nine and no others? What unique set of circumstances brought each of them to Minnesota and held them here for up to nineteen seasons? How did they change the Orchestra, and how did the experience alter them? What were their successes and failures, their proudest achievements and greatest disappointments? The answers to these questions have as much to say about the evolution of the Orchestra itself as about the nine very different men who have assumed its artistic leadership.

At the center of it all

A modern major American orchestra comprises 95 or so full-time musicians supported by an equally large staff that includes not only ushers and stagehands but large marketing and fundraising departments. Although performing is the orchestra's *raison d'être*, the organization is necessarily also in the business of selling tickets, writing program notes, designing season brochures, issuing press releases, maintaining a music library, negotiating contracts, and, in many cases, operating a concert hall. From the chief executive officer to the custodian who vacuums the lobby carpet, everyone has a job to do and must do it well if the orchestra is to thrive.

At the center of them all stands the music director. He (or, increasingly, she) is in charge of planning the subscription season—the orchestra's "A" series—from beginning to end, including repertoire and guest artists. He has the final (and occasionally the only) say on hiring musicians to fill vacancies in the ranks. He conducts roughly half the orchestra's subscription programs as well as special concerts, tour performances, and recording sessions. He attends social functions, makes public appearances, and spreads the gospel of classical music in the community.

Most important of all, he creates the very sound of the orchestra by the choices he makes when he conducts. Does the orchestra sound dry and passionless, as was sometimes said when Verbrugghen was on the platform? Does it have the luxurious string sound that Ormandy preferred? Does it have the "convulsive fire," as essayist Brenda Ueland described it, of a Mitropoulos-led ensemble?

Much has changed in the orchestral world over the last hundred years. Longer seasons demand more from everyone, from music directors to section players. Jet travel has made it possible for conductors, soloists, and even entire orchestras to have international careers. Strong musicians' unions have influenced every aspect of orchestra life. Recordings, broadcast media, and the internet have allowed orchestras to reach out to new audiences. Movies, television, professional sports, and other diversions have become major competitors for audiences. But through it all, this fact has remained constant: It is the music director who determines the orchestra's distinctive sound.

The term "music director" is of relatively recent origin: It arrived at this Orchestra with Skrowaczewski in 1960. In the following group portrait, however, we will extend the title retroactively to Oberhoffer, Verbrugghen, Ormandy, Mitropoulos, and Dorati, all of whom were music directors *de facto* if not in name. Likewise, we will

Antal **Dorati**
1949–1960

Stanislaw **Skrowaczewski**
1960–1979

Neville **Marriner**
1979–1986

Edo **de Waart**
1986–1995

Eiji **Oue**
1995–2002

1953   1963   1973   1983   1993   2003

generally refer to the ensemble they led as the Minnesota Orchestra, even though it was known as the Minneapolis Symphony Orchestra for the first 65 years of its existence.

Putting down roots

On November 5, 1903, when Emil Oberhoffer gave the first downbeat in the history of the Minneapolis Symphony Orchestra, only about 50 musicians raised their instruments. The season consisted of six orchestral programs, each performed once, spread over five months. The Orchestra had no paid administrators; its business affairs were managed by a committee of its parent organization, the Philharmonic Club. The annual guaranty fund was $10,000—a substantial sum for the time, but only a tiny fraction of what today's Minnesota Orchestra raises each year in contributions.

Oberhoffer was well equipped for the challenge that lay ahead. Born in Munich in 1867, he received a first-rate musical education at home from his father, a conductor and organist; at the Munich Conservatory, where he studied with the great organ pedagogue Josef Rheinberger; and in Paris, where he studied with Isidore Philipp. He reached New York in the mid-1880s and arrived in the Twin Cities about five years later, legend has it, as a member of a touring Gilbert and Sullivan troupe that suddenly disbanded, stranding him here.

Oberhoffer found work as a church organist, violist in a hotel orchestra, and freelance lecturer, recitalist, and conductor. He caught his first big break when Minneapolis's leading chorus, the Apollo Club, appointed him director in 1896. Four years later the rival Philharmonic Club lured him away, and soon he was leading the Philharmonic singers in ambitious performances of large-scale choral works. He was also urging the Philharmonic Club to establish its own permanent orchestra instead of relying on freelancers. In 1903, the club's officers consented, and the Minnesota Orchestra was born.

In his nineteen seasons on the podium, Oberhoffer built the fledgling ensemble into an important midwestern institution with a national reputation. Many of the activities that are a regular part of the life of today's

Minnesota Orchestra—including touring, Weekender Pops Concerts, and Young People's Concerts—not only date from his tenure but owe their very existence to his vision of what a professional American orchestra could be.

Once Oberhoffer set his sights on a goal, he was not easily deflected. Early on he decided that the Orchestra could not only expand its audience but actually generate revenue by touring. When the board of directors declined to put up the money for such a speculative venture, Oberhoffer underwrote the first three tours himself, beginning in 1907. All three made a profit. By 1910 the board needed no further persuasion, and the touring era began in earnest. The Orchestra made its Chicago debut the following year, reached New York in 1912 (with repeat performances in three of the next four seasons), played Boston in 1916, and went all the way to California in 1917 and 1918.

On the conductor's platform, Oberhoffer "was a picture of grace and authority pictorially blended," in the words of *Minneapolis Star* music critic John K. Sherman, whose 1952 book *Music and Maestros* (University of Minnesota Press, 1952) is the definitive account of the Orchestra's first half-century. "It was said that he practiced conducting before a full-length mirror, but whatever the means, conscious or instinctive, of attaining the visual effect, the figure on the podium was a persuasive and ingratiating portrait of a conductor in action."

Over time, Sherman adds, Oberhoffer became "a kind of civic symbol of musical culture. His ruddy hair made a misty aureole above a broad, high forehead and swept backward in the Paderewski style. Its color was a clue to his temperament and tenacity. He was a dreamer, but an energetic and purposeful dreamer. The touch of red in his mane and mustache was a visible sign of his inner fire; the far-gazing eyes spoke of imagination and vision."

In the later years of his tenure, Oberhoffer increasingly found himself at odds with Elbert L. Carpenter, president of the Orchestra's board of directors, and more than once he threatened to resign. Matters came to a head in 1922 when the board cancelled the Orchestra's spring tour. This time Oberhoffer carried out his threat. He announced his resignation on the day before the season's final concert—his farewell appearance with the Orchestra, for he never conducted it again.

THE MINNEAPOLIS SYMPHONY ORCHESTRA
EMIL OBERHOFFER, CONDUCTOR
WENDELL HEIGHTON, MANAGER
MAINTAINED BY AN ANNUAL GUARANTEE FUND OF $65,000 SUBSCRIBED BY THE PEOPLE OF MINNEAPOLIS

Seated in front of a northwoods backdrop on stage at the Minneapolis Auditorium, the Minneapolis Symphony Orchestra and founding conductor Emil Oberhoffer presented an impressive image in the early 1900s. The official photograph appears in several publications from the era, including this postcard, which announced the Orchestra's first appearance in Carnegie Hall, in 1912.

Emil **Oberhoffer**

*The renowned conductor Bruno Walter led
the Orchestra on several occasions, including
its first radio broadcast, in March 1923.
The following season he returned not only to
conduct the Orchestra, but also to perform in a
joint benefit recital with the Orchestra's music
director, Henri Verbrugghen.*

Enter a schoolmaster

The suddenness of Oberhoffer's resignation left the Orchestra with a difficult decision: either engage a permanent conductor sight unseen or entrust the 1922-1923 season to guest conductors. Carpenter chose the latter course and divided the season among five conductors, of whom only two—Bruno Walter and Henri Verbrugghen—were serious candidates for the permanent appointment. How the Orchestra's history might have changed had Walter received the nod will never be known. The season was scarcely two months old when Carpenter announced that Verbrugghen would be the Orchestra's next permanent conductor. (Walter's consolation prize was to lead the Orchestra in its first radio concert, on March 2, 1923.)

Born in Brussels in 1873, Verbrugghen was a violin prodigy who gave his first public performance at age nine and later became a prize pupil of the celebrated Eugène Ysaÿe. In 1888, he accompanied Ysaÿe on a concert tour of England and Scotland, and it was in Glasgow, four years later, that he landed his first professional job as a violinist with what is now the Royal Scottish National Orchestra. Over the next decade he performed with orchestras throughout the British Isles, but increasingly he was drawn to conducting and chamber music. He formed his own ensemble, the Verbrugghen String Quartet, which toured throughout Britain and subsequently followed him to Australia and America.

In 1915, Verbrugghen was offered the chance to found a new state-supported music conservatory in Sydney, Australia, to prepare young musicians for careers in a new symphony orchestra of which he would be conductor. He leapt at the opportunity. The Sydney Conservatorium of Music, as it is now known, was an immediate and overwhelming success; within a few years its orchestra was concertizing throughout Australia and New Zealand. But in 1921, when an overworked Verbrugghen asked to be paid separate salaries for his work as director of the conservatory and conductor of its orchestra, the government said no. Verbrugghen promptly took a leave of absence from which he never returned. (The Conservatorium did not forget him: Its main performing venue is named Verbrugghen Hall.)

Verbrugghen's eight seasons with the Orchestra witnessed a number of firsts. He introduced Twin Cities audiences to Bach (a composer Oberhoffer had all but ignored) as well as to works by Ravel, Honegger, Stravinsky, and Gershwin, whose *Rhapsody in Blue* and *An American in Paris* both received their Orchestra premieres under Verbrugghen's baton. It was during his tenure that the Orchestra hired its first professional manager (Arthur J. Gaines in 1923), made its first recordings (1924), launched its first regular radio broadcasts (1927), and abandoned the Lyceum Theater, its home since 1905, in favor of the University of Minnesota's new 4,800-seat Northrop Auditorium (1930). Verbrugghen also hired the first female Orchestra member, violinist Jenny Cullen.

Sherman, who began reviewing Orchestra concerts during the Verbrugghen years, describes the Belgian conductor as a colorful figure who "sported a pair of fiercely waxed mustaches, loved Beethoven, chamber music, and horses, collected old musical instruments, and smoked vile French tobacco in a meerschaum pipe." He spent his summers in Nevis, near Park Rapids, where he operated a sheep ranch.

On the podium, Verbrugghen was an entertaining sight. "He had a wide gamut of gesture, from the slashing swoop of his long baton to the neatest, most delicate motion of his small hands for the fine-tooled passages...," Sherman tells us. "In the roaring climaxes, [his] long hair would cascade over his eyes and his coattails would fly." For all his forcefulness, however, he often failed to win over the critics. Reviewing a Verbrugghen-led performance of Brahms's First Symphony, New York critic Pitts Sanborn wrote: "Never did conductor toss about more wildly, never did band appear to labor harder than in the celebrated finale, and never did that finale sound so small and so tame."

Those who admired Verbrugghen were inclined to praise what composer and critic Deems Taylor called the "almost architectural quality" of his performances. And Sherman notes that "it has been said that the orchestra had never been better technically than when it was under his baton." But the bottom line for Sherman was that "the schoolmaster had replaced the poet, and that care in crossing t's and dotting i's had taken some of the old spirit and glow out of the orchestra's playing."

Henri **Verbrugghen**

A dapper young Eugene Ormandy assumed leadership of the Minnesota Orchestra in 1931, when he was just 32 years old. During his five years with the Orchestra he established its reputation as an important force in the fledgling United States recording industry.

Two renowned music directors of the Minnesota Orchestra met in a rare moment that found them in the same town at the same time. In 1936 Eugene Ormandy left Minneapolis for the directorship of The Philadelphia Orchestra. The following season, Minnesota became the envy of the U. S. music world when it engaged the extraordinary Greek conductor Dimitri Mitropoulos, whose exciting twelve-year tenure with the Orchestra endured until 1949.

Verbrugghen's tenure with the Orchestra ended even more abruptly than Oberhoffer's. In October 1931, during a rehearsal of Strauss's *Ein Heldenleben*, he suffered a physical collapse. Although he eventually recovered sufficiently to serve as head of the music department at Carleton College, his conducting career was over.

The art of the music director
(Part I)

To be the music director of the Minnesota Orchestra in the early twentieth century was to have absolute authority over personnel decisions. After the Philharmonic Club agreed to establish the permanent orchestra for which he had been lobbying, Oberhoffer spent the entire summer scouting talent in Europe. He returned with four musicians whom he had hired to bolster sections where the homegrown talent was in short supply. No one questioned his right to do this; the decision was assumed to be his and his alone.

These days the procedure for hiring a new Orchestra member is spelled out in detail by the master agreement that governs all the dealings between the musicians and the Minnesota Orchestral Association, the Orchestra's parent organization. It's a complex process involving the formation of a committee of seven players (precisely which seven depends on the vacancy) that conducts as many rounds of preliminary auditions as necessary—five rounds is not unheard-of —to winnow the field to a handful of finalists. Only in the last round does the music director get involved, and it is he who selects the winner. But his choices are limited to the candidates advanced to the finals by the musicians.

There is an eminently practical reason for doing it this way: The number of applications for every Orchestra vacancy has grown far beyond the capacity of anyone to manage without help. When bassist Cliff Johnson joined the Orchestra in 1948, he was the only one who auditioned. The job was considerably less attractive in those days, of course. The season was only six months long, pay was low, and "it was a long, cold summer," Johnson says,

unless one was willing to teach or work a second job. Johnson himself played in dance bands and later turned to piano-tuning. As recently as 1964, says former Orchestra President Richard M. Cisek, "we auditioned for violas and only four people showed up." But no longer. By the end of the 1970s, the Orchestra was playing year-round, musicians' salaries had risen dramatically, and the competition for every opening had grown fierce. When Johnson retired in 1995, he says "there were two hundred applicants for my job."

The process of dismissing a musician has undergone a similar evolution. In Oberhoffer's day, Orchestra members had no security whatever; if the music director didn't like the way you parted your hair, he could fire you. This was undoubtedly a factor in the mid-century unionization of American orchestras. By the 1970s, the pendulum had swung in the other direction, and it was very difficult for a music director to dismiss a player—even one whose skills had eroded. One of the factors behind Skrowaczewski's resignation in 1979 was said to be a frustration over his inability to effect changes he felt were necessary to improve the Orchestra. Marriner, his successor, wasn't temperamentally inclined to fight personnel battles, so it was not until the arrival of de Waart in 1986 that a housecleaning took place.

Stepping stones

The Orchestra's third and fourth music directors, Eugene Ormandy and Dimitri Mitropoulos, were unknown in Minnesota when they arrived, made stupendous first impressions, and kept the magic alive for the duration of their careers here. Both moved on to prestigious orchestras—Ormandy after five seasons to the Philadelphia, Mitropoulos after twelve to the New York Philharmonic.

Verbrugghen's collapse early in the 1931-1932 season precipitated a crisis far more serious than Oberhoffer's end-of-season resignation nine years previously. In the intervening decade, however, two significant events had occurred: The Orchestra had started to employ professional managers, and Arthur Judson had emerged as the most powerful concert manager in America. The Orchestra's manager was Mrs. Carlyle Scott, who had replaced Arthur J. Gaines when the Orchestra moved its concerts to Northrop Auditorium. Judson in 1931 managed both the Philadelphia Orchestra and the New York Philharmonic and was also president of a new agency, Columbia Concerts Corporation (now Columbia Artists Management Inc.), which controlled the comings and goings of most of the important conductors and concert artists in America. As soon as she knew that Verbrugghen was in for a long recuperation, Mrs. Scott placed a call to Judson. Did he have anyone in his stable of conductors who might be capable of coming to Minnesota on extremely short notice and finishing out the season?

As it happened, he did: a young Hungarian named Eugene Ormandy.

Like Verbrugghen, Ormandy was a violin prodigy. Born in Budapest in 1899, he entered the Budapest Conservatory at age five, made his concert debut two years later, and received his diploma at fifteen. An international career beckoned—or so it seemed until he arrived in New York in 1921 to find that the agent who had promised him an American tour was broke. The aspiring young soloist settled instead for a job in the back row of the orchestra of the Capitol Theatre, a movie house that offered classical music between screenings. Within a week he had been promoted to concertmaster, which meant he was expected to fill in if one of the orchestra's regular conductors was indisposed. The chance soon came, and Ormandy made the most of it, conducting Tchaikovsky's Fourth Symphony without a score—on fifteen minutes' notice. Before long he was the Capitol's music director, a position he held for seven years before signing on with Judson in 1929.

In 1931, Ormandy made a sensational debut with The Philadelphia Orchestra, conducting six concerts as a substitute for the great Arturo Toscanini. It was during this stretch that Mrs. Scott placed her fateful call to Judson. Ormandy finished his Philadelphia engagement and took the next train to Minneapolis.

Ormandy's debut with the Minnesota Orchestra, on November 13, 1931, was an unqualified triumph. Reviewing the concert for the *Saint Paul Pioneer Press*, Frances Boardman described him as "a young genius" and the performance as "one of the most brilliant

Eugene **Ormandy**

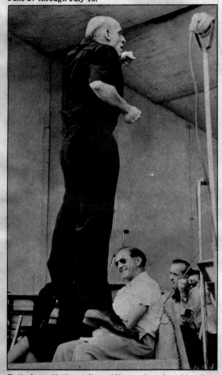

Dimitri the 'Gymnast'

Conductor Dimitri Mitropoulos' gymnastics on the podium, so familiar to Minneapolis symphony-goers, make him a very good camera subject. Among the best "action" pictures to be taken of him are these, snapped by free-lance photographer Ruth Orkin during a rehearsal in New York. The one at right appears in the May issue of Pageant magazine.

Although Mitropoulos has said his goodbye to Minneapolis, he still hasn't given way to Antal Dorati as conductor of the orchestra. He will direct the Minneapolis group at a series of concerts at Aspen, Colo., June 27 through July 16.

Both feet off the podium, Mitropoulos gives his all to build up a climax. Smiling is baritone John Brownlee.

People never tired of attempting to describe—and photograph—the Mitropoulos conducting style, which was unorthodox, to say the least. Mitropoulos's podium manner was not calculated to show himself off, but rather, to serve the music.

concerts of the Orchestra's history." Everyone agreed: The Orchestra had found Verbrugghen's successor. Within a week Mrs. Scott signed him to a one-year contract.

During his five seasons as music director, Ormandy completely overhauled the Orchestra, transforming it from "little more than an enterprising inland orchestra," as Sherman puts it, into a member of the "class group" of American orchestras with international standing. "But the greatest wonder to those audiences that heard him in the early thirties was the new kind of potency and persuasion of utterance he gave the Orchestra, wrought by painstaking preparation and a tense, concentrated platform style not lacking in dramatic gesture."

Ormandy's conducting style had "a lashing and athletic elasticity," Sherman writes, "compounded of youthful exuberance, intensity, and ardor." Adds musicologist William R. Trotter: The "slender, tense [conductor] with strong blue eyes and thinning blonde hair . . . was a volcano of energy—about as great a contrast as could be imagined to the placid conductor of the 1960s and 1970s, who often seemed content to put his fabulous chrome-plated ensemble [the Philadelphia Orchestra] on automatic pilot."

Offstage, Ormandy was charming, gregarious, and occasionally mischievous. Years later, on a rare return visit to Minnesota, he was asked by a reporter if he had any suggestion for improving Northrop Auditorium's acoustics. "Dynamite," he replied. After the interview, riding in a car with David J. Hyslop (later the Orchestra's president, but then its assistant manager), he smiled, and said, "I was a bad boy, wasn't I?"

That Ormandy would not grow old in Minnesota was a given. He was clearly on an inside track for a big-city orchestra; the question was not whether he would leave but how soon. He lasted a respectable five seasons, but the inevitable day finally arrived. In January 1936, Minnesota learned that Ormandy had been named to succeed Leopold Stokowski as conductor of the Philadelphia Orchestra, effective the following fall. Although his Minnesota contract still had a year to run, the Orchestra released him. "Those of us who have been intimately associated with Mr. Ormandy," Elbert L. Carpenter said, "have realized for some time that we could not retain his services permanently."

The monk in tails

Although Ormandy's resignation gave the Orchestra several months to find his replacement, the board—no doubt on the advice of Arthur Judson—decided not to rush into things. A season of guest conductors was planned, the first since the Oberhoffer-Verbrugghen interregnum of 1922-1923. Ormandy himself led the parade of seven guests by conducting the first three programs. Maestro number four was Dimitri Mitropoulos.

Among musicians and concert-goers old enough to have been there, Mitropoulos's twelve-year run as music director was a golden age. He was without a doubt the most inspiring leader this Orchestra has ever had, for Mitropoulos approached music-making with an almost religious intensity that has long been out of fashion in the orchestra world. His interpretations were thrilling; he had the power to bring music alive. Reviewing a 1938 performance of Schumann's Second Symphony, Sherman described it this way: "The impression you received was less that of [a] symphony being 'presented' than of a symphony living out its life before you, as if it were a living, breathing thing." That's high praise, indeed, from the leading music critic of the Orchestra's first hundred years.

Mitropoulos came by his intensity naturally. Born into a deeply religious Athenian family in 1896, he trained to be a Greek Orthodox monk but decided against it when he learned that the Church would not allow him to keep a musical instrument in his cell. Instead of becoming a musical monk, he became a conductor who viewed music, in Sherman's words, "as a religion, and the practice of it as a kind of worship."

Musically precocious, Mitropoulos began his lifelong habit of memorizing scores in childhood and entered the Athens Conservatory at the age of fourteen. His specialties were piano, at which he became a virtuoso, and composition, at which he excelled; but by the early 1920s he was being drawn to the podium, and his first real job was as assistant conductor of the Berlin Staatsoper. In 1924 he was named conductor of the Athens Conservatory Orchestra, the city's leading ensemble. By the early 1930s he was conducting throughout Europe, and in 1936 he made his American debut with the Boston Symphony.

Dimitri **Mitropoulos**

Mitropoulos's Minnesota debut, on January 29, 1937, was nothing short of sensational. In an ecstatic review, Sherman called it "doubtless the greatest performance" in the Orchestra's history. "It was really something close to a miracle," he wrote. "The Orchestra, under the flying fists and the shaking, quivering, and yet completely poised figure of Mitropoulos, evoked a splendor of tone, an incandescent brilliance of technique it has never summoned in the past. And yet it was no false stimulant that produced this phenomenon. It was sheer great music that enthralled the mind and gripped, vise-like, the emotions. The Orchestra was transfigured, the audience transported."

Within two weeks, with the help of Judson (who owed the organization a favor for letting Ormandy leave early), the Orchestra had Mitropoulos under contract.

Mitropoulos never used a score, even in rehearsals. "It was unbelievable," Cliff Johnson says. "Monday morning, the score was on the floor. It was all in his head. And he never made a mistake." Nor did he use a baton; he relied instead on a repertoire of expressive gestures that seemed to come straight from the heart. Sherman again: "His style is dramatic without being theatrical, positive with no hint of dogmatism. His gestures are the most plastic, the most expressive and unmistakable in meaning of any conductor's manual technique." His downbeat, however, was notoriously hard to follow. Johnson, who joined the Orchestra in Mitropoulos's final season, remembers asking an older bassist how to tell when it was time to start playing. "Pay no attention to the downbeat," the other bassist said. "But on the way back up, when his hands get to the fourth button from the bottom of his vest, *that's* when you begin to play."

Mitropoulos was unorthodox in other ways as well. For his first Sunday "Twilight" concert, he put together a program consisting entirely of overtures—seven in all. Unlike most of his professional colleagues, he was interested in popular music. "Benny Goodman told me how Dimitri loved jazz and would go hear him whenever he played the Orpheum," recalls *Star Tribune* columnist Barbara Flanagan. On one occasion the maestro went backstage afterwards and asked if he might examine the orchestrations on the music stands. "And of course there were no orchestrations," Flanagan says. "There were girlie magazines."

During World War II, Mitropoulos worked long hours as a Red Cross volunteer. Rosalynd Pflaum, one of the conductor's closest friends in Minneapolis (as well as a founder of WAMSO, the Orchestra's volunteer organization), often accompanied Mitropoulos on the "blood tours" that collected blood for the war effort in small towns around the region. Most of the tour stops were high school gymnasiums, and there was usually a piano nearby. "Mitropolous, of course, was a great drawing card," Mrs. Pflaum says. "He loved to play boogie-woogie on those old upright pianos. He was an absolutely howling success."

Mitropoulos's twelve years with the Orchestra were not without low spots. At times his interpretations struck listeners as mannered and artificial. A few were so eccentric that a new adjective, *Mitropoulized*, was coined to describe them; it was not meant as flattery. The Orchestra's overall skill level declined as well, in part because a number of outstanding young musicians were lost to the war, in part because Mitropoulos could not bring himself to fire a musician, even for cause. "He was not a good taskmaster because he was too kind-hearted," Mrs. Pflaum declares. "He'd take the shirt off his back for someone in the Orchestra. He was very much interested in the personal lives of the musicians."

Mitropolous also liked contemporary music and programmed considerably more works by the likes of Schoenberg, Sessions, and Křenek than most of the Orchestra's audience cared to hear. But he was such an inspiring conductor that they put up with it. No doubt some of the musicians felt much the same way. But others found the modern regimen stimulating. Johnson remembers playing Webern's Passacaglia for Orchestra "and laughing in the middle of it, it was so exciting."

Such was Mitropoulos's status in the community that in December 1948, when he announced his resignation at season's end to become music director of the New York Philharmonic, the Minneapolis *Morning Tribune* splashed the story across the top of page one under a banner headline: MITROPOULOS TO QUIT SYMPHONY.

Mitropoulos made an indelible impression on the community, and his departure in 1949 made front-page news.

The art of the music director
(Part II)

In the Orchestra's early years, it was a relatively easy matter for Oberhoffer to plan the entire season without assistance. Performances were few, guest artists were readily available, there was ample time to prepare. Even the advent of Sunday afternoon "pops" concerts in 1906 and Young People's Concerts in 1911 did not make the task onerous. Oberhoffer nevertheless had to walk a fine line between what most of the audience wished to hear—overtures, songs, and novelties—and what he and the musicians wished to play, which was symphonic music. He also had to take into consideration the tastes of the Orchestra's patrons, some of whom were not above expressing their repertoire preferences. Indeed, one major contributor went so far as to require an annual performance of Paderewski's *Minuet in G* as a condition of his gift. In the mid-twenties, during Verbrugghen's tenure, a proposal was floated to put all programming decisions in the hands of a committee of subscribers, but Carpenter quickly squelched it.

As late as mid-century, it was still possible for a conscientious music director to program the season by himself. Antal Dorati, who regarded programming as one of his most important responsibilities, began his tenure here by making a list of every piece the Orchestra had ever performed, so that his programs would consistently include works new to the musicians and audience as well as familiar standards.

Over the last four decades, longer seasons have made programming a more complicated process. In addition, major guest artists now fill their engagement calendars far in advance. In the 1960s, Stanislaw Skrowaczewski notes, "it was much easier, if you wanted an Oistrakh or a Rubinstein," to book him for the following season. "Now, if you want a special conductor or soloist, you have to plan three years ahead."

Among the Orchestra's recent music directors, Skrowaczewski and Edo de Waart held the strongest opinions about programming and guest artists, according to Richard Cisek, who worked with them both. "Skrowaczewski would discuss it with you," Cisek says, "but once he gave you a list of programs it was very dif-ficult to change his mind." He liked to work with established artists and had a special rapport with pianist Alexis Weissenberg; but he also introduced many other soloists during his long tenure.

De Waart was even more proprietary about programming, so if there was a soloist or conductor Cisek thought the Minnesota audience should have an opportunity to hear, he had to make the suggestion obliquely. Neville Marriner, on the other hand, was "very open" to ideas from colleagues and ready to compromise or adapt to accommodate other views.

Approaching maturity

The Orchestra's next two music directors, Antal Dorati (1949-1960) and Stanislaw Skrowaczewski (1960-1979), shared the podium for three pivotal mid-century decades during which the Orchestra enjoyed a heady reputation as a popular recording ensemble, changed its name (to the dismay of many), expanded its season to 52 weeks a year, and built a new home, Orchestra Hall, in downtown Minneapolis.

By his own admission, Dorati was a hothead who often lost his temper during rehearsals. "I used to be really terrible when I was young," he confided to a reporter not long after his arrival. "Now when I get mad, I excuse myself to the Orchestra and go back to my dressing room and kick the furniture around." He wasn't kidding. The first time he stormed off the Northrop Auditorium stage, many of the musicians, assuming the rehearsal was over, packed their instruments and went home. A few days later Dorati erupted again. This time, however, he had the presence of mind to bark "Don't leave!" before disappearing into his dressing room. Ten minutes later, composure restored, he returned to the platform and the rehearsal went on.

Like Ormandy, Dorati was a native of Budapest. Born in 1906, he studied at the Budapest Academy of Music, where his instructors included Zoltán Kodály and Béla Bartók, and began his career as a pit conductor for opera companies in Budapest, Dresden, and Münster. In 1934 he joined the newly formed Ballet Russe de Monte Carlo, and for the next decade he worked chiefly as a conductor for ballet companies on both sides of the Atlantic—including American Ballet Theatre in the early 1940s.

Antal Dorati had a human side that contrasted with his frequently high-dudgeon rehearsal style. Above: Dorati and his daughter shared a friendly moment for the photographer. Below: An accomplished artist, Dorati contributed many whimsical cartoons to a 1958 fundraiser cookbook published by WAMSO, the Women's Association of the Minneapolis Symphony Orchestra.

To supplement his ballet income, he took whatever guest conducting jobs were offered, and distance was no deterrent; during one summer he conducted orchestras in Los Angeles, Toronto, Havana, and Lima. In 1945 his hard work paid off: He was invited to take charge of reviving the Dallas Symphony Orchestra, which had shut down during the war. It was a rebuilding challenge of the first order, and by all accounts Dorati was up to it.

Four years later, the Minnesota Orchestra, too, had some rebuilding to do, and when Mitropoulos told the board he was leaving, it quickly settled on Dorati. Accompanied by his wife, daughter, mother-in-law, and two dogs, the new maestro settled into a house overlooking Lake of the Isles and went to work on reshaping the Orchestra.

While it cannot have been easy to follow a conductor of Mitropoulos's charisma, Dorati established his authority at the outset. Occasional outbursts notwithstanding, it was clear that he knew his way around the podium, and what the Orchestra's performances lost in emotional intensity they gained in clarity and detail. In a mid-season report in the *Sunday Tribune*, John K. Sherman itemized Dorati's achievements as follows:

- Interesting and diversified programs, striking a balance in the music he plays between the established old and the provocative new.
- Clean, clear and "open" orchestral sound, depth and richness of texture, definition of detail.
- A generally relaxed style of playing, with resultant absence of forcing.
- A notable gift for communication.
- Complete integrity of purpose.

In his eleven seasons with the Orchestra, Dorati had the opportunity to replace many of the musicians he had inherited from Mitropoulos. His experience as a ballet conductor came in handy. Touring troupes like the Ballet Russe rarely traveled with more than a conductor and perhaps a few key players; they hired freelance players in each city they visited. Dorati thus had musical connections all around the country, and when a vacancy occurred in his own orchestra he generally knew of someone qualified to fill it.

Dorati understood as well as any music director in the Orchestra's history the importance of touring and recording. During his tenure the ensemble generally spent at least seven weeks on the road each year. In 1957 he led the Orchestra on its first major overseas tour, an extraordinary five-week, 34,000-mile excursion sponsored by the U.S. State Department that included concerts in Eastern Europe, the Middle East, and India. And thanks to his connections with Mercury Records, he and the Orchestra began making recordings in a big way. "The LP had just come out," Cisek notes, "and everything was being re-recorded. Mercury's recordings were the state of the art technically, and we were one of the major orchestras on that label. The Mercury Records connection really put this Orchestra on the international map." Several of the Mercury recordings are still available on compact discs.

Unlike his two immediate predecessors, Dorati did not leave the Orchestra for a prestigious post. Worn down by the heavy demands of more than a decade at the helm, the Hungarian maestro stepped down at the end of the 1959-1960 season and took it easy for a year. But he was far from finished. In 1962 he became chief conductor of the BBC Symphony Orchestra in London, and he subsequently led orchestras in both Washington, D.C., and Detroit. He continued to make records, and at his death in 1988 left a legacy of almost 600 recordings, including the first complete edition of Haydn's symphonies as well as eight Haydn operas. His most celebrated disc, though, was his 1954 recording of Tchaikovsky's *1812* Overture with the Minnesota Orchestra, one of the best-selling classical recordings of all time.

"Do the hall."

No music director before or since has enjoyed a longer relationship with the Minnesota Orchestra than Stanislaw Skrowaczewski, who mounted the podium in 1960, stayed nineteen seasons, and as Conductor Laureate—a title created for him—continues to lead one or two subscription programs each year.

Born in 1923 in Poland, Skrowaczewski studied at conservatories in his home city of Lwow, and, later with Nadia Boulanger in Paris. He showed promise as a pianist, composer, and conductor. A wartime injury to his hands dashed his hopes for a career as a concert pianist, and in the decade after the war he focused on conducting—first in Poland, where he led orchestras in Wroclaw, Katowice,

Krakow, and Warsaw; then in Italy and France, after he won the first prize at the International Conducting Competition in Rome; and finally in the United States, where he made a notable debut with The Cleveland Orchestra in December 1958. Eighteen months later he was introduced as the new music director of the Minnesota Orchestra.

Skrowaczewski's tenure coincided with the Orchestra's greatest growth spurt. In his first year, the subscription season consisted of eighteen programs, of which he conducted fourteen. The Orchestra's 85 musicians were under contract for 28 weeks, which included the subscription season, touring, holiday concerts, and special events—but no summer season. The Orchestra's entire annual budget was $730,000. By the time he stepped down in 1979, the subscription season had grown by a third, and each of its 24 programs was being performed two, three, or even four times. The Orchestra itself had swelled to 95 musicians who were employed year-round, and the annual budget was approaching $7 million.

Although Skrowaczewski's international reputation today is that of a specialist in the large-scale, late-Romantic works of composers such as Bruckner (whose entire symphonic *oeuvre* he has recorded with the Saarbrücken Radio Symphony Orchestra of Germany), in his early years with the Minnesota Orchestra he was renowned above all as a champion of contemporary music. Perhaps because he was too busy to do much composing himself, he programmed new music with enthusiasm. For a five-year stretch during the 1970s, the Orchestra annually won awards from ASCAP (the American Society of Composers, Authors and Publishers) for its commitment to new music; by 2002 the total of ASCAP awards had reached eleven.

Early in his tenure, Skrowaczewski began campaigning for several ambitious artistic initiatives. More musicians were needed, he told the board, to perform the big symphonic masterpieces of the late-Romantic composers. A European tour was vital if the Orchestra hoped to build on the reputation established by Ormandy, Mitropoulos, and Dorati. Most important of all, the Orchestra needed a new home. Northrop Auditorium was an enormous cavern, and though several attempts had been made to improve its acoustics with shells and reflecting panels, it would never be good enough for a world-class orchestra.

Antal **Dorati**

Skrowaczewski on Orchestra Hall

THE BUILDING AND THE OPENING OF ORCHESTRA HALL was certainly a major, maybe the biggest event in the history of our Orchestra. My distinguished predecessors fought for it; so did I. But whatever was my role in making this dream real, my own happiness went far beyond the realm of the tangible. To express clearly my feelings about the Hall's inauguration, which are still vivid in me, I'd like to quote my own words, written in 1974:

"This is the resurrection of the invisible. For this Hall is the visible symbol of the never-ending search for the invisible, the infinite, which—pervading and ennobling all conscious and unconscious human desires—is the wellspring of artistic imagination and creativity.

"What I therefore find most important about the Hall is the enlightenment and the effort of the people who donated it. Their understanding of the priorities in life speaks for itself. Art is inherent in human nature and, together with religion and science, is a precondition of human transformation and ascent.

"To me, art is a dialogue with the unknown. This dialogue encompasses all fundamental human concerns—such as the meaning of life and death, love and cruelty, sacrifice and redemption—in the constant hope of knowing that which cannot be known.

"Art thrives on metaphysical ideas, which I believe are as old as human consciousness. Thus, art is a powerful antidote for the spiritual ills of our chaotic, violent, and troubled times.

"This hall will stimulate our awareness of art and sharpen our sense of life. We should regard this place not as an arena for competition between stars, but as a temple of mystery and contemplation in which the dialogue with the unknown will continue."

—*Conductor Laureate Stanislaw Skrowaczewski*

It says a great deal about Skrowaczewski's persistence and patience that he achieved two of these three goals. Despite the daunting prospect of adding salaries to a budget that was already growing rapidly, the board gave him the green light to begin enlarging the Orchestra, and over the next few years Skrowaczewski added ten musicians, including a fourth player in each of the woodwind sections. That left two issues on the table: a European tour and a new concert hall. "They said, 'We can only do one thing at a time,'" the maestro recalls. "I said, 'Do the hall.'"

The opening of Orchestra Hall in October 1974 was a watershed in the Orchestra's long history. It marked a new era in more ways than one, for with the new venue came such innovations as "coffee concerts"—morning performances for the nocturnally challenged. The Orchestra also appointed its first principal guest conductor: Leonard Slatkin, a talented young Californian (he had just turned 30) who remains the closest thing to an American music director the organization has ever had. Slatkin held the principal guest title for five seasons before relinquishing it to become music director—not in the Twin Cities, but in St. Louis, where he had begun his career as an assistant conductor in 1968. His formal association with the Minnesota Orchestra continued throughout the 1980s, however. As principal guest conductor beginning in 1974, and as artistic director of the Orchestra's summer season throughout the 1980s, he introduced such festival innovations as Rug Concerts, Beethoven marathons, and Sommerfest.

Toward the end of his tenure, Skrowaczewski grew increasingly frustrated over his inability to make personnel changes in the Orchestra. The recording industry had dried up, Orchestra Hall was no longer a novelty (though it remained sold out until well into the 1980s), and the long-sought European tour still hadn't materialized. Above all, he was eager to resume composing. During the 1960s his output had been limited to a single major work, a well-received Concerto for English Horn that he composed for Thomas Stacey, the Orchestra's English horn player, now with the New York Philharmonic. In the 1970s he took up the pen again, and the result was *Ricercari notturni*, a saxophone concerto that won the Kennedy Center's Friedheim Award in 1976. Now other musicians were asking him to compose works for them.

Since relinquishing the music directorship in 1979, Skrowaczewski has remained a Minnesota resident while pursuing a busy international career as a conductor and composer. Although he spent seven years as principal conductor of the Hallé Orchestra, of Manchester, England, it was a less labor-intensive assignment, and in spite of many offers, he has never accepted another music directorship. As he approaches his 80th birthday, he maintains relationships with several orchestras—including the Saarbrücken Radio ensemble, of which he is principal guest artist, and, of course, the Minnesota Orchestra. He has composed several more works, two of which, a Concerto for Orchestra (nominated for the Pulitzer Prize in 1999) and a Piano Concerto for the Left Hand, are on the Orchestra's centennial season schedule.

The art of the music director
(Part III)

In the Orchestra's salad days, the music director was expected to conduct every performance—and generally did. The practice of using guest conductors on a regular basis began with Dorati, who believed that everyone—conductors, players, and audiences—needs an occasional change of pace. Dorati's contract gave him the entire month of January to use as he pleased, and it pleased him to conduct other orchestras while guest conductors took his place here. In the 1960s and 1970s, as the seasons grew ever longer, more and more guest conductors began showing up on the Orchestra's schedule. Recent music directors have conducted about half of the subscription programs.

To be the music director of an American orchestra no longer implies an exclusive commitment. Indeed, many conductors hold two or more posts with orchestras on both sides of the Atlantic. Eiji Oue is a case in point: In the 2001-02 season, in addition to finishing his seven-year term as music director of the Minnesota Orchestra, he served as music director of the Grand Teton Music Festival

Stanislaw **Skrowaczewski**

in Wyoming, chief conductor of the Hanover Radio Orchestra in Germany, and professor of conducting at Hanover's Hochschule für Musik und Theater.

This proliferation of titled positions is largely the result of a proliferation of music-making. Today's busy orchestras need not only a music director but a staff of assistant and special-duty conductors. In the centennial season, for example, even though the Minnesota Orchestra has no music director, it has four staff conductors—Associate Conductor Giancarlo Guerrero, Assistant Conductor Scott Terrell, Principal Pops Conductor Doc Severinsen, and Conductor Laureate Stanislaw Skrowaczewski—in addition to the Orchestra's Music Director Designate Osmo Vänskä.

With so many slots to be filled, conducting has become a more attractive career choice than ever before, and "There are more and more talented conductors coming up through the ranks," Cisek says. "Ten years ago, we were talking about where the new conductors were going to come from. The challenge now is: Where are the managers coming from?"

The corporate era

By the end of the 1970s, the Minnesota Orchestra had embarked on the course it has maintained ever since: that of a large cultural institution serving both a metropolitan area and the surrounding region with a variety of programs designed to appeal to a broad spectrum of public taste. If that sounds a little corporate, why shouldn't it? Today's Minnesota Orchestra is a nearly $30 million annual operation. It is Minnesota's largest nonprofit performing arts organization by a considerable margin. It has a large administrative staff that has a great deal of leverage to influence any artistic decision with financial implications—as all artistic decisions do.

The time is long past when Mrs. Scott could place a telephone call to Arthur Judson and hang up with the name of the next music director. All three music directors chosen since the late 1970s—Neville Marriner (1979-86), Edo de Waart (1986-95), and Eiji Oue (1995-2002)—as well as Osmo Vänskä, who will become the Orchestra's tenth music director in 2003-04, were chosen by search committees.

The committee that selected Marriner was looking for someone on whose coattails the Orchestra could ride to international prominence. The several attractive candidates included Klaus Tennstedt, an East German émigré with a Mitropoulos-like talent for inspiring the musicians, and Slatkin, who was popular with both musicians and audiences. But Marriner offered something special: instant recognition and proven success in making recordings. As founder of the London-based Academy of St Martin-in-the-Fields, Marriner came to Minnesota as the most recorded conductor in the world. (Rather than lose their services entirely, the Orchestra engaged Tennstedt as principal guest conductor and Slatkin as artistic director of the summer season.)

Born in Lincoln, England, in 1924, Marriner studied at the Royal College of Music in London and the Paris Conservatoire, played professionally in a string quartet, and in 1956 joined the London Symphony Orchestra, then led by Pierre Monteux, as assistant concertmaster. He stayed with the LSO for twelve years. Meanwhile, in 1959, he founded the Academy as a vehicle for performing works by Bach, Handel, and other Baroque masters in the light, crisp style advocated by British musicologist Thurston Dart. Over the next two decades, under his calm and collegial leadership, the Academy evolved from a part-time ensemble into one of the world's best-known orchestras.

In Minnesota, Marriner proved charming, witty, and far more comfortable in the spotlight than Skrowaczewski had been. He was candid to a fault, which made for great copy. "Everybody liked him," says Cisek, who chaired the search committee. "He mixed well with everybody, engaged the community very well, and had a natural elegance that came across the footlights."

Marriner was the first music director of the Orchestra who did not establish residence here. Although he and his wife, Molly, kept a *pied-à-terre* at the Calhoun Beach Club, he was in essence "a commuting music director," Cisek notes, "and that took a toll. He would fly in on a Sunday and rehearse on Monday." Auditions, artistic planning meetings, and other activities requiring the music director's presence had to be timed to coincide with Marriner's trips to Minnesota, which meant that he rarely had time to relax. "It was a punishing schedule," Cisek says. "He had no light weeks."

Sir Neville Marriner (music director 1979-1986)
in rehearsal with frequent guest violinist Itzhak Perlman

Three successive music directors led the Orchestra
for more than one third of its first hundred years.
Pictured at a 1986 meeting in Orchestra Hall:
Stanislaw Skrowaczewski (1960-1979),
Sir Neville Marriner (1979-1986),
Edo de Waart (1986-1995)

Edo **de Waart**

Marriner was still learning much of the large-orchestra repertoire. The qualities he had brought to the Academy's performances of Baroque and Classical music—clarity of tone, nimble passagework, sprightly rhythms—needed to be augmented for the expansive romantic repertoire of Brahms, Tchaikovsky, and Strauss.

In his seven seasons on the platform, Marriner presided over a number of firsts, including the Orchestra's first composer-in-residence program (with Libby Larsen and Stephen Paulus) and a star-studded gala in 1982 attended by members of several Scandinavian royal families. He led the Orchestra on two international trips, to Australia in 1985 and Hong Kong in 1986, that set the stage for its European and Japanese tours in the late 1990s. And in 1985 he achieved a distinction unique in Orchestra annals by being the first of the Orchestra's music directors to be knighted.

Because Marriner was so closely identified with the Academy, however, there proved to be relatively little interest in having him record with any other orchestra; over seven seasons he made only half a dozen recordings with the Minnesota Orchestra. His successes lay rather in his live performances. In the words of Luella Goldberg, chairman of the board in the Marriner years, "The vitality and warmth that Neville Marriner and his wife, Molly, brought to their years in Minnesota captured the hearts of audiences and the community both inside and outside Orchestra Hall."

Rebuilding the Orchestra

The Orchestra that Skrowaczewski inherited from Dorati in 1960 was a relatively young one. The Orchestra that de Waart inherited from Marriner in 1986 was considerably more advanced in years, in part because many of Dorati's hires were still members. Some were still capable of performing at a high artistic level, but others were not. As a result, the Orchestra was due for an overhaul.

The search committee that recommended de Waart —the first on which there was as many musicians (five) as board members—was looking for an experienced music director with a large repertoire and the toughness to deal with the musicians' union. In addition, he had to be willing to move to the Twin Cities, for it was generally agreed that Marriner's portmanteau leadership

had been unduly hard on both the maestro and the Orchestra.

In de Waart they found a candidate who met all their criteria. Still in his mid-40s, the Dutch conductor had already proved his mettle as music director of the Rotterdam Philharmonic and the San Francisco Symphony and he was widely credited with having turned the latter around after years in the artistic doldrums. Born in Amsterdam in 1941, de Waart started out as an oboist and in his early twenties spent two years in Amsterdam's renowned Concertgebouw Orchestra. But what really interested him was conducting. In 1964 he won the Mitropoulos Competition for young conductors in New York, and his career path was set; when he returned to the Concertgebouw in 1966, it was as assistant conductor. A year later he was music director at Rotterdam.

De Waart immediately set about transforming the Orchestra from one with intonation and other problems to one that consistently played well. It was not an easy transition, and the maestro's brusque personality had a way of making tempers rise. "He had to pull teeth to begin with," Cisek recalls. "He brought a different kind of temperament to the institution, which created some pretty tense situations. But the Orchestra could tell they were improving, week by week and season by season, as a result of his changes."

While Edo de Waart's greatest contribution to the Orchestra during his nine seasons at the helm was undoubtedly his makeover of the ensemble itself, he was also responsible for establishing a tradition of concert performances of opera, opening with a triumphant *Das Rheingold* in 1988 and closing with a magnificent *Otello* at his farewell concert in 1995. And by the end of his tenure, he had the respect if not the affection of the players. "Edo was certainly responsible for reorganizing the Orchestra," says retired violist John Tartaglia. "He was a harsh authoritarian, but you have to give him credit for that."

Unlike the gregarious Marriner, de Waart wanted no part of the social scene. "One-on-one, he is an engaging and witty conversationalist whose personality blooms as one gets to know him," observed *Saint Paul Pioneer Press* critic Michael Fleming in a 1994 article. "But the public persona is undeniably cool. . . ." Another writer put it

During his tenure, de Waart's love of opera manifested itself in memorable concerts featuring singers with the Minnesota Orchestra—the great symphonic repertoire with voice, as well as performances of entire operas. Here, de Waart, Orchestra, and soloist Leontyne Price acknowledge the audience reception.

more bluntly when he declared that de Waart had "the charisma of a porcupine."

De Waart told Fleming he was disappointed that he hadn't made many recordings with the Orchestra (a promising relationship with Virgin Classics withered on the vine) and that the one major foreign tour he was scheduled to lead was cancelled by the outbreak of the Persian Gulf War. About the Orchestra itself, however, he had no regrets. "It's like watching a plant grow. You get so involved in whatever goes on that you don't see it yourself. But I do think the Orchestra plays with a lot more panache and pride now."

"I think history will treat Edo well," Principal Clarinet Burt Hara told *Star Tribune* music critic Michael Anthony just before de Waart's farewell concert. "I think

as time passes, people will look back and see that he did a lot of good in his time here. I have a lot of respect for the man and the musician."

At long last Europe

When de Waart announced his resignation, a new search committee went to work. Like the previous search committee (and search committees generally, perhaps), it was looking for someone who offered qualities his predecessor was deemed to lack—in this case, an engaging personality, a cheerful demeanor, and a willingness to participate in the marketing and educational activities of the Orchestra. A conductor, in short, with people skills. It found what it was looking for in Eiji Oue.

*In May 2002 Minnesota Orchestra Life
Director Nicky B. Carpenter (chairman of the
board of directors when the Orchestra engaged
Oue) presented a bouquet to retiring Music
Director Eiji Oue at the conclusion of the final
concert of his seven-year tenure.*

The announcement of Oue's appointment took the music world by surprise and shock. "Eiji who?" asked Michael Anthony in the *Star Tribune*. A headline in *The New York Times* put it more delicately—"The Minnesota Makes an Unexpected Choice"—but the underlying question was the same: Why had a major American orchestra selected a virtual unknown to be its next artistic leader?

Oue was not really unknown, of course. When the Hiroshima native's appointment was announced in late 1993, he had already been in America for fifteen years. Oue had studied at Tanglewood and the New England Conservatory, and, significantly, had been a protégé of Leonard Bernstein. But he had held only two named conducting posts: associate conductor of the Buffalo Philharmonic and, for four seasons, music director of the Erie Philharmonic. In snaring the music directorship of the Minnesota Orchestra, Oue was leaping several rungs up the career ladder.

The organization recognized that "there is a risk in going with someone with a lesser name," Hyslop told a *Times* reporter. "But when he has conducted our Orchestra, the response from the players and the audience has been tremendous. I would say he's one of the most talented conductors I've worked with in my 29 years in the orchestra business." And in any case, the Minnesota Orchestra had had pretty good luck with "virtual unknowns" over the years.

Those who hoped Oue would be the second coming of Ormandy, however, were destined to be disappointed. While he was clearly a popular choice, some critics questioned the depth of his musicianship.

For many of the musicians, however, Oue was a

refreshing change who brought out the best in his players. After nine seasons under the demanding, difficult-to-please de Waart, it was "very encouraging," Associate Principal Cello Janet Horvath told Anthony, to see Oue on the podium "with a smile on his face, loving the music and loving what we were doing. . . ." Principal Timpani Peter Kogan agreed. "There was just a collective sigh of relief," he recalled, when Oue took over. "There was all this pent-up energy and desire to play well, and it was all being let out. By the first European tour, we were really opened up. We played great, and the audiences felt that."

Oue's tenure will be remembered for three major international tours—its first trips to Europe and Japan, both in 1998, and a second European tour two years later. By leading the Orchestra abroad, Oue fulfilled the ambitions of music directors going all the way back to Skrowaczewski and gave the Orchestra splendid exposure in a number of foreign music capitals. He also accomplished something no music director since Dorati had achieved by getting the Orchestra back into recording in a major way. The Orchestra under Oue turned out seventeen recordings in seven years—including four that were nominated for Grammy Awards—for the Reference Recordings label.

Oue will be remembered, too, as a champion of outreach. He visited elementary schools, nursing homes, and community centers. He turned up at public events of all kinds—including a Minnesota Vikings game for which he composed a special fanfare and conducted the Orchestra in the National Anthem. Oue conducted many high school orchestra rehearsals. He was photographed wearing Vikings' braids. It was all part of being music director. Not since Mitropoulos, perhaps, has the Minnesota Orchestra had a maestro as active in the community.

Looking ahead

This season (2002-2003), for the first time since 1936-1937 and only the third time in its history, the Minnesota Orchestra has no music director. The search for Oue's successor lasted a year and a half—almost twice as long as the one that brought Oue here—and by the time the Orchestra settled on Osmo Vänskä, chief conductor of the Glasgow-based BBC Scottish Symphony

In May 2001, Osmo Vänskä was named the Orchestra's tenth music director beginning in September 2003. Here, Vänskä applauds cello soloist Truls Mørk (not in photo) at a November 2001 concert.

and of the Lahti Symphony, he was unavailable until 2003-2004.

The Orchestra has turned the centenary season into something of a retrospective: All four of its living former music directors, former principal guest conductors Leonard Slatkin and Charles Dutoit, and former Associate and Resident Conductor Henry Charles Smith will appear as guest conductors—as will Vänskä. But in a sense, the Vänskä era has already begun, for the decisions he is making as music director designate are determining the shape of seasons two, three, perhaps even four years down the road.

How will Vänskä transplant to American soil the practices that have brought him such great success in other countries? How will his proven gift for exciting programs influence the repertoire of the Minnesota Orchestra? For how long will Orchestra audiences and musicians have the privilege of his leadership? For five seasons? For ten? For nineteen? The answers to these questions lie in the coming decades of the Minnesota Orchestra's second hundred seasons.

On the Road to Fame
Our Touring Orchestra

*Cellist Joseph Johnson warms
up backstage on tour.*

MARY ANN FELDMAN

*Mary Ann Feldman wrote the program
notes for the Minnesota Orchestra from
1968 to 1999—the longest annotatorship
among American orchestras.
A well-known Twin Cities commentator
on music, she introduced pre-concert talks at
Orchestra Hall upon its opening in 1974.
She has also served as* Showcase *editor,
associate director of public affairs, and vice-
president of the Metropolitan Opera in the
Upper Midwest. Feldman toured with the
Orchestra on five foreign tours.*

WHEN THE CARNEGIE HALL stage lights abruptly went off without so much as a flicker of warning, soprano Kathleen Battle continued to sing her aria from Verdi's *Attila*, and the Minnesota Orchestra was right with her. Performing from a darkened stage on the night of February 15, 1998, Eiji Oue and his musicians carried on as if nothing had happened. In the hall's faint glow, the startled New York audience listened in disbelief as the show went on. For an Orchestra delivering the New York prelude to a long-awaited tour of Western Europe (virtually a debut, for on a Middle East tour 41 years before, the Orchestra had touched down to play only in Greece and Yugoslavia), the worst was over. Confident that such a mishap would not strike twice, the musicians boarded the plane for London the next day in high spirits.

Rolling through the Rhine Valley on our way to a concert in Düsseldorf a week later, Principal Bass Peter Lloyd looked up from the book on Oriental rugs he and I were sharing and reflected: "This is a bona fide, authentic historical moment in the evolution of the Minnesota Orchestra. We've never toured Europe before, and no matter how many times we come back, we'll never experience it the way we are experiencing it right now."

Whether they realized it or not, these 95 artists proved as capable of dealing with adversity as had their hardy orchestral forefathers. Back in the neophyte days of the Minneapolis Symphony Orchestra—for that was its famous name from 1903 to 1968, during which it emerged as the travelingest orchestra in the world—the lights often failed in the school gymnasiums, cow palaces, lodge halls, and jerry-built theaters of the prairie towns where it was awakening the American heartland to symphonic music. The Minneapolis Symphony Orchestra's founding music director, Emil Oberhoffer was determined to carry on where an earlier touring conductor, Theodore Thomas, and his famous orchestra had left off. Oberhoffer always came prepared: His band of 50 musicians cultivated a repertoire of pieces to be played by heart in an emergency.

*The Minnesota Orchestra in its debut with Music Director
Eiji Oue at Vienna's Musikverein, March 4, 1998*

A tour flyer from 1912

Publicity of the Best Kind

BEFORE LONG, THE ADVANTAGES OF A SUCCESSFUL symphony orchestra from a purely commercial point of view were unmistakable. As noted in the *St. Louis Times* after the MSO played there in 1913, this Orchestra was "backed by hard-headed businessmen on hard-headed grounds. It is carrying an excellent impression of Minneapolis to all parts of the United States." Advertising pays, "but the symphony carries the message."

By the time the Orchestra attained its 100th anniversary season in 2002, it had performed in 659 different cities and towns—mostly across the United States, but in 59 cities in 21 foreign countries as well. Other symphony orchestras may have accumulated more mileage, making repeated European trips and traveling to distant places like China, but none can match the Minnesotans' number of venues as they helped to develop the nation's audiences for great music.

Gentlemen, on this long trip, I beg of you one thing. Let us give our temperament full swing, and let us leave our tempers at home.

—Emil Oberhoffer to his musicians,
about to depart on tour

Across nearly two-thirds of its first century, the orchestra launched in 1903 as the Minneapolis Symphony packed up its instruments and took to the rails more than any other orchestra in America. Soon it was known as "The Orchestra on Wheels." Before this risk-taking organization turned 50, it had performed 3,168 concerts in a total of 442 cities in the United States, Canada, and Cuba. Fame was assured.

The astonishing tour chronicle dates back to 1907 when, with funding from his own pocket, Oberhoffer led his musicians on a maiden trip to Moorhead, Grand Forks, and Duluth. By 1910, the visionary Oberhoffer had proven his point, and the orchestral association headed by Elbert L. Carpenter—music lover and persuasive fund raiser—bought into the idea and sponsored the tours.

Traveling to the isolated towns and growing cities of what then was customarily called "The Northwest," the determined Oberhoffer had taken up the mantle abandoned by Theodore Thomas and his orchestra, whose odysseys across the U.S. and Canada, including fifteen appearances in Minneapolis/Saint Paul, dated back to 1869. Their visits abruptly ended in 1891, when Thomas settled permanently in Chicago to head the new Chicago Symphony Orchestra, which absorbed most of his personnel. Contemplating the void left by the Thomas Orchestra, Oberhoffer lost little time in taking his

fledgling Minneapolis Symphony on the road. These jaunts not only extended the weeks of employment for the musicians in those days of short symphony seasons, but consistently netted a profit—more than $1,000 a week for a six-week tour in 1909.

In its sixth-season "Spring Festival Tour of 1909," the Orchestra traveled the bands of steel uniting isolated places to bring Dvořák's *New World* Symphony, Beethoven overtures, and period bonbons to eight states and one Canadian province—30 cities in all. Each welcomed the Minneapolitans time and again, annually when possible.

In addition to one-night stands, separated by Pullman car journeys rendered sleepless by the clickety-click of rails, the Orchestra and its entourage of soloists collaborated in festivals crammed with events. Following a breakfast cooked in a baggage car set up with a stove (Oberhoffer was praised for frying ham and eggs), the musicians would hasten to a three-hour rehearsal or roam the host town before playing a matinee geared to students and adults, typically in a ratio of 800 to 400. Then would come an evening concert at 7:30 or 8:00, while the next day posted a rehearsal with the local chorus or soloist, capped by an evening finale—Mendelssohn's *Elijah*, perhaps, or an operatic program.

From the start, Omaha demanded five concerts for its festival. Thanks to the indefatigable tour manager, Wendell C. Heighton, who before long was logging 40,000 miles a year selling the MSO, Omaha scored a triumph in capturing "a fashionable and discriminating" audience. Meanwhile, the college town of Grinnell, Iowa —one of five campuses on the itinerary, the others being large state universities—concluded that the MSO "was fully as interesting as the Theodore Thomas Orchestra" (*Scarlet and Black*, May 18, 1910). Net for this tour: more than $10,000.

Young as it was, the Orchestra was already earning coverage in national periodicals. The *Musical Courier*'s Western correspondent, reporting Denver's three-day festival of April 1910, declared that "those who have heard other traveling orchestras do not hesitate to place the Minneapolis Symphony Orchestra in the category of the few really great orchestras in the country."

As the ambitious 1909-1910 season wound to a close, the poorly paid ensemble tallied a record of 30 concerts at home (ten on Friday nights, twenty on Sunday

In 1918 a train wreck delayed the Orchestra as it crossed the state of Nevada en route to a concert in Utah. No one was injured.

afternoons) and 111 concerts on expeditions to thirteen states and 46 cities. That summer, a Minneapolis *Tribune* feature by Oscar Hatch Hawley, representative of *Musical Courier*, bannered the opinion that "Twin Cities Form the Most Important Musical Center of the Entire West." Reporting his adventures west of the Alleghenies, Hawley wrote:

> I found everywhere that the fame of the Minneapolis Symphony orchestra had preceded me. Minneapolis is looked upon with wonder and admiration by musical people the country over, when they learn that its orchestra of 80 men, giving upwards of 30 concerts [at home] a year, was organized only seven years ago. The recent spring tour . . . did more to advertise Minneapolis as a city of culture and high artistic standards than columns of published publicity could have done.

Hardly content to adventure only out to the prairies, Oberhoffer set his sights on the big time, invading

Thomas territory to debut in Chicago on March 9, 1911—the first of 39 visits, plus twenty appearances at suburban Evanston's North Shore Festival. Postcards announcing the event were circulated to all Minnesota guarantors and subscribers, with Elbert L. Carpenter's request to forward these advance souvenirs to their Chicago friends. Boxes were reserved for Twin Cities VIPs who did not want to miss the event. This was the first Western orchestra to play in Thomas's own sanctuary—a worthy risk, for not even a powder mill explosion that shook Chicago's Orchestra Hall that night, forcing a "brief pause," spoiled the Windy City debut.

Heighton filled his portfolio with the kind of press raves that have always motivated tours and inspired local pride. Glenn Dillard Gunn in the *Chicago Tribune* reported, "Not since the last visit of the Boston Symphony Orchestra has a foreign body of players been accorded a reception that equaled in cordiality that extended to the organization from the Northwest." He pointed out that "the Minneapolis orchestra is a direct

Touring as a Way of Life

A PATTERN DEVELOPED: PLAY A SUNDAY AFTERNOON HOME concert as the kick-off, and then head for the train station, departing at 5:50 p.m. on the Great Northern if the first stop was Winnipeg, as happened 31 times by 1952, racking up 89 concerts in all. The English-flavored city deferred the founding of its own orchestra until 1948. Long before Winnipeg, other cities used the MSO as a model when launching homegrown orchestras. All recognized that a symphony orchestra bolsters a city's image, becoming an asset to trigger business support. No one ever dreamed that an orchestra actually would pay for itself, even in the no-frills wanderlust days of the MSO, when audiences often packed to the doors. After the concerts, cellist Carlo Fischer recalled, "there was always a pail of beer on ice waiting for us," which may account for the rollicking party in Deadwood, S.D., in 1910, which witnessed Oberhoffer riding a drowsy old nag to the train station in the wee hours.

. . . if praise were a detriment to an orchestra instead of a benefit, one would rather dread the effect of the tour upon Mr. Oberhoffer and his men. City after city hailed the orchestra with acclaim and pronounced it the greatest body of musicians in the West; and a great many critics placed this young orchestra, now only seven years of age, upon a par with any of the older organizations of Eastern cities.

—*Minneapolis Tribune*, June 6, 1910

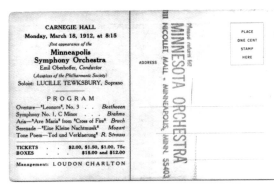

Postcards proclaimed the Orchestra's first appearance in Carnegie Hall: March 1912.

descendent of our own Thomas orchestra . . . fired to emulate the example of their great work in American music." Gunn predicted that Minneapolis was "destined to play an important part in the musical development of the United States."

All the critics were present. The next day they lavished praise on the "dramatic" Oberhoffer, not just a drillmaster but a "conductor of the virtuoso type," comparing him favorably to such giants as Felix Weingartner and Arthur Nikisch. A program of Beethoven, Tchaikovsky, and Wagner was calculated to test the mettle of any orchestra. Under the headline "Orchestra Achieves Triumph in Chicago," the *Chicago Daily News* reported that volleys of applause followed the opening movement of Tchaikovsky's *Pathétique* Symphony "and would not end until the members of the orchestra rose at Oberhoffer's signal to join him in acknowledging the ovation." Departing Chicago in victory, the nomadic Orchestra boarded two private Pullmans, catching a night's sleep en route to the next stop.

That season they spent a total of eleven weeks on the road—120 cities in all. Next year: Carnegie Hall.

With Carpenter's blessings, Oberhoffer and Heighton not only re-booked Chicago for 1912, but set their sights on the East. Going to New York 85 strong, according to a Minneapolis *Tribune* editorial, would be a "genial invasion" of a sacrosanct place, for New York by then was the nation's musical capital. Cincinnati, Buffalo, and other cities that had cultivated a musical life long before Minneapolis figured on the itinerary. Oberhoffer's programs for that season's expeditions totaled 35 in all, with 50 different compositions—an uncanny abundance by today's norms, especially since he included both the Verdi *Requiem* in Winnipeg and a concert performance of *Aida* in Galesburg, Illinois. The board was anxious to put its "Western" orchestra on display, showing, in the words of the *Tribune*, that "Its men have made their home beyond the Mississippi [not all, to be sure, for some resided in St. Paul], a response to local demand and the fruit of local experience." Capitalizing on laurels earned in Chicago, the hometown paper proclaimed that the MSO

had already earned its rank among the top half-dozen orchestras in America—a boast affirmed everywhere.

Plumbing the Chicago reviews for all their worth, a barrage of advance publicity—plus ticket hand-outs—produced a near-capacity house at Carnegie Hall. While the audience was enthusiastic, Gotham's press was condescending, sneering at this import from the West. Nevertheless, Oberhoffer was hell-bent on returning the following year, whereupon the *New York Times* in 1913 sarcastically observed that the MSO seemed to have a "mania for traveling far from home," even though New York "is more than fully supplied with all the orchestral concerts it needs."

Back then, big crowds gathered in small cities, thanks to the frequent trains linking them. The *South Bend Times* reported that people flocked from all the surrounding cities to award Oberhoffer "salvos of applause which would have gladdened the heart of the most expectant of prima donnas." Out in Aberdeen, South Dakota, the lights failed and never popped on again, as Oberhoffer led his band through works played from memory; at the end, everybody, players included, exited through a single darkened doorway. "Rare Display of Cool Minds at Last Night's Concert," reported *The Aberdeen Daily News* on June 3, 1912.

Orchestra lore is a chapter in itself, a saga of concerts in unlikely places. When Edmond, Oklahoma, could not provide an adequate facility, the Minneapolis Symphony played in a circus tent jammed with 2,000 listeners, while others sat in their automobiles and honked their horns in lieu of applause. A favorite story profiles the colorful Oberhoffer. Talking with John K. Sherman in 1946, as the critic was undertaking to write *Music and Maestros* (University of Minnesota Press, 1952), Carlo Fischer—not only cellist, but manager, program annotator, and general factotum from 1903 until the 1950s—described an early concert at the Corn Palace in Mitchell, South Dakota:

> It was an old and rickety structure and has since been replaced by a new building. During the progress of the concert a bad storm came up and the roof began to leak. Emil Oberhoffer conducted with an umbrella in one hand and a baton in the other. But the really funny part of the concert was the gradual shifting of

the orchestra men to avoid being rained on. Before the concert was over everyone was in an unaccustomed place with the sections all mixed up, and Oberhoffer had a hard time conducting.

In 1916 the Orchestra made its longest trip yet: eight weeks, spanning twelve states to play 98 concerts in 49 cities. (Small wonder that by its 50th anniversary, the MSO had played nearly 65% of its concerts out of town, a figure that goes a long way in explaining its extraordinary fame.) The kingpin of that trip was Boston —even more intimidating than New York and Chicago, for the very name Boston Symphony invited reverence. Headlined "Great Triumph of Western Visitors" (February 1, 1916), Arthur Elson's *Boston Review* account was a great relief: "The advent of Emil Oberhoffer's Minneapolis orchestra, which performed in Symphony Hall last evening, proved to be an important event in Boston's musical annals. . . . We have had visiting orchestras from many outside cities—New York, Philadelphia, Chicago, etc.—all apparently desirous of being measured by the yardstick of our own great organization. The Minneapolis orchestra came fully up to any of those famous visitors."

Adding a touch of Boston chauvinism, Elson asserted that the Orchestra's personnel might be judged by the fact that its concertmaster (one of Oberhoffer's preferred tour soloists) was Boston's "own former symphonic artist, Richard Czerwonky; the first viola is Karl Scheurer, also a Boston graduate," whereupon the critic bestowed praise on other principals, "even though they are not Boston transplants."

For the year 1917, the MSO aimed to go as far to the southwest as possible: Los Angeles. Then in its fourteenth season, the Minneapolis Symphony traveled south to Texas before crossing to California via Arizona; proceeding up the West Coast to San Francisco and Oakland, they returned home by way of Salt Lake, Laramie, Denver, and other Western cities. In Los Angeles, which did not form its own L.A. Philharmonic until 1919, the evening *Express* commented ruefully that Minneapolis people "seem to have more of a realization of the value of an orchestra as a civic asset."

High demand spurred the Minneapolitans to head West again the following year. In autobiographical papers tucked into his scrapbook, Heighton noted on November 11, 1917, that he had in hand more requests for the Orchestra than could be met. By then, he had booked the Orchestra in nearly every major city from coast to coast. Even though it was wartime, the schedule filled up quickly, and audiences of 2,500 or 2,600 were realistic expectations in armories, ice arenas, and big halls. Interviewed by *Musical Courier* (June 20, 1918), Heighton noted that the Orchestra had already done thirteen aggregate weeks of touring in the six months since the start of the year. His words may inspire concert promoters of the turbulent 21st century:

> Music fills a deeper need at this time than it ever has before. The psychological reason, as I see it, is that music supplies, as does nothing else, a relief from emotional tension, and a spiritual uplift, and serves to promote the poise and confidence so much needed at this time.

Winnipeg, which had suspended its festivals in the anxiety of the First World War's outbreak, resumed them in 1918. "There have been difficulties—great ones—but they have been surmounted," said Heighton. Speaking for Oberhoffer and the musicians, the tour manager emphasized that "We are trying to sustain the morale of the people"—this even though a war tax on railroad fares and Pullman accommodations was eroding the profit.

Thus the Orchestra on Wheels continued its mission throughout the Oberhoffer days, building momentum in its second decade. A falling-out with Carpenter, who had been treading on artistic turf, resulted in a final concert of the 1921-1922 season that turned out to be Oberhoffer's farewell. He was never invited back as guest conductor. Shocked at the last-minute news of his departure, many in the audience wept. They recognized that he had not only enriched their lives, but left the Minneapolis Symphony's imprint on the national map.

Three original members of the Orchestra: Carlo Fischer (cello, 1903-1952), E.M. Schugens (bass, 1903-1933), and William Faetkenheuer (timpani, 1903-1941)

I found everywhere that the fame of the Minneapolis Symphony Orchestra had preceded me. Minneapolis is looked upon with wonder and admiration by musical people the country over, when they learn that its orchestra of eighty men, giving upwards of thirty concerts a year, was organized only seven years ago.

—Oscar Hatch Hawley, *Musical Courier*, 1910

As a national asset, the Minneapolis Symphony Orchestra has arrived, and that city will be called upon more and more to divide its musical glory with other cities.

—*Kansas City Journal* (February 8, 1924)

Following an interim season of notable guest conductors, Henri Verbrugghen assumed the Minneapolis podium in 1923. At 50, the Belgian, arriving by way of his Australian career, was an experienced music director, orchestral craftsman, and crusader for chamber music. A suave figure who sported waxed mustachios but was also at ease in his fishing camp dungarees, Verbrugghen may not have rivaled Oberhoffer in the charisma department, but he was a genial leader, and no less dedicated to touring. The big difference between them: Oberhoffer built his orchestral career in this community, while Verbrugghen came from exotic places and with impressive credentials.

Verbrugghen took charge in heady times, the bullish twenties, when inventions like radio and recordings were changing the musical world forever. Already in the interregnum season, the MSO, conducted by Bruno Walter, had its first rendezvous with audiences across America: a March 1923 national broadcast that prompted letters and telegrams from half the states in the nation.

Scarcely a year later, while again invading the East, the Orchestra showed off its new maestro at Carnegie Hall and the next week remained in New York to make four milestone recordings for the Brunswick-Balke-Collender Company. Carpenter's signal to go ahead with this venture was delayed until the last possible moment: not until the New York press—then generating six or seven reviews—delivered an affirmative judgment of the new maestro. (To this day, when a visit to Carnegie seldom brings out more than one or two critics, the New York verdict rattles orchestral nerves.) Lawrence Gilman in the *Herald Tribune* wrote that "Any hidebound Easterner who may fancy that all the good orchestra conductors in America live and operate on this side of the Alleghenies is in need of enlightenment." On the same day, April 15, 1924, William J. Henderson in the *New York Sun* noted that the MSO was supplying the musical demands of more than half the states in the U.S. and, although only in its 21st season, had already traveled "a distance equal to six times the circumference around the world."

When its first recordings were released in September, the name Minneapolis Symphony Orchestra stood out in print ads all over the country. Astute local businessmen responded by beefing up the Guaranty Fund goal to $450,000. The much-hyped wax novelties promoted tour sales, which flourished throughout the decade. (Nowhere is there a more symbiotic relationship than that between tours and recordings, as the Minnesota Orchestra discovered on its 1998 trip to Japan, where widely praised Reference Recordings of the Eiji Oue era sold as prized souvenirs of the concerts.) Tours, recordings, broadcasts—this is the triumvirate that cements an orchestra's fame.

The touring MSO became an Orchestra on Water not only in its ferry crossings of Lake Michigan, but also on jaunts to what now seems an unlikely destination: Havana, Cuba, reached by boat from Miami. There in 1929 the Orchestra played to three sold-out houses of fashionable people enjoying their new hall. Happily, the MSO was invited back, for Florida and the Gulf Coast have long been midwinter antidotes to the ice storms and plummeting temperatures of home. Yet a third Cuban visit, in 1931, was cancelled at the last minute. The MSO's manager, Mrs. Carlyle Scott, revealed only that the decision was made "on account of conditions there."

Verbrugghen's tours were full of color and adventure. A Palm Beach audience of snowbirds in 1930 drew financiers Otto Kahn and John D. Rockefeller, who, observed one wag, did not fling dimes onto the stage. A year later, a 3:30 matinee in Washington, D.C., was briefly delayed when the White House called to advise that Mrs. Herbert Hoover would be late in joining her box of notables. After the Orchestra had won accolades in eleven states, Mrs. Scott boasted back home that "it was all very thrilling . . . the boys brought new honors to the name of the city in three sections of the country."

Conductor Henri Verbrugghen (center, with bow tie) surrounded by Orchestra musicians

Henri Verbrugghen (second from left) was the first music director to travel by airplane; his companions in the photo are not identified.

Boarding a ship in Havana at the end of their 1929 Cuban tour: violinist and Personnel Manager Max Schellner; Music Director Henri Verbrugghen, violinist Jenny Cullen, Orchestra Manager Arthur J. Gaines, trombonist Fred Molzahn, cellist Chris Erck, and violist Russell Barton

First Women

EXITING AUSTRALIA WITH VERBRUGGHEN WAS A GIFTED pupil and colleague, violinist Jenny Cullen, the first woman to hold a regular Minneapolis Symphony chair. The presence of the tiny figure midst that sea of gentlemen players astonished the tour cities, especially in the genteel South. "Aunt Jenny" was virtually a member of the Verbrugghen family, and long after this sturdy Scotswoman's orchestra career ended in 1949, she remained in the Twin Cities as a beloved teacher. Pupils and friends cherished the musician who made local history as "one of the boys," to quote the pet phrase of Mrs. Carlyle Scott, the Orchestra's first woman manager, herself a pathbreaker.

Early 1930s tour flyer

The "Touringest" Orchestra

NOT ONLY WAS MINNESOTA TOUTED NATIONALLY through its symphony, but this Orchestra—like none other in American musical history—whetted the country's nascent thirst for great music. Not since the touring Thomas Orchestra in the previous century had there been such a role model for other cities. The San Francisco Symphony, for instance, was founded in 1911, but did not make cross-country tours until the 1950s; the Saint Louis Symphony, founded two decades before our own, did not perform at Carnegie Hall until 1950, trailing the Minnesota Orchestra by nearly 40 years.

~

MINNEAPOLIS SYMPHONY IS PICTURED AT THRESHOLD OF GREATEST PERIOD

Dynamic Vigor and Youthful Enthusiasm

Will Carry Orchestra to New Heights, Asserts

Tribune's Music Critic

—Minneapolis *Tribune*, May 29, 1932

Nothing could stem the excitement generated by the 31-year-old Eugene Ormandy, an ambitious promoter who took over in the 1931-1932 season when fate dealt a tragic blow to Verbrugghen: On an unseasonably warm October day in the season's second week, he collapsed while rehearsing Strauss's *Ein Heldenleben*. A musical hotshot ready at the gate, Ormandy swiftly responded to Mrs. Scott's summons. His first appearance at the University of Minnesota's Northrop Auditorium (where the Orchestra performed its home concerts from 1930 to 1974) set off an explosion of excitement, launching the Orchestra on a wild ride that buoyed it through the Depression, when bankruptcy was always just around the corner. He would depart almost as fast as he came, for The Philadelphia Orchestra nabbed him in 1936. The youthful Hungarian may not have been exactly lovable, but subscription audiences regularly topped 4,000, and students responded to ticket campaigns geared to them. The campus was a breeding ground for new audiences.

Within weeks of arriving here, Ormandy and the MSO set off on the 1932 annual winter tour—7,248 miles in all. First stop: Chicago, where the Brahms First Symphony earned the headline, "Ormandy Thrills Chicago Crowd." In New Orleans, which had carried on an affectionate relationship with this northern orchestra since 1916, the crowds went wild, and in Jacksonville, Florida, the audience recalled Ormandy to the stage twelve times. Despite that year's economic crisis only one date was cancelled, when Nashville could not muster up the guaranteed fee. Back home, the entire season was preserved, for the "Dollar-Up" plea of the SOS campaign—"Save Our Symphony"—plus the willingness of musicians to take cuts in already pitifully small salaries

(ranging from $5,500 down to $800 for 26 weeks of employment)—carried the Orchestra intact through the toughest of times. Speaking at the Woman's Club, Mrs. Scott compared her job to "sitting on a keg of blasting powder while smoking a cigarette."

Even in the most threatened of seasons—a stricken music director and the darkest period in the nation's economy—the Minneapolis Symphony carried on. A 1933 *Star* editorial commended the decision not to cut back on touring, but to persist in "its happy habit of crusading to other parts of country, visiting places that have learned to couple the finest symphony with the name of our city."

Host cities everywhere expressed the wish to tie up the MSO and keep it for themselves. And fortunately, classical music broadcasts in the 1930s whetted the appetite. Radio slots under Ormandy, soon paralleled by milestone 78-rpm recordings sold across the oceans, spread the name of the Minneapolis Symphony over the globe. Ormandy scarcely had unpacked his batons here when he led a November 12, 1931 concert that spanned the nation's airwaves. By the time he left town in 1936, the MSO had reached ten million listeners across the nation.

The Minneapolis Symphony had not yet turned 30 when it was categorized as one of America's top five. And when Ormandy returned from a 1932 summer holiday in Europe, he fired up local citizens worried that the economy was threatening the very existence of the MSO by telling reporters that "our Orchestra beats Europe." Touring was slightly abbreviated in 1933 (5,000-mile circuit to fourteen cities, with just one day off), but fund-raising parties and broadcasts—big time, when the Orchestra was heard coast to coast the night Radio City opened—kept everyone preoccupied. Then, in 1934, Victor sent a crew to Minneapolis for ten full days of recording, announcing plans for more than 50 releases. These would carry the MSO name all over the world. "It did my heart good," said MSO librarian Herman Boessenroth after hearing his Orchestra's recordings on German radio in 1936. "It was a sign we are being recognized for something besides wheat."

By 1935, the cumulative impact of tours, records, and radio hook-ups was touted by a resplendent *Tribune* headline: "Symphony Wins World Praise." "Its recordings are played everywhere—second only to the Philadelphia

Eugene Ormandy,
music director
(then called, simply,
"conductor") from
1931 to 1936, and
Mrs. Carlyle Scott,
first female manager
of the Orchestra

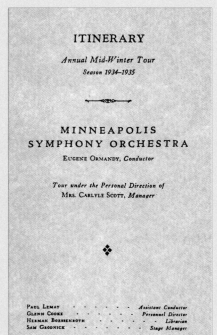

ITINERARY

Annual Mid-Winter Tour
Season 1934–1935

MINNEAPOLIS
SYMPHONY ORCHESTRA

Eugene Ormandy, *Conductor*

Tour under the Personal Direction of
Mrs. Carlyle Scott, *Manager*

Paul Lemay	Assistant Conductor
Glenn Cooke	Personnel Director
Herman Boessenroth	Librarian
Sam Grodnick	Stage Manager

*The only difference between a man
and a woman in [this] business is that a
woman is more interested in details.*

—Mrs. Carlyle Scott,
while on tour as MSO manager,
Memphis Press Scimitar, January 23, 1932

33

*Tuba player Lester Booth, memorialized by
the cartoonist and mis-identified as a bull fiddle
artist, went into Orchestra history for his
misadventure on a 1935 tour.*

Orchestra," the article explained. In Florida that February, musicians found icicles on the palm trees, forcing them to forego beachcombing. Among the vast tour lore is an account of the near suffocation of musician Lester Booth, who had snuggled into a bass case for a backstage nap. Rescued in the nick of time, he played the concert.

Returning from Europe after another summer jaunt, Ormandy reported that Minneapolis Symphony recordings were in high demand. "Europe knows our Orchestra," he exulted. But the liaison with the third music director was shattered when, on January 2, 1936, the dailies broke the news: "Ormandy Named New Philadelphia Symphony Leader."

Plans for touring were not shelved, for the assignment was eagerly undertaken by Russian-born composer Daniele Amfitheatrof (1901-83), who aspired to the director's post. (Going on the road was still profitable, costing around $1,000 a day, while fees generally reaped $1,500 to $2,500. Places like toney Palm Beach paid more, but some small towns en route got a bargain, the concert offered for expenses only.) Who would replace the Twin Cities' meteoric leader? Since Ormandy agreed to fill in for part of the 1936-1937 season, the board freed him from his contract. Their search was on.

**All the obstacles and the inescapable effects
of the Second World War notwithstanding,
Mitropoulos raised the orchestra into one of
the best and most famous symphonic ensembles
of the States. He realized with it fifteen
tours in cities of the States and Canada.
The nationwide radio networks transmitted
his concerts, which included a great number
of first world performances...**

—From a tribute to Mitropoulos
by the Greek community

Twin Citians first encountered Dimitri Mitropoulos on the wind-whipped night of January 29, 1937. To them he was "a question mark," said John K. Sherman, for he was not yet famous in America. At first they did not know what to make of the "bald, lithe, and rawboned" man who virtually exploded from the wings to draw glorious sounds from the 90 figures before him. As Orchestra benefactor Kenneth N. Dayton once remarked, "When Mitropoulos conducted, we didn't know Northrop had acoustical shortcomings."

Just weeks later, Elbert L. Carpenter announced from the stage at intermission that Mitropoulos would become the Minneapolis Symphony's new music director. A whoop went up, and resonates still, for Mitropoulos—mystic, visionary, a non-disciplinarian but inspiring leader—is still the Orchestra's iconic conductor. All who have followed are judged by his standard. Even before the Orchestra's Mercury LPs under Antal Dorati and Stanislaw Skrowaczewski circulated around the world, Mitropoulos had put the crowning stamp of fame on the Minneapolis Symphony Orchestra.

Mitropoulos was the Orchestra's wartime conductor. A deeply religious and socially committed man, he participated in the community's volunteer efforts, working for the Red Cross Blood Bank. The government encouraged performers to travel, so long as they didn't impede more vital journeys, and the Orchestra set out on dusty day coaches teeming with servicemen en route to new bases. Rhadames Angelucci, the legendary principal oboe from 1937 to 1982, recalled the time when the only seat he could find was a pile of duffel bags to perch on for five or six hours.

Every year from 1939 to 1949, the Orchestra played in Chicago, whose critics had a hard time making up their minds about this dynamic maestro, so different from any other they had experienced. The *Chicago Tribune*'s formidable music critic Claudia Cassidy described "a virtuoso's orchestra created in the image of music as conceived by its conductor, Dimitri Mitropoulos."

Everywhere the Greek's benevolence and spiritual demeanor resonated with audiences. In mighty Boston, the Minneapolitans in 1948 were bravoed by the largest-ever audience to greet a visiting orchestra in its Symphony Hall. Meanwhile, the San Francisco Symphony (under Pierre Monteux, 1947) and The Philadelphia Orchestra (with Ormandy returning) performed here, allowing Twin Citians to make comparisons.

*During the Orchestra's 1949 spring tour, members of the Orchestra gathered for a light-hearted photo.
The horn player in the second row is actually violinist Mischa Bregman, who has traded instruments with Waldemar
Linder, eighth from left. The top row consists of Samuel Flor, violin; George Kurz and William Bagwell, viola;
James Greco, trumpet; Emil Opava, flute; Bregman, violin and librarian; Henry Denecke, timpani; Linder, horn;
James Mackay, trumpet; Ray Fitch, bass; Paul Binstock, horn (making devil's horns with his left hand over the head of his
neighbor); Samuel Segal, percussion; Max Schellner, violin; Herman Boessenroth, librarian; Arthur Randall, stage manager
Front row: Emil Niosi, flute; Dimitri Mitropoulos; Fred Molzahn, trombone; Arthur Kurtz (holding oboe), bassoon;
Jack Bass, trumpet; Irving Winslow, violin; Egon Plagge, violin*

*Conductor Daniele Amfitheatrof
led the 1937 fall tour.*

Audiences may have chafed under Mitropoulos's programming of twentieth-century music, but they were not likely to trade him off for another maestro. Travels to 88 cities under him, adding new states like Maine and New Jersey, only spread their Orchestra's fame. But because Mitropoulos was in high demand, engaged twice by the New York Philharmonic in three months of the 1946-1947 season, it became harder to schedule the tours.

A glimpse of the future is found in a *Tribune* article (December 19, 1947) headlined ORCHESTRAS FACE RISING TOUR COSTS. The biggest factors were travel and hotel accommodations, which together explain why later touring required underwriting, and even then could trigger deficits. Going on the road was eating the profits. The saving grace at mid-century came from the Columbia Community Concerts flourishing throughout the land, when practically every city or town of any size worked with New York booking agents who offered concerts in a bundle at a discount rate. After World War II, most of the great orchestras began crisscrossing the country, paying scant attention to each other's dates. When sales of recordings soared to new heights upon the advent of the LP, record companies played a strong hand in the continuation of touring. Competitors abounded.

The plum booking of 1949 fell to the Minneapolis Symphony just as its cherished leader, Mitropoulos, was about to depart for the New York Philharmonic: Aspen called. After logging more than 12,000 miles on the road to 79 cities that season, the MSO was the featured orchestra at the international Goethe Bicentennial Festival

*. . . for the excellent job it has done
in selling Minneapolis as a cultural
center to music enthusiasts throughout
the United States on its concert tours.*

—Chamber of Commerce citation to
the Minneapolis Symphony Orchestra,
March 31, 1949

Minneapolis and its symphony are gaining new advocates who, by their high positions and wide geographical spread, will help make our city's name more than ever an international symbol of cultural enterprise and excellence.

—John K. Sherman reporting to
The Minneapolis Star from Aspen, 1949

Mitropoulos conducting an Orchestra rehearsal in Aspen, 1949

Value to its Community

WITH THE ASPEN RESIDENCY, WHOSE ONLY CRISES WERE late-afternoon thunderstorms that poured down on the concert tent and halted performances, the city of Minneapolis realized how much it owed to the Orchestra. SYMPHONY BOOSTS CITY BEFORE WORLD AT ASPEN, ran the headline.

held that July in the historic silver-mining town in the Colorado Rockies. Not yet the glamorous ski-celebrity-music festival scene of the 1950s and after, this was the place the best minds of the world were going in 1949. Across the three-week celebration, the Minneapolis Symphony, collaborating with guest artists like Arthur Rubinstein, Nathan Milstein, and Gregor Piatigorsky, performed for an international press and public. Reports were transmitted everywhere, even to cities like London and Cologne, where the Orchestra would appear in person nearly 50 years later.

Already three months before this Aspen high, *Tribune* columnist George Grim had reminded his readers: "World Knows About City, Thanks to the Symphony!" Having just returned from overseas, where people were hearing MSO recordings on the short-wave, Grim wrote: "It would be an eye-opener for many a Minneapolis—or Minnesota—booster to travel around our world, as I've been able to do, and see what we mean to a person in Madras, Paris, Rome, Prague, Hobart, Hong Kong, Athens, Copenhagen or where

have you. You'd soon discover that most notions about us are wildly off base, except where the Minneapolis Symphony is concerned. THAT, I've thanked heaven many a time, is known . . ."

Dimitri Mitropoulos departed to the New York Philharmonic, never to be heard here in person again. But the year 1949 marked the threshold of a boom time in the musical world. Just as the Minneapolis Symphony was gearing up to its 50th anniversary, yet another temperamental Hungarian came on the scene: Antal Dorati.

∾

Minneapolis, Minneapolis? Just where in the United States is Minneapolis?

—A woman in Bombay after cheering the
Minneapolis Symphony, 1957

Nobody was better at sniffing out an opportunity than Antal Dorati. Except for him, as the late Boris Sokoloff explained on a stroll through Philadelphia one day

Minneapolis Symphony Orchestra in London en route to the Middle East, 1957

Personal Memories

HENRY KRAMER, FORMER PRINCIPAL SECOND VIOLINIST who, approaching his 90th birthday, finished his unpublished memoirs, has written:

> For me, Athens was the triumph of the Near East tour, both musically and personally. The MSO had not played together since the end of the season in April but I think the spirit of our beloved "Maestro" [Mitropoulos, of course] was guiding us that first night in Athens. The sight of the marble columns shining high above . . . was enough to make us play like Apollo himself. Dorati was just the vehicle guiding us, and I cannot recall another time when playing in a symphony orchestra gave me such an utterly sublime, beautiful, and powerful impression. Perhaps this was the way Mitropoulos envisioned music in his mind as he conducted a symphony orchestra, for I felt lifted far above my earthly body.

(where this former MSO manager had gone to head The Philadelphia Orchestra), the Minneapolis Symphony might not have captured the Mercury recording contract that cemented its fame—a glow rekindled when these incomparable discs were reissued as CDs in the 1980s. Sokoloff explained how it all came to happen and spoke of cross-country and Western Canadian touring, encouraged by the recording company, even though costs were escalating at an alarming rate.

Above all, the Dorati epoch marked the 1957 tour of a lifetime: a four-week, 45,000-mile journey across the Middle East, with a preludial stop at the Athens Festival and a postlude in two cities of Yugoslavia—the only time the Orchestra played on European soil before 1998. This is the best-documented tour in our archives, though to examine the folders of correspondence that detail exasperating changes of plans and thorny obstacles—like getting Jewish musicians into Iraq—is to wonder why Sokoloff and the British management didn't throw up their hands in despair and simply trundle off to Texas one more time.

At a time of Cold War cultural exchanges, geared to promoting good will, the State Department offered invitations to several orchestras. To the MSO came the most challenging of all: the already troubled Middle East. ANTA, the American National Theater Academy, served as the sponsoring organization, but there was little time for the complex arrangements. As late as June 14, 1957—less than three months before departure—Boris Sokoloff told ANTA that a looming deficit here made it impossible to raise an extra $16,000 requested: "That is quite final, and I must necessarily ask you where that leaves us."

Plans proceeded even though snags turned up throughout the routing efforts: A trade fair at Damascus ruled out Syria, while the threat of terrorism eliminated Israel. At last came the memorable night: a concert at the 4,000-year-old Herodicus Atticus Theater in Athens, with a full moon rising as the musicians played their hearts out.

At the two Athens concerts, each attended by 3,000 listeners, audience members hugged Americans in the crowd to convey their excitement. The Orchestra also took the Beethoven *Eroica* and the rest of its opening program

Amateur Hour Antal Dorati, conductor of the roving Minneapolis Symphony, tries out a Pakistani sarangi, ancient stringed instrument, during a visit to musicians of Radio Pakistan. The orchestra played two concerts in

Antal Dorati tries out a "sarangi" in a Radio Pakistan studio.

38

to a less glamorous place, the American Farm School at Salonika. There the musicians slept in barracks on cots, but were grateful for fresh milk, rare on this trip.

Next stop: Baghdad, after crossing one of numerous mountain ranges in a non-pressurized aircraft cabin. Consider the bravado required for such a tour in the pre-jet age, when some of the players had never flown before. Runways were short, and flights were bumpy. As the Orchestra had been warned, the sterilized American stomach was at high risk; at one time a third of the players were ill. Fortunately, the management had engaged twenty additional musicians for the expedition, all from prestigious orchestras; five came on leave from the Metropolitan Opera. Baghdad's outdoor concert, third stop on the journey, was a low point. *Time* magazine quoted Principal Bass Ray W. Fitch, who said that the stop might have been "a pleasure except for the concert: Yelping dogs competed so successfully that at the concert's end Dorati fled from the podium in a huff, a case of dogs beat man."

At the Golestan Palace in Teheran, Shah Reza Palevi and his sister sat in the front row with the American ambassador, attentive to Henry Cowell's *Persian Set*, commissioned by the MSO for its premiere there. The Orchestra played on a special platform erected over a lily pond. Greeting Dorati at the end with his program book in hand, the Shah asked the ambassador for a pen. Reaching out for a pen with which to sign his own name, Dorati was flustered when he realized that it was the Shah who intended to do the autographing.

Karachi was another hit of the tour, featuring a Mozart, Beethoven, Bartók, Ravel program plus a rendition of Pakistan's national anthem orchestrated by librarian Herman Boessenroth. (When Dorati discovered that none of the host cities could provide more than piano renditions of their anthems, Boessenroth quickly produced resplendent orchestrations, which were taped for each government and authorized for re-use.) President Iskander Mirze was so moved by the Pakistani anthem that he asked Dorati to repeat it. The crowd rose to its feet. As Fitch was departing he heard an old Pakistani woman tell Dorati: "You have not brought guns or tanks or planes. You have brought genius. Please come again."

The evening stretched on as five members of the orchestra—names almost as well-known at home for jazz as for the Orchestra, including Elliot Fine on drums and Cliff Johnson on string bass—joined the band at Karachi's Hotel Metropole for a jam session. "For two hours, this capital city was the hottest jive center outside New Orleans," said Fitch. The next morning Karachi's radio station musicians introduced the travelers, including Dorati, to native music, featuring the lute-like sitar and various percussion instruments; they improvised endlessly in the changing rhythms of their native musical language. One can only conclude, Henry Kramer wrote in his diary, "that music is innate in human beings, reaching the same universal level wherever it is given a chance."

After Lahore, where musicians were entertained in small groups, the Orchestra advanced to Bombay. There the outdoor concert was the experience of a lifetime for its citizens. Many sat in branches of the surrounding trees. Although musicians in every section were contending with "Delhi belly," all "performed manfully," according to *Time* magazine's correspondent. Paris-styled Beirut offered both respite and a Mediterranean beach, where a couple of wind players drew all eyes when they turned up in bright purple boxer shorts, the only suitable swim clothes they could find.

The first day of October brought the Orchestra to Turkey, its final Muslim destination before the journey's coda in Yugoslavia. This first major symphony orchestra ever to perform in their country astounded the Turks. A Turkish official told the American ambassador, "There would be no problem of Turkish-American harmony if you would continue to bring groups like this." Another said, "One such concert is worth a hundred miles of highway."

Translations of the enthralled Turkish press covering two concerts in Ankara and three in Istanbul (where a shortage of hotel rooms forced the players to stay on a ship moored in the harbor) fill seventeen pages of single-spaced copy. In the *Yeni Istanbul* of October 6, 1957, Pertev Taner summed up the amazing tour: "To conquer hearts is more difficult than to conquer countries, and Dorati and the Orchestra he conducted won our hearts in a success that is never to be forgotten."

The Shah of Iran (center, in suit) at attention during the Orchestra's performance of the Iranian National Anthem

The elegant program book from the Orchestra's 1957 concert in Lahore

Minneapolis Symphony performs at Golestan Palace, Teheran, Iran, 1957.

The Orchestra in an outdoor performance at the Herodicus Atticus Theater in Athens, 1957

Language barriers, bacteria, bureaucracy, scary flights —if the Middle East odyssey seemed like the tour from hell, only recall that by the late 1950s the Minneapolis Symphony was full of what broadcaster Tom Brokaw has dubbed "our greatest generation." Not long before, many of these musicians had survived the Depression, and some had undergone such World War II experiences as fighting at the front, travelling in dangerous zones to play in military bands that entertained the troops, or even crewing on B47s.

On the return flight across the Atlantic, with 15,000 pounds of instruments and baggage inflated by souvenirs, KLM feted the weary musicians with a special "Minneapolis Symphony Orchestra Menu." At 5:10 p.m.

on October 9, 1957, their plane rolled up to the gate at Wold Chamberlin airport, where a civic reception cheered what *Newsweek* (September 21, 1957) had hailed as "this crack American orchestra."

∾

This 37-year-old Polish conductor is precisely what the doctor ordered to return the Minneapolis Symphony to the eminence it enjoyed a dozen years ago under Dimitri Mitropoulos. The Minneapolis musicians will benefit as much from Skrowaczewski's presence as he will from theirs.

—*Seattle Times*, October 17, 1960

When Stanislaw Skrowaczewski came on the scene as the Minneapolis Symphony's sixth music director at the start of a nineteen-year tenure, not only had he never conducted this Orchestra before, but he had never set foot in Minnesota. What is even more surprising is that he led his first concert not in the big city, but at the newly refurbished high school gymnasium up in fishermen's paradise, Brainerd, Minnesota. The next morning he and the 93 musicians set forth on a month-long tour cast in the venerable MSO tradition. "From the beginning, I liked to tour very much," says Skrowaczewski. "The first tour—Brainerd, then immediately off to the West—was so exciting for me. I was getting my first feeling for the Orchestra, and they were getting to know me. This was all very positive—full of hope as I began a new time in my life."

The Orchestra performed almost every night in a different city. In Eugene, Oregon, they presented four concerts in as many days for an audience of mostly university students, before proceeding to eleven dates in California. That year the Association also launched a ten-year, $5-million endowment drive in the newest effort to keep the Minneapolis Symphony Orchestra flourishing as a top-flight institution.

Like Mitropoulos, Skrowaczewski was known for his bold programming of the newest music. Probably no

A visit to a Montana copper mine on Skrowaczewski's first tour, in 1960: (from left) Ron Hasselmann (trumpet), Joseph Roche (violin), Robert Feit (violin), David Abel (violin soloist), Boris Sokoloff (general manager), Music Director Stanislaw Skrowaczewski, Fritz Scheurer (assistant principal bass), Norman Carol (concertmaster), and Rose Marie Baker (violin)

name was getting more attention in the world press than that of Krzysztof Penderecki, a strong new voice from Poland whose *St. Luke* Passion found a wide audience in the mid-1960s, earning him diverse commissions. The American premiere performances of the Passion took place in Minneapolis on November 2 and 3, 1967, just before the Orchestra was slated to introduce it at Carnegie Hall. Fate intervened when Skrowaczewski, suffering a detached retina, could not conduct. The New York premiere was postponed until March 1968, when, as part of a two-week eastern trek, the maestro at last brought Penderecki's sacred work to Carnegie, with four vocal soloists and three top-rate Minnesota choruses.

At the start of the 1968-69 season, the Minneapolis Symphony metamorphosed into the Minnesota Orchestra (a name change that had been broached in 1914, when the St. Paul Symphony Orchestra, after eight seasons, gave up the ghost). The Penderecki delay could hardly have been better timed, but it was only a first step in establishing the Orchestra's new name.

Music Director Skrowaczewski in front of Carnegie Hall

*Minnesota Orchestra at the United Nations,
December 10, 1968, Skrowaczewski on
podium far right*

The following season, yet within the same calendar year, another highly visible opportunity presented itself when the Orchestra was invited back to New York for the Human Rights Day celebration at the United Nations in December—a videotaped event featuring the premiere of Spanish composer Cristobal Halffter's cantata *Yes Speak Out Yes*, based on a text by Norman Corwin. Alas, this type of *pièce d'occasion* does not appeal to music critics; the stirring event drew less press coverage than anticipated. More disheartening, Peter Davis, in *The New York Times*

(December 12, 1968), got the name wrong: "Minnesota Symphony," he reported, one of many instances in which this Orchestra has been labeled by a confusing hybrid of its historic and new names.

Dust had scarcely coated the chandeliers at the Kennedy Center, Washington D.C.'s cultural showpiece on the Potomac, when the Minnesota Orchestra played in the new concert hall on April 21, 1972. A lively contingent of Orchestra supporters and fans went along, eager to hear their musicians in the shoe box-shaped environment prophetic of the Orchestra Hall about to be built in Minneapolis, and ready to celebrate with political notables in the Kennedy Center atrium afterwards.

Annals for the late 1960s and '70s record more regional events than for any other period. Categorized as Tour Series (at both Rochester and the Benedicta Fine Arts Center near St. Cloud), and Run-Out Concerts,

the touring of these days composed the Lake Wobegon circuit, so to speak, by which the Minnesota Orchestra was living up to its name in a big way. Add to this the outdoor Symphony for the Cities programs in the summertime, and the Orchestra was demonstrating its priority attachment to the community. Old-style touring was becoming a thing of the past. As Richard M. Cisek, who as chief administrative officer ushered the Orchestra through this period, explains:

No more trains from city to city, increasing—and expensive—travel by airplane, and new terms in the musicians' contract made it impossible to tour on the same scale as before. Regional touring represented a stop-gap period before Orchestra Hall was built. It gave us time to get through the political hurdles, mount a funding campaign, and carry out the archi-

Concert Tours: What the Audience Never Knew

THE MINNEAPOLIS SYMPHONY, KNOWN AS THE "ORCHESTRA ON WHEELS" during its early years, was commonly on the road for four or five weeks at a time, often touring more than once during a single season. My story of recognition, sacrifices, humor, and lasting friendships describes life as a member of a touring professional orchestra.

The Orchestra played most of its concerts in small towns, and the musicians were housed in motels that ranged in quality from A (the best) to B and C (lower-grade accommodations). The first-chair players and senior members of the Orchestra stayed in the A motels, while the section players and newer members were relegated to B and C. Sending mail to touring musicians was difficult during this period, as motel assignments were not posted until our arrival in a town. To counter this obstacle, I volunteered to be Postmaster (no one else wanted the job), with the duty of retrieving the mail at General Delivery and distributing it to the members. For this honor I received a bonus of ten dollars a week and free taxi rides to and from the center of town to pick up the mail. This helped my popularity with fellow musicians, who tagged along for the free rides.

During the 1960s when we were traveling by train, with our own separate sleeping cars, the train would pull into a station, the Orchestra cars would be disconnected and placed on a siding off the main track, and the rest of the train would continue on its regularly scheduled run. On a typical day we walked around town, saw a movie, or played basketball at the local YMCA. After dinner we played the concert and retreated to our train cars, where we played cards or just relaxed. Sometime during the night another train would pull into the station, hitch up our cars and travel to the next town, where the procedure would be repeated day after day until we reached the West Coast.

In later years, we traveled by train but stayed in hotels. This created a new set of difficulties, for after we exited the train in a new town, we had to find the means of getting to our hotel on our own, as the Orchestra did not furnish buses. Our per diem allowance was eleven dollars a day, out of which we had to pay for meals, hotel fees, and taxis. We had to decide whether to walk the one or two miles to the hotel, carrying our suitcases and instruments—in order to save our per diem— or wait with 100 other people for one of the few taxis.

For the evening concerts our tour manager would charter one city bus for the entire Orchestra to ride to the concert. He would stand outside the bus with a coin changer and charge us 25 cents for the privilege of being jammed into a bus among 100 people. I remember on one occasion standing by the back door of the bus with my face crushed up against the glass so tightly that the door could not be opened until everyone in front moved off the bus.

Our tour manager seemed to improvise some of our travel arrangements. Occasionally I saw him studying train schedules during our concerts. Once, after a concert, we boarded buses, drove for an hour, and disembarked on a lonely road that crossed a railroad line. We waited for 45 minutes in the dark, standing along a single track; a train stopped, we boarded, and we traveled to the next town . . .

We endured many harrowing experiences throughout the years, from blizzards and landslides to flooded bridges and automobile accidents. Somehow we rarely missed a concert.

—*From the memoirs of Ron Hasselmann, retired associate principal trumpet player and associate personnel manager*

tectural process for the downtown facility we needed. Fortunately, foundation grants supported our regional efforts, but these typically were provided on a diminishing basis over a three-to-five-year period, with the most funding at the start. When the Hall at last opened in 1974, we were able to accommodate the long orchestra season by expanding the subscription events to 24 weeks and offer Summer Pops, the Rug Concerts, and eventually Viennese Sommerfest.

Former Associate and Resident Conductor Henry Charles Smith (who merits accolades for serving as a respected voice in the effort to stem the erosion of music education in the schools) remembers those days of traveling the local roads and interstates, establishing connections with the State that would be the envy of other orchestras. Smith reports:

> Between 1968 and the opening of Orchestra Hall six years later, we would often be packing up the Orchestra van and heading out in buses to towns all over the state, living up to our name as the Minnesota Orchestra. I conducted in places like Annandale and Worthington, or towns "Up North," as we like to say. Often I would repeat the very programs that Skrowaczewski had presented at subscription concerts the week before. We drove out, so to speak, but when Orchestra Hall opened in 1974, they drove in—people wanted to come to the new Hall, and so the regional concept continued to fade.

National touring was never entirely abandoned. Out in Ohio, young Richard Marshall (later co-principal violist) heard the Minnesota Orchestra on tour in Columbus, performing the Rachmaninoff Symphony No. 2, a longtime tour staple: "Little did I know," he says, "that it was to be the first piece I would play with the Orchestra when I won my job as violist with it in 1984." Carnegie Hall remained the coveted site for every major orchestra. New York critics, weary of all the orchestra visitors, long ago had pondered why these institutions insisted upon crowding the schedule with their appearances. The answer is the same now as it was then, as Skrowaczewski has explained:

> I always fought for an annual tour to Carnegie, even though the board's executive committee questioned

that—and I especially argued the case after the change of name. It was important also that our players be challenged by performing in the same place where all the great orchestras of the world appear. Not everyone on the board understood this, which is why I liked to have them come to concerts at Carnegie or Kennedy Center.

"The heyday of touring is probably past. But it's still important on an international level, for audiences abroad get an idea of what the total picture of American life is."

—Leonard Slatkin, 2001

After a fifteen-year gap, the Orchestra at last made a foray outside the United States—this with the generous support of the late Northeast Minneapolis banker Walter C. Rasmussen. Marking its 70th anniversary in 1972-1973, the ensemble set out for Mexico in midwinter.

Because the name "Minnesota Orchestra" had not yet registered in the public mind, only a minuscule audience came to Mexico City's Bellas Artes hall on February 26, 1972 for the first of the Orchestra's four concerts. Abundant and favorable press was triggered by the stunning concert, at which the players gave Skrowaczewski every ounce of their musicianship, as if to compensate for the disappointing house. Nearly every Mexican critic said something like this: "If only the music lovers of Mexico City had known that it was the famous Minneapolis Symphony Orchestra performing at Bellas Artes last night!" In Mexico City, frequently a destination for touring university ensembles bearing state identities, the concertgoing public had confused the Orchestra with non-professional visitors and stayed away in droves.

Seldom afterwards in the twentieth century would the name "Minnesota Orchestra" fail to appear without an identifying tag, "Founded in 1903 as the Minneapolis Symphony Orchestra." Both names appeared together on the cover of a photo history circulated as a press book for the three foreign tours of the late 1990s.

The Orchestra Hall loading dock: Only a capacious vehicle can hold the one hundred-plus trunks with which the Orchestra tours.

If you're top-notch, you want to show yourself off to the world! There is the feeling that we're all pulling together—that we're there not only to play our best but to be ambassadors.

—Bassoonist Norbert Nielubowski, chairman of the Minnesota Orchestra Members Committee

Londoner Neville Marriner took charge of the Minnesota Orchestra podium in 1979 as the most recorded conductor in the world. His recognition soared when, two years later, he served as music director and conductor for the film version of Peter Shaffer's *Amadeus*, a smash hit everywhere. He came to this most toured of American orchestras as one of the touringest of all conductors. Founder of the Academy of St Martin's-in-the-Fields, he had behind him twenty years of traveling with his famous chamber orchestra. No one could better empathize with the musicians' frustration as they had watched the erosion of major touring.

"The importance of touring for an orchestra is really just to remind yourself what your current standard is," Sir Neville says. "Touring provides an atmosphere that certainly gives an edge to the performances. Touring around the world has also been one way of propagating your gramophone recordings, which is of immense value to the recording company and to the orchestra."

By this time, Orchestra touring had become a drain on the budget, and was replaced mostly by "run-outs" and short regional jaunts. Expansion to the year-round season, and the more equitable salaries at last won by the musicians, contributed to skyrocketing costs. Touring was less viable. Moreover, the proliferation of regional orchestras following World War II had changed the market. Like recordings before the advent of the compact disc, orchestra tour schedules were contracting, except for a handful of mega-budget groups dispatched to Europe and such destinations as China and Latin America.

In the background were persistent doubts about the name, even among the newest and youngest members of the Orchestra. The globe-savvy Marriner, with the grit of a Yorkshireman in his veins, lost no time in confronting the issue, which all had hoped would go away. At his urging, the MOA board formed a blue ribbon committee to examine both sides of the twelve-year-old controversy. Pros and cons of the new name were debated at a final committee meeting. Decision: to retain Minnesota Orchestra. Another change might only compound the perceived difficulties.

President Jimmy Carter greets the Minnesota Orchestra at the White House: Vice President Walter F. Mondale (next to the President), conductor Robert Shaw with his young son, Joan A. Mondale, Concertmaster Lea Foli, and Principal Viola Clyn Dee Barrus.

Smooth Moves

Except for one year of Army service, Minnesota Orchestra Stage Manager Timothy Eickholt has worked in his profession since the age of fifteen. During his studies at the University of Minnesota, Eickholt continued to accept stage calls part time. Working full time for the Orchestra since 1968, he was named stage manager in 1993, following Sam Grodnik, Art Randell, and Bob Gubbins as only the fourth person to hold the position in the first century. Eickholt has played an invaluable role in ensuring smooth touring operations for this well-traveled Orchestra.

"I heard my first Orchestra concert in the mid 1950s at Northrop Auditorium. Music Director Antal Dorati conducted Young People's Concerts then, and the Orchestra played *Boléro*. I was mesmerized. In high school I worked part time as a professional stage hand. My favorite place was Northrop Auditorium—I loved working for the Minneapolis Symphony. I also worked for the Metropolitan Opera at Northrop from 1962 until 1985—one intense, exhausting, thrilling week each May. The Met stage hands—the best in the world—taught me how to think, plan ahead, move onstage, how to organize a stage and backstage to insure a smooth performance, how to get along with people. In the mid 1990s I read a study of American venues that named Avery Fisher Hall at Lincoln Center as the busiest and Orchestra Hall, Minneapolis, as second busiest in the country. It is not unusual to have two or three—sometimes four—completely different events on the same day. We have a great crew at Orchestra Hall: Terry Tilley, Dave McKoskey, and Gail Reich—to my knowledge, the first woman stage manager in a major symphony orchestra. (It's important to have a woman on the stage crew. After all, 30 percent of the Orchestra musicians are women.) My crew and I treat all people alike and with respect, whether we're dealing with a youth orchestra or with the Berlin Philharmonic. This profession takes patience, good humor, flexibility, and level-headedness. We have to be sensitive to the pressures that performers experience back stage and onstage.

"How lucky I am to be the stage manager of this grand old Orchestra."

—*Timothy Eickholt*

Musicians Bruce Rardin, Kendall Betts, and Ross Tolbert on a 1985 tour with Music Director Sir Neville Marriner that took the Orchestra to Melbourne, Australia

Despite visits to Carnegie Hall and public radio broadcasts that took the sound of the Orchestra across the nation (and still does), something was missing: foreign touring. Now, as then, Marriner insists that "touring should go on, as a yardstick for the players," but adds realistically, "*if* economically viable."

Marriner came up with a plan: Why not test the Orchestra's touring skills in some distant place like Australia? For its first international tour in nearly 30 years, Marriner in the spring of 1985 could not have taken his Orchestra to a more receptive place—the Commonwealth's "Down Under" outpost. Our conductor was well known by music-loving Aussies.

The journey was arduous. These travelers—many of whom had not been outside the United States before—landed in Sydney after the long flight via Honolulu, only immediately to board a plane for Melbourne, first stop on an eight-concert, five-city tour. Joining the Orchestra were two young artists on the threshold of major careers: violinist Cho-Liang Lin, known to all as Jimmy, and pianist Cecile Licad.

Producer-writer Jason Davis of KSTP/Channel 5 Television went along to produce an extraordinary musical travelogue chronicling the Minnesota Orchestra's pilgrimage to the beautiful continent and its welcoming people. Davis's hour-long narrative is one of the

Minnesota Orchestra with piano soloist Yefim Bronfman and Music Director Sir Neville Marriner at the 1986 Hong Kong Arts Festival

In 1986, Associate Concertmaster Roger Frisch worked with a violin student in Hong Kong.

treasures of the Orchestra's substantial video archive. The Australian Broadcasting Company aired three of the concerts.

Going to Australia was like a honeymoon after years of searching for a spouse. Luckily for the travelers, "the people spoke almost the same language," says librarian Eric Sjostrom. "What a great place Australia was—and still is. The people, only fifteen million back in 1985, love music. We were told that while they had a handful of quite good orchestras in Australia, the quality of the Minnesota Orchestra was superior. All the musicians were excited: The adrenaline to play was very high."

Next came an invitation to the spectacular British colony of Hong Kong, where Marriner was a celebrity. With the cooperation and generosity of Minnesota companies doing business in Asia, the proposed residency at the 1986 Hong Kong Arts Festival proved economically feasible.

Sprung from the North American continent for a second consecutive year, the musicians had a splendid time adventuring and performing. The *Hong Kong Standard* reported that the Minnesota Orchestra "lived up to its billing as one of North America's finest" and "did not disappoint the packed house" on opening night, the first of five concerts. Along with the lustrous cello playing of Miklós Perényi, the Orchestra brought the fireworks of a Russian program with pianist Yefim Bronfman playing the Prokofiev Piano Concerto No. 3—a sensational performance prophetic of the young Israeli's impact years later when he joined the Minnesota Orchestra on its European debut tour.

One thing became apparent, as I went along for Minnesota Public Radio to tape adventures with musicians in exotic street markets, apothecary shops, and mahjongg parlors, and interviewed members of the audience at intermissions: No one had ever heard of the Minnesota Orchestra, nor could anyone articulate an image of Minnesota, only guessing that it was a cold place, yet good for agriculture.

Three months later, the Orchestra was set to go again, this time to the Festival Casals in Puerto Rico—a third jaunt outside the U.S. in just thirteen months. Players were warned that the tropical sun in June would be their biggest hazard, especially since accommodations were on the Caribe Hilton's golden shore, where guest conductor David Zinman and Conductor Laureate Stanislaw Skrowaczewski were among the avid beachcombers. Zinman led two colorful programs featuring works that had been favorites with audiences everywhere since the Oberhoffer days, including Dvořák's *New World* Symphony. Skrowaczewski crowned the Festival with Mahler's Symphony No. 2, joined by the University of Maryland Chorus and soloists Phyllis Bryn-Julson and Florence Quivar.

On an island where everybody assures you "No problem" no matter how dire the situation, the Orchestra management handled everything capably, especially since they'd been forewarned that a little tip makes all the difference. The players, eager to repay Medtronic's generosity as a sponsor, presented a special chamber music event at the company's Humacao plant. Meanwhile, other musicians conducted master classes, as they often have done on domestic tours. Music was made every day, despite a telling archival receipt: a purchase order for $200.33 worth of "Nature's Glow Sunblock Lotion."

In the three long-distance journeys of Marriner days, compressed into two seasons, the musicians developed a spirit of touring and were raring to do more. Europe, however, remained elusive. A dozen years would pass before the musicians were asked to update their passports.

Principal Trumpet Manuel Laureano in session with student musicians in Puerto Rico, June, 1986

This orchestra is in terrific condition.

—Richard Dyer in the *Boston Globe*, following a Tanglewood appearance under David Zinman on July 9, 1994

Edo de Waart entered the scene known as an orchestra-builder. Behind him were nine seasons as music director of the San Francisco Symphony (1977-1986, plus two preceding years as principal guest conductor) and an international reputation as an opera conductor. At age 45, the Dutch conductor brought a wealth of experience to this Orchestra. As a disciplinarian he did not aim for popularity.

Like his predecessors from Dorati on, de Waart knew the value of foreign touring for a major American orchestra. In a recent conversation, he ruminated:

> Touring is great. Orchestras like the Berlin Philharmonic and the Concertgebouw tour a lot, and have always toured a lot historically. It generates the feeling, "At eight o'clock we need to be at our best." You feel that at home, of course, but when you're in strange situations you have to depend even more on each other, and the need to be an ensemble is magnified. That sense of relying on each other—that faith in each other's craftsmanship and willingness—is very important, and it happens on tour.

Why then didn't de Waart push for international touring? His first priority, he says, was orchestra-building. He wasn't ready to take them to Europe. And when finally he was, the times were wrong. Deficits threatened, as costs were escalating beyond the worst expectations.

When it came to going on the road, however, de Waart was no slouch. Midway through his first season, he led the Orchestra to Florida before swinging up the coast to Washington, D.C. There the Washington *Post* reported that Mahler's Fifth Symphony under de Waart was "a rendition rich in lyricism and marked by glowing string sections"—a compliment prophetic of the rave press this Orchestra's strings would elicit all over Europe and Japan ten years later.

The following year, on Carnegie Hall's Great American Orchestras series, the Orchestra performed

Sommerfest Artistic Director David Zinman conducted the Orchestra in its Tanglewood debut in 1994.

Since its debut there in 1912, the Orchestra has performed at Carnegie Hall 43 times, including this concert on January 19, 1995, with Music Director Edo de Waart.

with the stellar soprano of the day, Kathleen Battle. Like Skrowaczewski and Marriner, de Waart fought the case for Carnegie appearances and sometimes brought big (read: costly) works, like Janáček's brassy Sinfonietta, which required lots of extra players, and a concert performance of Verdi's *Falstaff* featured at Carnegie's 100th anniversary celebration in 1990.

The span of these latter-day domestic tours was short, often touching only four or five cities. Meanwhile, the St. Cloud and Rochester series continued to be valued state outposts until Rochester, hampered by its hall, plus the

willingness of its music lovers to drive to the Twin Cities, finally gave up. A touring association forged in 1909 ended after the 1991-92 season.

In the same year that run-outs to Mayo Clinic territory ended, the Orchestra had plans for a third trip across the Pacific. Japan was the destination, but upon the sudden outbreak of the Gulf War, the tour was cancelled. Instead, the Orchestra substituted a festival dedicated to "The Power of Music—Celebrating the Human Spirit"—seven concerts spanning two weeks. Japan would have to wait for the Eiji Oue era.

Retired Stage Manager Bob Gubbins and Assistant Stage Manager Gail Reich on the Orchestra's tour of Europe, November 2000.

Gubbins was the stage manager for earlier international tours—the 1957 tour of the Middle East, for example—and countless domestic tours that took the Orchestra throughout the United States and into Canada, to university auditoriums, and to Carnegie Hall. Gubbins's successor, Tim Eickholt, with Orchestra Operations Manager Beth Kellar-Long and their staffs, took over the complex logistics of planning and executing the Orchestra's traveling schedules and they carried out the century-end tours of Europe and Japan.

∾

What was the mood of the Orchestra at the start? They were focused, really focused, though maybe some players were a bit nervous. I was relaxed, and didn't feel any tension. Here was London, and we were playing the Barbican. But no more than five minutes into the program, the Barber Symphony, they seemed to feel truly at home. This was not only the first concert of our European tour, but one of the best.

—Eiji Oue

In the booming dot-com 1990s, the time for Europe was ripe. "The Campaign for the Minnesota Orchestra," an extraordinary fundraising success, chaired by Douglas W. Leatherdale (later, chairman of the board) and led by Mary Ellen Kuhi (vice president for development), came in over goal in less than five years. Recordings under Eiji Oue on the Reference label were winning accolades everywhere. Nobody could restrain the passion to introduce Europeans to the Minnesota Orchestra in person. President David J. Hyslop accepted the mandate. Hyslop, who had trained here in orchestra management under Cisek three decades earlier, was highly experienced in touring. He had returned to Minnesota after serving as executive director of the Saint Louis Symphony in its 1980s heyday under Music Director Leonard Slatkin, when that orchestra was riding the crest of its fame on several foreign tours. Minnesota Orchestra Vice President and General Manager Robert R. Neu also had requisite experience, having arranged tours of the Cincinnati Symphony Orchestra. Costs would be high, but these managers—with input from an affirming board—knew how to pull it off.

The money was there, the staff was confident, and the musicians consistently were playing in top form. Moreover, technology-savvy Karl Reichert, director of

public affairs, devised the best of all possible ways for a touring Orchestra to relate to its own community. He and the Orchestra's education staff exploited the relatively new World Wide Web as a tool for involving the folks back at home in the daily excitement of the Orchestra's next expedition, a tour of Europe in 1998.

Everybody could be "On Tour with the Minnesota Orchestra," as the project was labeled. The staff prepared to expedite daily reports, and the touring musicians participated by responding to questions submitted by school children from all over the state. A new generation, raised on the computer, connected with a great symphony orchestra, learning about music, geography, history, and more. The "Virtual Tour" received up to 10,000 hits per day as people of all ages logged on to participate in this historic journey.

The musicians were raring to go. Suspense built, until at last came the thrilling moment when the Orchestra filled the stage at London's Barbican Centre to show the near-capacity house and well-primed British press what it could do. The Minnesota Orchestra, featured on an Inventing America series, unfolded the lyricism of Samuel Barber's Symphony No. 1 and offered a work commissioned especially for the tour, *Reflections on a Hymn Tune* by Dominick Argento, the Orchestra's Pulitzer Prize-winning composer laureate. Following the expressive union of guest artists Gil Shaham and Nobuko Imai in Mozart's Sinfonia Concertante for violin and viola, Oue and the musicians left a powerful impression with Bartók's Concerto for Orchestra, a showpiece connected with the Orchestra since the Middle East tour. Strings that surged forward "with a brash glamour more reminiscent of Hollywood than chillier Minnesota" impressed *The Financial Times*'s Richard Fairman.

From that night of February 19, 1998 onwards, the tour proceeded without a hitch. Three double basses damaged in overseas transport had been repaired in time for the concert, returned by the expert London instrument maker in even better shape than before, said their owners. The double bass scare had been traumatic for Stage Manager Timothy Eickholt and his predecessor, the long-experienced Bob Gubbins, out of retirement to assist with the toughest part of touring—getting millions of dollars of equipment from place to place and

Minnesota Orchestra onstage
at Leeds Town Hall with
Music Director Eiji Oue

51

My memory of touring with the Minnesota Orchestra in 1998 is wonderful. It was their first tour of Europe, and it was simply amazing to me that an orchestra of their caliber, already 95 years old, was visiting Europe for the first time. This was really incredible! Everywhere the audiences were so enthusiastic, the receptions so glamorous, and the critics always raving. Above all I will remember the excitement of the players that helped make it such a success.

—Pianist Yefim Bronfman

setting up almost daily in unfamiliar halls. Speculating that a dropped palette had caused the damage, Eickholt devised a system of even thicker special foam padding for future trips.

After an enthusiastic reception in Nottingham, a picturesque city bordered by Robin Hood's Sherwood Forest, the Orchestra headed north to play in Birmingham's Symphony Hall, acclaimed as one of the best modern halls in Europe, acoustically resonant and architecturally spectacular. "This excellent American orchestra made the most of Samuel Barber's first symphony," reported Norman Stinchcombe in the *Evening Mail*.

But the most stirring moment of this British Isles debut occurred at the tour's northernmost point, the city of Leeds, where the Minnesota Orchestra became the first American orchestra ever to appear in Leeds Town Hall, an imposing 1857 relic of the Victorian age. The capacity audience in this university hub was not only youthful, but as intent on listening as the riveted public encountered in Japan later that year. Hundreds sat on the steep steps encircling the Orchestra, some only a foot or two behind the brass and woodwinds. In the set-up, every single piece had to be carried up the sloping makeshift stage. David Denton, in the *Yorkshire Post*, commented:

> They are an extremely fine ensemble with a brass department of refined quality, soft-grained woodwind, and a string section who produce such a weight of tone that, even in the Town Hall's lopsided acoustics, they never became swamped.

What he neglected to report was the memorable response to an encore, the "Nimrod" movement from Elgar's *Enigma Variations*. Emblematic of England, these strains had been heard at the funeral of Princess Diana not long before. A prolonged hush sealed the fading cadence, whereupon these Brits unleashed their cheers in as heartfelt an ovation as any orchestra could earn. "Playing 'Nimrod' there was a challenge," says Eiji Oue, "for everybody knows that melody. It was like a European orchestra going to New York and playing a Gershwin piece."

Following Sunday afternoon in Reading, it was off to Paris, where the reviewer for *Le Monde de la Musique*

Principal Flute Adam Kuenzel, Assistant Principal Second Violin Julie Ayer, violinist Carl Nashan, and violinist Celine Leathead in Europe, February 1998

noted that our Orchestra, "formerly the Minneapolis Symphony," was known exclusively for recordings under the batons of Mitropoulos, Dorati, or Skrowaczewski. "Its homogeneity, its flexibility, its fullness of sound class it among the ten best American orchestras."

In Robert Schumann's Rhineland city of Düsseldorf,

review: "Where passages could be threatened to slide into banality, Oue gave them refreshing emotions. He performed the Largo's rhythmical atmosphere so well rounded that it seemed as if no other interpretation is valid for the moment."

A throng of concertgoers accustomed to hearing the world's best orchestras in Cologne's magnificent new hall came out with a detectable "show-me" attitude. This American Orchestra, whose chairs had once been filled by German immigrants, seduced the public, and subsequent concerts in Frankfurt, Stuttgart, and Mannheim triggered equal enthusiasm. Cologne could scarcely wait to re-engage the Minnesota Orchestra. In the prestigious columns of *Die Welt*, Detlof Gojowy summed up the impression: "a highly sensitive orchestra . . . colorful precision in the winds, and as soloists they gained special applause. But above all: the orchestra was able to handle a huge excitement in their performance and transferred it to the audience spontaneously."

The journey's surprise was the twelfth stop on the thirteen-city tour, Llubljana, Slovenia—a beautiful city graced by Baroque and Art Nouveau architecture that had survived the Iron Curtain era intact and now was thriving. All agreed that the Llubljana audience, like the place itself, was the most enchanting of the trip. In its chief daily, *Dnevnik*, Peter Kušar mirrored the compliment: "I have never heard a better orchestra than the Minnesota Orchestra and there cannot be any better, just different. And even then I am not completely certain that of all those superb, yet different orchestras, I would not still prefer the Minnesota Orchestra."

Buoyed by this boost to self-esteem, the Minnesotans re-crossed the Alps to the Mecca of the orchestral world: Vienna's hallowed Musikverein, which, says General Manager Robert Neu, is like Carnegie used to be backstage, before they renovated—"the horrible load-in, load-out, and there's no room backstage, nor much onstage, but nobody cares. Just to go there and say, 'Mahler stood right here where I'm standing'—that's incredible." Nearly every seat was filled for the tour's grand finale on March 4, 1998. Hard-to-impress Vienna came out in full force. Adrenaline was pumping as the Orchestra concluded its virtuoso program with Tchaikovsky's Fifth Symphony. Hugs, smiles, and tears of joy prevailed among musicians

the *Neue Rheinische Zeitung* hailed Yefim Bronfman as the conquering lion of the keyboard and praised the Shostakovich Fifth Symphony under Oue, who earned many laurels in Germany, capped by an appointment later that year as chief conductor of the Hanover Radio Orchestra. Patrick Starbatty concluded his Cologne

Tour poster, Japan 1998

The Orchestra's 1998 Japan Tour included this performance with Music Director Eiji Oue at Tokyo's Suntory Hall.

and supporters who had flown in for the supercharged event. "This is the happiest night of my life," remarked a notable patron.

The Minnesota Orchestra had accomplished its mission, returning with press enough to fill a 100-page booklet. Europeans who paid attention now knew that one of America's greatest symphony orchestras can be found up north in the state of a thousand wolves—and of only one Minnesota Orchestra.

༆

It has been a joy for the Minnesota Orchestra to experience the honesty, friendliness, and warmth of the Japanese people. May each of you get a chance to visit Japan during your life!

—Violinist Pamela Shaffer
to school children on the Internet

Bulls continued to outpace bears as an escalating economy ushered the century to its close. Another foreign tour in 1998 was on the planning boards: Japan, to which Robert Neu and his operations crew, along with two musician representatives, had already made an advance trip to scrutinize the travel details and forge links with host concert halls. As luck would have it, the sponsor was Kajimoto Concert Management, whose clockwork efficiency guaranteed a hassle-free experience.

What no one counted on was a Northwest Airlines strike just days before departure. Last-minute booking for an entourage of well over a hundred (family members, even small children, often go along on modern-day tours) is no easy matter. But Northwest management saved the day when they found seats on Brazil's Vasp Airlines, one of the oldest in the world. The Orchestra connected with Vasp in Los Angeles after flying a Champion Airlines charter from home. Everyone trusted to fate that the NWA strike would be over by the time of the Orchestra's return at the end of September. Once again, the tour's single glitch had struck at the start. From then on the trip went smoothly, despite wind-driven downpours of the monsoon season.

Fortuitous though it was to have Eiji Oue as the Orchestra's conductor, no one assumed that success in Japan was a given. He was not yet well known there, for he had not lived in his native country since first coming to the U.S. in 1978. A decade before, when he had suddenly conducted in Tokyo as a substitute for the ailing Leonard Bernstein, the Japanese were disappointed to find on the podium an unknown conductor instead of the musical hero they had paid many yen to see. Some demanded a refund. Returning now at the head of a famous American orchestra, Oue would have his day at Tokyo's Suntory Hall, offering some of the same works that had been programmed at the near-fiasco concert of the past.

After landing along the Sea of Japan, just outside Osaka, the September 17-28 excursion comprising nine cities/ten concerts (two in Tokyo) started by riding a bullet train that sped past villages of blue-tiled roofs all the way to Tottori, famous for its sand dunes. The Orchestra appreciated Tottori both for its welcoming audience and its sushi bars.

Then came the city that had arisen from the ashes of World War II: lovely Hiroshima, Oue's hometown. The mayor hosted a formal daytime reception that featured an exchange of gifts, with media on hand to capture the return of the native son. Later that afternoon, Oue led a solemn entourage of musicians, staff, and accompanying patrons along a tranquil path to ground zero—the very spot where thousands of Japanese had been incinerated by the atomic bomb of August 6, 1945. All stood by in silence as he placed a wreath on the monument—one of the trip's most emotional episodes.

Only hours later Oue conducted the Orchestra's performances of Symphonic Dances from *West Side Story* and Mahler's Symphony No. 5 before the most vested crowd of all: family, friends, and a hometown audience curious to see if he'd live up to expectations. That he did was confirmed by applause stretching across a half hour, after which concertgoers formed long lines to purchase Orchestra CDs.

At Ibaraki on Sunday afternoon, September 20, the Orchestra played a concert celebrating the 50th anniversary of the founding of this sister city of Minneapolis. Mayor Sharon Sayles Belton came for the occasion, which culminated in a feast for the entire Orchestra and audience. But the most satisfying stop for the musicians was an engagement at Nagoya's Aichi Prefectural Art Center Concert Hall. At rehearsal, Concertmaster Jorja Fleezanis expressed her delight in the acoustics of the 1,786-seat hall, one of the best in Japan. Later the big audience, comprising all ages, responded to the performances with hearty ovations.

Sprawling Tokyo intimidated no one, but all were grateful for calming stops afterwards in two serene northern cities. With a pair of Suntory Hall dates, Oue was able to display in Tokyo the entire tour repertoire—works of Mozart, Beethoven, and Stravinsky, along with Bernstein and Mahler. A top-notch local video crew assisted in recording segments of these memorable concerts. Thanks to the Virtual Tour, Minnesotans were once again following along on the World Wide Web.

The press was as enthusiastic as the public. On the Internet's *Classic News*, Minoru Okamoto noted that "Oue brought to life the magnificent sound of the Minnesota Orchestra." For the record, the strike was settled, and NWA flew the wanderers back home. Thus, in a single calendar year, the Orchestra debuted on two foreign continents—fulfillment of decades of wishing.

The kids thought it was great! Thank you for all your work in bringing the Minnesota Orchestra closer to our schools and students.

—Faribault teacher Shirley Burkhartzmeyer, responding to the Virtual Tour of 2000

A little more than ten months into the new millennium, the Minnesota Orchestra undertook a second trip to Europe. The four-country, ten-city return was identified as The Jules Ebin Memorial Tour, named for an avid concertgoer whose closest friend contributed a substantial portion of the costs. Once again students were

included in the world of classical music via the Internet's Virtual Tour.

With a repertoire of a dozen works, and encores to meet the high demand everywhere, the Orchestra set out via London and returned to chief cities of the 1998 tour before making its debut at Berlin's Philharmonie. Following a flight to play for an appreciative audience at Friedrichshafen, on the shores of Lake Constance, the Orchestra made its repeat foray to Vienna, this time for a pair of concerts on November 8 and 9, 2000. The *Neue Kronen Zeitung* had this to say: "At the end came Beethoven's Fifth: luscious, emotionally passionate, with gleamingly polished sound. Great cheering."

The year 2000 marked a double debut in Spain, first in Barcelona's glittering Palau de la Musica Catalana, whose colorful tiled walls and tinted windows afford a striking concert site. Next day the Orchestra moved along to the capital city for its final tour concert. In typical Madrileño style, the concert did not begin until after midnight. That timing would have made this the only event in the Orchestra chronicle that spanned two days, were it not for a 1918 concert in Logan, Utah: Delayed by a train collision in eastern Nevada, but walking away from the crash unscathed, the Minneapolis Symphony had begun the Utah concert, too, close upon midnight. But the music-starved Westerners waited for them—a reminder that across its long touring history, the Minnesota Orchestra—once the peripatetic Minneapolis Symphony—has done more than any other comparable organization to light the fire for the orchestral sound in America. It took up the mantle of Thomas, and has carried on the challenge.

Reflecting on the Orchestra's recent tours, Association President David J. Hyslop has this to say: "Until orchestra musicians perform in the musical capitals of Europe, they feel that they are pretenders, not contenders, in the world musical tournament. You can be one of the finest orchestras in the world, but you need to be judged in places like London, Berlin, Vienna, and Tokyo. Foreign touring is the price of doing business at the top level, and it puts you in line to engage the greatest conductors and guest artists. Tours are reputation-building. Music is an international language, and an orchestra has to be heard on the world stages."

Assistant Conductor Scott Terrell and percussionist Kevin Watkins in Europe, 2000

∽

One of the world's finest symphony orchestras is at your doorstep. Open the door and let their music in.

—*Minnesota Daily*, encouraging students to buy tickets

In April of its centennial season, this renowned "Orchestra on Wheels and Wings" will reprise its long practice of bringing symphonic music to towns around the state: Pipestone, Monticello, Perham, Bemidji, Grand Rapids, and Moorhead—this last the very city visited on the debut tour of 1907, to which it returned 49 times more. Meanwhile, plans for further international tours are under way.

Numbers reveal a lot: The Minnesota Orchestra has played more than 4,200 documented concerts outside its home base. Some took place in communities as small as Florence, Alabama (1912), Moose Jaw, Saskatchewan (1950), and Nacogdoches, Texas (1964). College and university towns repeatedly brought the Minnesotans to their campuses: For instance, 84 concerts at the University of Wisconsin (Madison) and 76 at the University of Iowa (Iowa City) enriched the lives of young people who would form the nucleus of future audiences and support. And for a long time, cities like Birmingham and New Orleans in the South, and Winnipeg in the North, regularly welcomed the Orchestra, which offered the brightest moments on their musical calendars.

Add to these the big venues—armories, arenas, and concert halls on four continents, with 43 Carnegie Hall dates and nearly as many large cities—and it is safe to say that this Orchestra on tour has played for more than five million people.

Touring from its fourth season, first broadcasting to all corners of the country in its twentieth, and releasing a stream of recordings along the way, the Minnesota Orchestra—once upon a time the Minneapolis Symphony—has won fame for itself and a luminous place in the American musical chronicle. Visionary leaders and gifted musicians have helped assure that in this musical nation the Orchestra ranks with the best. The touring that holds an illustrious place in its history has an assured role in its future.

Concertmaster Jorja Fleezanis in Vienna's Musikverein, November 2000

They are very interesting, these large American orchestras. Here are artists of all nationalities and races, sitting peacefully one besides the other and still playing with such a perfect harmoniousness. One unconsciously starts to wonder: What is possible in music, why should it be impossible anywhere else?

—Newspaper of *Radio Zagreb*,
following the Orchestra's 1957 Middle East tour

Musical Values—A Community's Pride

Elbert L. Carpenter, a founder of the Minneapolis Symphony Orchestra and chairman for 40 years

PAMELA HILL NETTLETON

Pamela Hill Nettleton is editorial director of Minnesota Monthly *magazine. Her work has appeared in* Redbook, Sports Illustrated for Kids, *and other magazines. She is author of* Getting Married When It's Not Your First Time *(HarperCollins) and librettist of* The Underwear Opera. *Three of her Young People's Concert scripts have received Minnesota Orchestra premieres:* Nutcracker: The Untold Story *(winner of both the Parents' Choice Gold Medal and a Gold Parenting Publication Award),* Shostakovich, *and* Alma Mahler on Mahler.

THERE MAY BE INSTITUTIONS WHERE VOLUNTEERING means donating a few hours of dispassionate work a year, where community involvement means writing a check with only a vague notion of what it affects, and where serving on the board means gathering quarterly for meetings that are largely social affairs.

Not this Orchestra.

This is an institution whose volunteers have invented innovative educational programs copied by orchestras nationwide, created the first season ticket packages and sold them, hosted competitions to encourage and nurture young musicians, and grappled directly with the most challenging problems facing the Orchestra each season. This is an institution whose board members get tears in their eyes when they speak of a memorable concert, describe goose bumps from listening to a conductor's groundbreaking interpretation, and serve with dedication for decades in roles as demanding as positions in the competitive business world. This is an institution with a long tradition of volunteers who have taken the organization's success—and the music—very seriously.

Because they loved music and wanted to hear it in their own city, business leaders, citizens, and musicians joined forces to create something no single person or business could finance, and a community came together to build an orchestra.

One of the Minnesota Orchestra's founders and its first orchestral association president—a post he held for 40 years, from 1905 to 1945—Minneapolis lumberman Elbert L. Carpenter was himself an amateur musician (at the tender age of thirteen, he temporarily ran away with a traveling orchestra). Carpenter's passion for music was key in creating and nurturing the young Minneapolis Symphony, and his sheer personal drive and his own checkbook kept the organization alive through difficult times.

Board members—and all, at one time, board chairs—Kenneth N. Dayton, Judson "Sandy" Bemis, and John Myers, invaluable leaders of the Minnesota Orchestra for many decades

59

In *Music and Maestros*, a history of the first 50 years of the Minnesota Orchestra, writer John K. Sherman describes Carpenter's unique and striking devotion to the Orchestra: "It was a case . . . of a man finding his dearest hobby and playing at it harder than most men work." Carpenter's involvement was so personal that it eventually contributed to strain between himself and the Orchestra's founding music director, Emil Oberhoffer, who broke their friendship off and resigned in 1922.

Elbert L. Carpenter leads a 1939 Symphony Ball grand march.

Carpenter's son, Leonard (board member from 1938 to 1972, vice president from 1945 to 1965, and life director from 1970 until his death in 1994), had his own deep devotion to the Orchestra, one that inspires fond stories in those who knew him. Kenneth Dayton, Minneapolis businessman and longtime board member, says that "he served the Orchestra so well and passionately. But the one position he would not accept was that of chairman of the board. In spite of that, every chairman consulted him before taking important actions, and his was always the strongest voice on the executive committee. He was wise and learned and had more musical knowledge than other committee members. No one wanted to stand up against him. Furthermore, I always thought he was right when he voiced his opinions. He attended every concert with his wife, Geraldine, sitting ramrod straight in his chair. He closed his eyes throughout the concert—never to fall asleep, but always to concentrate better on the music."

The Carpenter family history with the Orchestra has endured through the entire century. Leonard's son, Thomas, served on the board from 1971 to 1977, and Thomas's wife, Nicky, was chair from 1990 to 1995.

Countless other families, too, committed time and resources to the Orchestra throughout generations. Among the many families involved with the Orchestra were individuals of singular commitment throughout board history.

Why? What brought and even drove people to come together for such an intensely demanding purpose—a century ago, and through the years since then?

One hundred years ago, E. L. Carpenter and his colleagues were not simply creating an orchestra in Minnesota. They were part of a handful of pioneers who were inventing a fresh and uniquely American way of funding and presenting classical music. Historically and until the turn of the last century, the tradition of opera and symphonic music was a European one. Operas and orchestras were state-supported organizations, funded by royalty and governments. European orchestras did not rely on the community for operating funds and support—these music-making organizations simply *were*.

But no such "automatic," state-funded orchestras existed in the late 1800s and early 1900s in the United States. When the then-called Minneapolis Symphony completed its first, four-month-long season in 1903, the city had become only the eighth in the country to establish its own major orchestra, after Chicago, New York, Saint Louis, Portland, Cincinnati, Philadelphia, and Boston. (San Francisco, Cleveland, Los Angeles, and others would follow.)

The creation of the Minneapolis Symphony was part of the founding of a new American tradition. Because they loved music and wanted to hear it in their own city, Twin Cities business leaders, citizens, and musicians joined forces to create something no single person or business could finance, and a community came together to build an orchestra—and, eventually, a hall, a catalog of respected recordings, and a rich tradition of excellence.

Times were not always easy, and board members and volunteers recall stresses that occasionally must have seemed insurmountable. The earliest years of the Orchestra were certainly lived hand-to-mouth, and E. L. Carpenter was known for filling his pockets with fund-raising materials and setting out to tackle the toughest-sell donors himself. During World War I, when anti-German sentiment in this country was at a peak, the heavily German Orchestra with its German-born music director, Emil Oberhoffer, and its repertoire of German music (Beethoven, Bach, and Wagner) presented challenges to management, which countered negative public feeling by publicizing that Oberhoffer forbade German to be spoken backstage and asking musicians to sign loyalty pledges and buy Liberty Bonds. When the Orchestra's performing space in the Lyceum Theater doubled in rent, the organization struggled under the burden, and the board had to look for and find new space—the 4,800-seat Northrop Auditorium, which became the Orchestra's home from

An Auspicious Time

The twentieth century in America dawned with optimism and energy. In 1903, when the Wright brothers took to the skies over North Carolina, out in Detroit Henry Ford founded the Motor Company that shaped the country's destiny. The Dayton Company had just come on the scene to be the retail anchor of Minneapolis and produced a family that established a model for corporate and individual giving. Meanwhile, over in St. Paul, the 3M Company took root, soon growing into one of Minnesota's giant enterprises. And also in St. Paul, on the very day that the Minneapolis Symphony Orchestra played its first concert—November 5, 1903—twin daughters were born to the pioneering Hamm family, of brewery fame. Marie and Theodora Hamm grew up to become music lovers known as Mrs. DeWalt Ankeny, Sr., and Mrs. Theodora Lang. Thus the mighty currents of invention, business, philanthropy, and culture merged to create the climate in which this Orchestra has thrived.

The Twin Cities community and the Minnesota Orchestra have depended upon each other for support for an entire century. In October 2001, in the aftermath of the September 11 disasters, the Orchestra created a massive concert of healing music led by conductors Andreas Delfs, of The Saint Paul Chamber Orchestra, and Minnesota Orchestra Conductor Laureate Stanislaw Skrowaczewski.

1930 until the opening of Orchestra Hall in 1974. Its location on the University of Minnesota campus forced the board to forge a unique agreement for a non-university organization to hold fee-taking concerts in such a space. In the 1930s, the Depression made attendance at the Orchestra seem an expensive luxury. The board arranged numerous social and musical appearances for Music Director Eugene Ormandy and Orchestra musicians—anything to help raise funds—and initiated an aggressive fund drive based on a brusque question: "Do you favor the continuance of the Minneapolis Symphony Orchestra?" Volunteers launched "Save Our Symphony" efforts at schools.

World War II pulled many experienced musicians from the Orchestra's ranks, and the number of women players rose to its highest point in history. Concertgoers were asked to toss change into baskets passed at intermission, volunteers promoted children's concerts and fund raising events, and the board struggled to conceive of potentially successful ventures, such as pops concerts and informal ways of presenting the Orchestra to wider audiences. Those who led the Orchestra through the 1940s, says Dayton, "had done yeoman service, holding the Orchestra together during the war."

Board members at the beginning of the present century struggle with problems that are echoes of the historic ones that faced the Minneapolis Symphony, such as concert attendance and tight funds, and they face problems of the new millennium: intense competition from new media for leisure time, population shifts to outlying suburbs, and the easy availability of symphonic music on recordings. Still, the passion for the demanding job of Minnesota Orchestra board member or volunteer endures.

An extraordinary level of community involvement is "essential to an orchestra's survival," says Minnesota Orchestra President David J. Hyslop. And in that, this Orchestra is extraordinarily blessed.

During its first century of music making, the Orchestra was guided, assisted, expanded, and nurtured by literally countless friends and patrons. Some took on projects and worked side-by-side with staff or musicians.

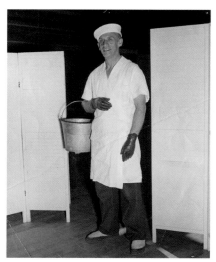

Conductor Dimitri Mitropoulos, a familiar figure at Red Cross blood centers, volunteered in Hutchinson, Minnesota, during World War II.

The history of the Minneapolis Symphony
Orchestra is not only a Midwestern story.
In a real sense it is an American story,
the oft-repeated one that tells of free citizens in
a free land who, wanting to do more than
thrive and be comfortable, have willingly
assumed the obligation to build for themselves,
their neighbors, and their children,
the good life.

—John K. Sherman
*Music and Maestros, The Story of
the Minneapolis Symphony Orchestra,*
University of Minnesota Press, 1952.

*On August 15,
1927, looking for-
ward to the 25th
anniversary season
of the Orchestra,
the* Minneapolis
Daily Star *urged
community
support.*

Some served on committees, were appointed to the board, or led other volunteers. Some gave generously of their days, some generously of their resources. Some served for decades, some served for weeks. They sat on boards or stood as ushers, guided as teachers in educational programs or acted as chairs of prestigious events. Whoever they were and whatever they gave, each hour of time, each creative idea, and each individual gesture became a richly valued treasure to the Orchestra, each as cherished as the next, each deeply meaningful because it came from the heart.

Over its 100-year history, the Minnesota Orchestra has benefited from the focused attention of a wide-ranging, broad-based band of board members and officers, WAMSO and YPSCA volunteers, and community supporters. And there are four things those individuals name over and over again as the reasons they give so freely of their time and commitment with such devotion. Goose bumps. Tears. Passion. And pride.

THE LIST OF THOSE who have shared their talents and dedication with the Orchestra stretches across the years and knits together a statewide community of music lovers. The sheer breadth and depth of such a list honors the Orchestra and humbles anyone seeking to record and mark it. These pages afford only limited room for the stories and memories of a few good friends, but they speak with an awareness of the exponential numbers of community members they represent.

Nicky B. Carpenter, who joined the board in 1977 and chaired it from 1990 to 1995, ultimately became a life director in 2000. Her rich memories of Orchestra life span from childhood, through her years as chairman, to the present, as she serves as chair of the Orchestra's centennial celebrations.

"I remember going Friday evenings to Northrop Auditorium," she says. "My parents had three seats, and I can remember being the little one sitting on the aisle. The first thing I remember was Mitropoulos's bald head —the spotlight would shine on it!"

When Music Director Edo de Waart stepped down in 1995, Board Chair Nicky Carpenter presented him with a Richard Strauss autograph letter.

She recalls that much later, Orchestra President Richard M. Cisek and board member N. Bud Grossman "came to me at one point and asked if I would chair the Orchestra. I thought long and hard, being advised by everyone to say no!" She accepted, helping to steer the organization through a $2.5 million annual structural deficit, a $50 million fund drive, a music director search, and a musicians' strike, "which was sad for everybody and proved nothing for anyone." At her retirement as chair, she retained a strong sense of the Orchestra's importance to the community. "There is more interest in the Orchestra out in the community than we might believe," she says. "Sometimes Minnesotans are nice, not pushy, and they don't necessarily volunteer, but when we asked for help, many were willing and said, 'We wish you'd asked sooner.' We have wonderful board members who are extremely committed."

Carpenter believes that "concert goers and patrons have to be ambassadors for the Orchestra. You have to talk to people about how wonderful the Orchestra is and get them to go and try it. Supporting an Orchestra isn't just financial—it's the fact that you attend concerts."

Minneapolis Tribune columnist and
Orchestra board member Barbara Flanagan
with board member George H. Grim
at a 75th anniversary celebration

Mrs. John Myers (Betty) and Mrs. Louis Zelle (Ann)

Grim remembers a particular post-concert "gathering" with a chuckle. "It had rained and frozen into a thin sheet of glare ice during the concert, but you couldn't see it on the roads," he says. "We all drove out of Northrop Auditorium's parking ramp, and when we hit the Third Avenue bridge, why, the cars just started to slide. Nothing you could do about it, it was ice. Everyone slid into each other, and then we got out and tried to stand up and walk around, holding onto the cars. And no one was mad; we all knew each other, and had just been to the concert together. The next week, we were all comparing insurance estimates during intermission."

Influential *Star Tribune* columnist and Minneapolis icon Barbara Flanagan wrote the book *Ovation* on the occasion of the Orchestra's 75th anniversary. For the last 36 years, she's been a regular Wednesday night concert-goer; both she and her husband, Earl Sanford, have served on the board—Flanagan from 1969 to 1973, Sanford from 1973 through 1995, acting as vice president from 1973 to 1974. Before she became involved in the Orchestra board, she recalls being assigned as a reporter to cover a board meeting on a hot summer day. "I had on a cotton dress and espadrilles, and I told

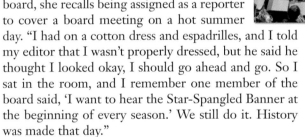

my editor that I wasn't properly dressed, but he said he thought I looked okay, I should go ahead and go. So I sat in the room, and I remember one member of the board said, 'I want to hear the Star-Spangled Banner at the beginning of every season.' We still do it. History was made that day."

She marvels at the vision of the early Orchestra pioneers. "Imagine Carpenter starting the Orchestra here; it was quite rustic still, you know," she says. "He did it, in part, because Oberhoffer needed a job, and what he ended up doing was to build the beginnings of a 100-year-old Orchestra. The Orchestra needs those kinds of people." A tremendous proponent of what are now Minneapolis institutions—sidewalk cafes and Nicollet Mall—Flanagan marks as "significant and remarkable" the community accomplishment in getting Orchestra Hall built. "This building says, 'Here we are, we're going to stay,'" she says. "I hope the Orchestra has another 100 years in it. I think it does."

"It was a way of life, Friday nights at Northrop," says George H. Grim, board member from 1959 to 1969, and 90 years old during the Orchestra's centennial year. "Each week, everyone sat in the familiar places, you saw the same faces. There was a collegiality. The Orchestra belonged to you and you to them." Concerts conducted by Music Director Dimitri Mitropoulos were especially "magical," recalls Grim. "Somehow the music went from the score to his heart to his innards to his hands. Friday after Friday night it was wonderful." The night in 1949 when Mitropoulos said his farewell was memorable, too. "It was very brief, and touching," says Grim. "He went to the side of the proscenium arch at Northrop, and said 'I must say goodbye, there's a mountain I have to climb. . . . And I hope I haven't caused you to suffer too much.' I've been going to the symphony 70 years or more; I started going with my mother and father. The symphony becomes part of the fabric of your life. It's a hole in my life not being able to hear it each week."

Vice President Hubert Humphrey danced with WAMSO President Dorothy Gaucher at the Symphony Ball in 1966.

Former Minnesota Orchestra
Board Chairman and Life Director
Judson "Sandy" Bemis.

A board member from 1959 to 1977, Judson "Sandy" Bemis was on the executive committee for two periods (1961-1985 and 1991-1992), served as vice president (1964) and president (1964-1968), and was named a life director in 1978. Bemis provided support for key Orchestra endeavors, such as a 1990s children's video project, MOVE, which showcased the Orchestra and matched classical music to children's books and themes. His crowning achievement was the impetus he provided in funding and building Orchestra Hall. Bemis died in February 2001; his widow, Barbara Bemis, and his son, Judson "Kim" Bemis, continue the family involvement in the Orchestra. Kim served on the board from 1993 to 1999 and the executive committee from 1995 to 1996. Barbara has had a lifelong love of classical music and the Orchestra.

"I've been going since I was a child," she says. "The concerts happened at night, of course, so going along meant I got to stay up late, which I thought was peachy."

Her husband's involvement was energetic, to say the least. No sooner had he concluded a major fund raising drive, says Barbara, than Sandy was on to his next Orchestra project. "His fund raising was so successful, and everybody was so pleased and slapping him on the back—but only a few days later he came to me and said, 'Now, we're going to have a new hall. Stan is miserable and so is the Orchestra and it's time.' And Sandy did it!"

Barbara remembers the day she first heard a note played in the Hall. "We went to the Minneapolis Club for lunch—Ken Dayton organized a party—and then we walked to Orchestra Hall. They played the Bach Toccata and Fugue. So many of our friends had tears in their eyes." Since the Hall opened, she's had the same seats: first tier, first two seats on the piano side.

She has also had a long time association with the Metropolitan Opera and recalls an associate there who once asked her, "How is it possible for you in Minneapolis to raise so much support for music and the arts?" Barbara says, "The same people give and give again, and so many people choose to give. We are just blessed with a very, very generous population."

Young People's Symphony Concert Association (YPSCA)

THE YOUNG PEOPLE'S SYMPHONY CONCERT ASSOCIATION organized in 1911 in order to assist, augment, and promote Young People's Concerts of the Minnesota Orchestra. In the beginning, men and women volunteers in the community worked with the Orchestra's founding conductor, Emil Oberhoffer, who expressed extraordinary commitment to bringing the concert experience to young people. The program that they established together has continued throughout the Orchestra's history, changing only to adapt to current needs. YPSCA organizers sold tickets to the first YP Concert, November 24, 1911, and helped to create additional performances when the first one proved so popular that hundreds of children were unable to get tickets. During the Depression, YPSCA established a Free Seat Fund to supplement inadequate public school budgets, and in the 1930s YPSCA volunteers met with Orchestra personnel and school educators to create a music curriculum to accompany YP Concerts. In 2002-2003 YPSCA's ongoing programs include financial support for school groups who attend YP Concerts, volunteers who go into schools to prepare children for YP Concerts, YP Concert ushers, and annual School Music Auditions to identify and honor young instrumentalists.

Board Chair Luella Goldberg and Music Director Sir Neville Marriner

Marriner with Scandinavian royalty and dignitaries, including (center, back row) the soprano Birgit Nilsson and the pianist Victor Borge, at gala Tonight Scandinavia concert, 1982

Elinor Watson Bell is a grande dame of the Orchestra, a trained concert pianist, board member from 1962 to 1968, and 91 years old as of May 2002. She has met all but one of the music directors of the Minnesota Orchestra. "My parents always brought me to the symphony," she says. "I learned to appreciate it and loved to go." Concerts Friday night are a "habit I'd rather not miss," and she's attended through the Lyceum and Northrop and now Orchestra Hall years. She remembers opening night in the new Hall. "On its opening concert, everyone was waiting with bated breath for the first note to be played in the Hall. When the sound came out, it . . . felt like a great occasion. I couldn't believe the sound."

Bell offered both resources and time as a board member, but also made very hands-on commitments to the Orchestra. During a period of significant financial stresses for the organization, she "stood on the corner of 8th and Nicollet holding a sign that said 'SOS—Save Our Symphony,'" she says. She also served as usher during concerts. "My children went to the children's concerts, and I can still see [my son] Fordie walking in with his class, looking up into the tiers for me."

When Bell served on the board, she remembers, she asked honorary director and executive committee member Stanley Hawks (1954-1966) a provocative question. "At one meeting, I asked if it was by design or accident that no women were on the board's executive committee. I just couldn't resist—it seemed so obvious to me." Hawks, she recalls, was not particularly pleased with the query. "Soon after that," she says, "Several women moved through the ranks of the executive commitee."

In a move that surely pleased Elinor Bell, Luella Goldberg became the first woman chair of the Orchestra in 1980. She was Junior WAMSO president in the late 1960s, WAMSO president from 1972 to 1974, and vice president of the board from 1975 to 1979. After three years as chair, Goldberg served as director for more years and became a life director in 1998. "It was particularly meaningful to me to be the first woman chair," she says. "I was delighted that the Orchestra was opening up the possibility of the responsibility of chair being assumed by a woman. It was a very exciting time to be chair of the Orchestra—many wonderful things were going on at that time: Sir Neville Marriner was music director, the hall was full-to-overflowing, the Orchestra went abroad to the Hong Kong Arts Festival, toured Australia . . . it was extremely thrilling to be in that beautiful Sydney Opera House, standing under a starlit sky, overlooking that harbor, hearing our Orchestra play so beautifully."

During Goldberg's tenure as chairman of the board, Marilyn Carlson Nelson organized the 1982 Tonight Scandinavia telecast, an Orchestra concert attended by various Scandinavian dignitaries and royalty. That's a memory Goldberg particularly cherishes, along with her time working on the dedication concert of the opening of Orchestra Hall. "I remember standing in the Hall when the very first note was played," she says. "There was just a handful of us. The Orchestra was on stage, and it was an amazing moment. There was a wonderful concert for the people who worked on building the Hall; that preceded the public concert. It's been a lifelong involvement with the Orchestra, and a lifelong love of it."

But one which began through happenstance. "Someone who knew me and my twin sister, just after we graduated from college, asked if we would work on a WAMSO project called Twin Town Tours to raise money for the Orchestra. At the first meeting, they said, 'We trust you all are members,' so my sister and I looked at each other and signed up. One thing led to another."

An understatement, but Goldberg is characteristically modest about her ground-breaking election as chair. "It was satisfying to have such a wonderful opportunity for responsibility and leadership," she says—and immediately moves the subject on to what she loves the most about this work. "Music is such an international language. It speaks across all cultures and differences. It unites people. In this day and age, where, to an even greater extent than ever before, people are frantic, rushing around, and almost isolated due to technology, live concerts bring people together.

"One hundred years is an enormous accomplishment. I think the next hundred will be very challenging, but a community that is caring and committed to quality will find a way to meet those challenges."

∽

Working to create an approximately $12 million expansion in funding for the arts, Minnesota Governor Arne Carlson, who served from 1990 to 1998, is credited with changing the way arts are supported and funded in Minnesota. "We wanted to expand what we already had and try to create more exposure through the state," Carlson says. "Part of that effort was to take our orchestras in St. Paul [The St. Paul Chamber Orchestra] and in Minneapolis [Minnesota Orchestra] and move them around a bit, getting them out into the state and bringing arts access to more people."

The Governor is particularly proud of the outreach efforts of the Minnesota Orchestra, performing in Rochester, St. Cloud, and other greater Minnesota communities. These statewide efforts have deep roots in the Orchestra's history—a tour of Duluth, Grand Forks, and Moorhead was undertaken as early as 1907. "The arts can no longer be sustained exclusively by private donations," Carlson says. "The arts nourish our souls, reflect our community, broaden how we think. When the Orchestra plays out in the state, that's when people say, 'Isn't this a great quality of life we have?' We should never allow ourselves to get to the point where we don't think the arts are necessary to life."

Carlson credits his father, a Swedish immigrant, with instilling a love of music in his son. "He loved opera, adored opera," says Carlson. "He had me believing Enrico Caruso was really Swedish."

∽

Another Carlson, unrelated to Arne, is long-time board member Marilyn Carlson Nelson. A member from 1974 to the present, she served as secretary from 1978 to 1979, vice president from 1979 to 1983, and vice chair from 1986 to 1989. The WAMSO president from 1972 to 1974, Luella Goldberg, asked Nelson to chair the Symphony Ball, and the two women together served as co-chairs of the 75th anniversary of the Orchestra, in 1978.

"It's rewarding to serve on the board of the Orchestra, because it's an institution that is truly committed to excellence," says Nelson. "The Orchestra has had such important aspirations and has had people who were willing to make the commitment and the sacrifice necessary to propel the organization to that level of performance and artistry."

Nelson includes board members in her list of individuals who are deeply involved. "The people who support the Orchestra and who take the time out of very busy lives to provide leadership to the Orchestra represent a very interesting and enlightened group of people who are not self-interested but who have a commitment beyond themselves." Among fellow board members she found peers and friends, says Nelson. She also found something else. "I found many role models when I was a young woman involved in the Orchestra. Many of the leaders were role models in terms of philanthropy, building community, commitment to the arts, musical sophistication . . . it was educational and inspiring, but it was also fun. One of the thrills in my life was when my daughter-in-law, Margie Nelson, became involved in the Orchestra, chaired a ball, and went on to be on the board. It's a thrill when our children have some of the same priorities and passions that we have."

The importance her own family places on its Swedish roots sparked in part her interest in the unique 1982 Orchestra project Scandinavia Today. "I come from a school that thinks a lot about multiple generations and about heritage. We go back to Sweden in order to understand and have a perspective about our place in history as a living link to the past and the future." The Orchestra, she says, "is multi-generational . . . it is a culture transfer that is very important. It transfers values and enhances our lives and carries that message beyond the boundaries of a metropolitan region or even an entire state. "A really fine orchestra that travels throughout the world is not only . . . representing the best of us, the beauty of the music, the skill and discipline of the musicians, but also is a marketing tool for the community."

*St. Paul Mayor George Latimer
and Orchestra hornist Frank Winsor
volunteering at the telephone bank*

*Board member Marilyn Nelson and
President Richard M. Cisek (right) greet
composer Gunther Schuller (far left)
at a 75th anniversary celebration.*

*Life Director John S. Pillsbury, Jr.,
and Mrs. Pillsbury (Kitty), 2002*

*President David J. Hyslop, Board Chair
Douglas W. Leatherdale, outgoing
Chair Thomas M. Crosby, Jr., and
Principal Trumpet Manuel Laureano
at board luncheon December 2000*

Nelson also sees music as a way of strengthening communities. "I think that music has to do with something that is spiritual, that is transcendent, that can be unifying. It's a language somewhere between the heart and mind. We've been using music to express our deepest emotions, whether of celebration or of sadness, loss, love, excitement. . . . Having an orchestra in a community gives us one more level of shared experience. Whenever we can have common experiences we build bridges between each other and create a stronger community. The key to the longevity of the Orchestra is in the hearts and minds of the community."

∾

The Pillsbury family also has significant, time-honored ties to the Orchestra. A board member from 1914 to 1959 (when he became a life director), John S. Pillsbury set an example that five family members have followed. Philip W. Pillsbury, a member from 1940 and president from 1955 to 1958, also became a life director upon his retirement. Eleanor Pillsbury served on the board in the mid 1940s, and John S., III, "Jock" Pillsbury was a board member from 1969 to 1979. John S. Pillsbury, Jr., a board member from 1958 through 1992, was chairman from 1961 to 1974 and has been life director since 1976.

Thomas M. Crosby, Jr. (nephew of John S. Pillsbury, Jr.) joined the board in 1969 and has held various offices through the years, including the chairmanship from 1998 to 2000. "I'm the third generation of involvement in the Orchestra, on each side of my family," he says. "On the Crosby side, my grandfather, Franklin M. Crosby, was a board member for 33 years, and my grandparents were season ticket holders, as were my parents."

The continuing commitment of generations of families and of ex-board members strikes Crosby as particularly noteworthy. "The Orchestra has had very good volunteer leadership," he says. "Look at some of the past chairs—Nicky Carpenter, Bud Grossman, Luella Goldberg, Ken Dayton. They all continue to be very supportive of the organization.

There's important continuity." In addition, he emphasizes the new look of the board. "At the same time, we're in a new era. Early in the Orchestra's history, leadership was in the hands of relatively few individuals and families. Today's board is reflective of today's society, with broad-based support from many parts of the community at large."

Such leadership will be needed, Crosby feels, in facing today's pressures and challenges. "Back in 1965 when I first came back to this community, the Orchestra was a part-time profession for musicians—one performance a week, Friday night. There was one charity ball in town—the Symphony Ball. Now we've gone to three or four concerts a week and 52 weeks of employment [for musicians]." Keeping Orchestra Hall filled for so many performances a year is difficult, not only due to programming, but due to the demands of modern life, says Crosby.

"I view the Orchestra's competition as extremely varied. It's competing with a night at home . . . or a movie, or the Vikings. Two working professionals with young children: Will they go to the Orchestra if it requires getting a sitter? It's not a question of going to this orchestra or that orchestra. It's a question of going out at all. And, given the fact that younger people may have less music education in school . . . you cannot assume, as you once could, that people will necessarily gravitate towards the Orchestra."

Crosby's enthusiasm for the Orchestra epitomizes his family's long involvement in its support. "The most memorable part [of my board involvement] has been getting to know members of the Orchestra. My wife and I heard the Orchestra on tour in Barcelona. To be able to spend some time with musicians, to hear them there, in a fabulous hall . . . wonderful!"

∾

Kathy Cunningham, an ex-officio Orchestral Association board member as WAMSO's president in 1980, has been on the board for all but one year since then through the present. "I first got involved with WAMSO in their educational projects," she says. "I really enjoyed the education part of it, and the fact that young children were learning about music at early ages. I could encourage my children to go on and be interested in music."

But soon, Cunningham found another strong Minnesota Orchestra interest: its history. Now the chair of the Orchestra's archives committee, Cunningham has led the effort to organize the massive collection of historical materials that the Orchestra had stored in the Performing Arts Archives in the Manuscripts Division at the University of Minnesota. Recently, the University built a new, state-of-the-art storage and access facility, the Elmer L. Andersen Library. Cunningham and the committee used the Orchestra's approaching centennial as motivation to seek funding to hire a professional archivist to sort and describe the Orchestra's materials.

"I've been involved with the Orchestra for 40 years, and it's fun for me to go back into the history," Cunningham says. "The more I get into the history of the Orchestra, the more I find out what an important form of art this is for this community and the great love people have for the Orchestra."

∾

Jevne Pennock's husband, George, joined the board in 1966. He served as vice chair from 1975 to 1976, chair from 1967 to 1978, and was named life director in 1984. George died in 1998. Pennock describes her husband as a good musician in his own right. "He played sax, and he really knew how the halls were to play in," she says. "He wouldn't go to the Ordway, he didn't like the sound, but in Orchestra Hall, it's good sound.

"I started going to the symphony when I was nine years old," she says. "I'm 89, so I've been going a long time."

Pennock remembers sitting in the first tier at Northrop Auditorium on Friday nights, and now sits in the first tier at Orchestra Hall. "I go every Wednesday night, opening night. I love the opening night. It's exciting. And then I hear it again Friday [on Minnesota Public Radio] when I'm home. It sounds good both times."

She worries, though, that students today are not receiving the same quality of classical music education as they did in generations past. "We need to get the young ones interested, but they aren't doing enough music in the schools," Pennock says. "If they get into music, they'll love it forever."

∾

Deborah L. Hopp, publisher of MSP Publications in Minneapolis, has served on the board since 1997 and was Symphony Ball Chair in 2001. Her involvement in the Orchestra stems from a desire to support community arts endeavors. "I'm not a live theater person," she says. "Music hits me more personally; I'm more drawn to it." As a mother of two, Hopp nurtures a keen interest in the education efforts of WAMSO, YPSCA, and the Orchestra. "The WAMSO and YPSCA programs are fabulous. And serving on the board is a link with the community, a way to feel and be involved in its development."

And it's a community that doesn't need to be convinced of the importance of the Orchestra, Hopp says. "Even if people don't attend regularly themselves, they regard the Orchestra as a community asset. The people who volunteer are the ones who take action on that. I've found when asking for dollars or time that people are flattered and feel it's a privilege to help."

Minnesota Orchestra patrons Jevne and George Pennock with Music Director Sir Neville Marriner

∾

Douglas W. Leatherdale, chairman during the centennial season, joined the board in 1980, served as vice chair (1988-1996 and 1999-2001) and vice president (1990-1991), and assumed the chairmanship in December 2000. "I remember exactly how I got involved," he says. "I had just moved here from Canada and went to a couple of concerts at the University [Northrop Auditorium]. My boss at the St. Paul Companies asked me to help the Orchestra on the investment committee. I grew up when young corporate executives were expected to participate in the community." A long and rewarding relationship had begun.

"Filling the Hall, balancing the budget, securing the endowment—I like these challenges. They're intriguing." As chairman of a major and highly successful endowment drive in the mid-1990s, Leatherdale has left his mark on the Orchestra.

"This is a great Orchestra," says Leatherdale. From the first, he found the business side of an arts organization

Leonard Slatkin (formerly Minnesota Orchestra principal guest conductor and artistic director, Viennese Sommerfest) presents 1997 ASCAP Award for Innovative Programming to President David J. Hyslop (left) and board members Kathy Cunningham and David Ranheim.

Douglas W. Leatherdale, vice chairman at time of photo (1995), later chairman of the Minnesota Orchestra board of directors

Governor Harold Levander proclaimed an official Stanislaw Skrowaczewski Week, as Skrowaczewski and wife, Krystyna, looked on.

to be an engaging challenge, and finds it so, still. "In this community, we are overwhelmed with an abundance of riches, a plethora of arts, museums, theaters, sports. . . . There's just plain more for people to do," he says. "The environment has changed fairly dramatically over the last ten or fifteen years."

"Even though we're dealing with factors that didn't exist years ago, the Orchestra still touches the community in meaningful ways." Leatherdale also clearly responds to the Orchestra's devotion to excellence. "We are a global Orchestra," he says. "The reception this Orchestra gets around the world is so rewarding."

∾

Stanislaw Skrowaczewski was more than music director of the Minnesota Orchestra from 1960 to 1979—he is the man whose energy helped make the drive to build Orchestra Hall a resounding success. "I came here in 1960, and from the very beginning, I was starting to talk about [a new] hall, like my predecessors—but seriously," he says. "Because of my experience with recording, and because the level of the Orchestra was excellent, I felt to play in Northrop was difficult—the qualities of the Orchestra, they cannot come through." He remembers that when the Orchestra toured to New York City and played at Carnegie Hall every year, "certain board members went to hear, and they'd ask, 'Why don't they play so beautifully here?' Well, they play the same; the hall is better."

Though the acoustics and the sheer size of Northrop Auditorium had been complained about for years by many, a campaign to raise the funds necessary to build a new hall would require a special commitment from the community—not just the board, WAMSO, and YPSCA, but from the larger community, as well. Skrowaczewski says he started by complaining. "It took ten years of my hammering of letters. My crying, my shouting, my imploring got an answer from people who were very wonderful, powerful, who understood: Kenneth and Judy Dayton, Sandy Bemis, who was chairman at the time, and many others—too many to name."

"The Daytons set the tone for the hall fund raising with a generous gift," says Skrowaczewski, which influenced others to see the project as possible and to give on their own. "Kenneth started the whole avalanche of

donors." Ground was broken in spring of 1973; the new Hall opened in October 1974. Skrowaczewski's dream had come true, and he credits the generosity of a community determined to host and hear world-class music.

"In twelve or thirteen months, we got this wonderful Hall built," he says. "Without those persons [who first gave] and many others around them, we couldn't have done it. We cannot forget the role of WAMSO. WAMSO raised money in millions. It was all volunteers connected with this. It was a common effort. It was magnificent.

"This community was particularly wonderful and just understood the art of music—before I came—how important is culture, what is really substantial to a human being. We may develop marvelous technology, but it is a danger to forget about art as food for human beings."

∾

N. Bud Grossman joined the board in 1971 and, except for one year in the mid-1990s, has served on the executive committee continuously from 1977 to the present time. He was chair from 1987 to 1990 and was named a life director in 1995. "I was fortunate," he says. "I wanted to concentrate my efforts—devote myself to one board, so that over time my efforts would have an effect." Although Grossman has served on many boards in the community, his more than three decades of service to the Orchestra have, indeed, had an effect.

A lifelong businessman, Grossman says he found working with the Orchestra intriguing. "It's similar to business, but very, very different, in that it's a not-for-profit organization and particularly complex. There's a high labor content, an aggressive market, and lots of union activity. As a result you find yourself much more challenged for economic viability than in other businesses."

Grossman feels that the challenge attracts the best and the brightest. "The quality of the people is amazing," he says. "It's a big board, bigger than most, and yet it functions very well. We've always had great support from the business community—many of our most prominent business leaders have served as chairs."

Grossman credits that leadership for a significant change. "Some years ago we looked at the Orchestra's modest endowment fund and decided to broaden the base. We undertook a professionally assisted, well-organized effort to strengthen the endowment and to create big community involvement. Since that time, we've had another couple of major endowment efforts. This has had a good influence in the survival of the Orchestra. The transition was smoothly made, from the older method, where only a few leaders played a key role, to the present one, where we have strong community participation. The leadership was critical in making that smooth transition.

"You look at that roster and you're pleased at the quality of the people, and that people take that time. The community has been very supportive of the Orchestra throughout the years—in good times and in difficult ones."

Future challenges the community and board will need to face? "I think music is so much a part of human nature that it will always be there," Grossman says. "I think the question is, 'How will it be delivered?' I think the community will continue to meet the challenges, and that the Orchestra will continue to serve the community far into the future."

Their first date was a Minnesota Orchestra concert, and their dedication to the Orchestra has been a great, shared love in their lives. Kenneth N. and Judy Dayton have both served as directors, Judy ex-officio as president of YPSCA from 1967 to 1969, Kenneth nearly continuously from 1947, with two rotations off the board to concentrate on the first endowment fund campaign and, later, the Orchestra Hall drive. He was vice president from 1952 to 1953, president from 1953 to 1955, and was named life director in 1983. On the 50th anniversary of his joining the board, Dayton quietly resigned. He now (2002-03) holds the title Emeritus Director.

"I started going to the Young People's Concerts in about 1929 to avoid manual training [in school]," says Dayton. "At that time, the Orchestra was under the direction of Verbrugghen at the old Lyceum Theater. I then attended concerts after the Orchestra moved to Northrop Auditorium, particularly with my mother. . . . During the war, the Orchestra ran out of directors, so they asked my father, who was a donor to the guaranty fund. He said, no, I can't do that, but I have a son who loves Brahms, and he'll be back from the war shortly. So I joined the board and executive committee at the same

time in 1947 and have been involved in one way or another ever since."

Dayton remembers past music directors of the Orchestra vividly. He attended concerts at the old Lyceum with Verbrugghen and at Northrop with Ormandy. But his real love affair with the Orchestra started with Dimitri Mitropoulos. "Mitropoulos had the most incredible ability to electrify the Orchestra and was one of the most exciting conductors I have ever seen . . . when he played the piano and conducted the Orchestra as well, it was not to be missed." About Dorati: "I was on the committee that brought him here. In those days, we all leaned very heavily on the great manager Arthur Judson, the most powerful influence in the music world at the time. He said, 'I think you should have Dorati'—and we had Dorati! Although not a flashy conductor, Toni was an effective music director and he strengthened the Orchestra. In many ways he was the exact opposite of Mitropoulos."

Dayton was also on the committee that searched for Dorati's replacement. He and other committee members traveled to Cleveland to hear Stanislaw Skrowaczewski conduct The Cleveland Orchestra in his American debut.

About Skrowaczewski, Dayton says, "Almost the moment we saw Skrowaczewski walk on stage, [we knew] he was the man. We met him backstage, and he could hardly speak English, but it didn't matter. We just knew that we wanted him. The result was nineteen years of the most glorious music-making this community has ever had."

After Skrowaczewski's term Dayton was asked if he'd like to serve on the search committees for finding two subsequent music directors, but turned them down "in the hope that the new generation of Orchestra leadership would take over"—a value he has maintained throughout his involvement with the Orchestra. During his chairmanship he worked "to get a [board] rotation system going so the Orchestra wouldn't end up in the hands of the old goats."

(continued on page 75)

Minnesota Orchestra Life Director
N. Bud Grossman

In May 2001 Minnesota Orchestra musicians performed chamber music in honor of the gift of The Michael Leiter Bass Violin Collection, made possible by the generosity of Kenneth N. and Judy Dayton and Douglas W. and Louise Leatherdale. From left: musicians Richard Marshall, Joseph Johnson, Kerri Ryan, Vali Phillips, Sarah Kwak; Douglas Leatherdale; musician Peter Lloyd; Judy Dayton; musicians Aaron Janse, Kenneth Freed; Kenneth N. Dayton

Community efforts on a large scale created Orchestra Hall. Minnesota Orchestra Music Director Stanislaw Skrowaczewski ("conducting" the ground-breaking ceremonies, far left) inspired everyone with his artistic guidance. Creative planning and generous support came from private sources, families, corporations, and foundations, whose names are inscribed on 141 plaques in the Orchestra Hall lobby. Public officials such as Mayor Charles Stenvig provided necessary municipal support for the project. Begun in 1973, Orchestra Hall opened on October 21, 1974, after only sixteen months of construction, supervised by contractors Naugle-Leck Associates. Dr. Cyril Harris served as acoustician, and Hugh Hardy, architect, led a team of colleagues from Hammel Green and Abrahamson, Inc., of St. Paul and Hardy Holzman Pfeiffer Associates of New York. Cost of the project: $13,570,000.

The WAMSO Collaboration

IN 1949, LONGTIME MINNESOTA ORCHESTRA PATRON ROSALYND PFLAUM, wife of board member Leo Pflaum (who served from 1945 to 1964, vice president from 1948 to 1955), and personal friend of Music Director Dimitri Mitropoulos, gathered together a small group of women to discuss the idea of founding a volunteer organization for the Orchestra. "I didn't think there would be many challenges establishing a volunteer group for the Minnesota Orchestra in the later 1940s," she is quoted in a WAMSO 50th anniversary publication in May 2000. "I presumed that there would be many women who would feel privileged to be asked to do something for the Orchestra."

She presumed correctly. For more than 50 years, WAMSO—Minnesota Orchestra Volunteer Association, originally named "Women's Association of the Minneapolis Symphony Orchestra"—has done a wide variety of "somethings" for the Orchestra, including enormously successful and highly innovative fund raising, and education programs, recognized and emulated by orchestras across the United States.

Rosalynd Pflaum (left) founding president of WAMSO; Mrs. Ernest F. Dorn, Jr., WAMSO president in 1954; and Mrs. John Carroll, vice president

WAMSO members have raised funds for the Orchestra through balls and parties, raffles and fashion shows, have sold concert tickets, have organized concerts to benefit musician pensions, and have guided custom tours through the Twin Cities. In 1956 WAMSO originated the annual Symphony Ball, successfully run completely by volunteers for 45 years and netting more than ten million dollars for the Orchestra. Another major fundraising effort resulted in the endowment of the WAMSO Principal Percussion Chair in 1986.

WAMSO members have also organized award-winning education programs. Music in the Schools brought Orchestra ensembles to area schools beginning in 1954; Young Artist competitions provide prize money and performance opportunities to advanced music students in an eleven-state region; Young Audiences of Minnesota, a now-independent organization that WAMSO initiated, brings artists and musicians into schools; Kinder Konzerts offer four- and five-year-olds their first concert experiences in Orchestra Hall; and Gear Your Ear© provides a listening curriculum and statewide listening contest for fifth- and sixth-graders.

Four recent WAMSO presidents explain the organization's strengths:

"Collaboration!" says Jane Gregerson (1994-1996). "WAMSO has always fostered collaboration between musicians and community and staff and schools."

"The common thread through all WAMSO members," says Mary Schrock (1992-1994), "is a genuine love of music, a heartfelt passion. We are in WAMSO for the same reasons people go to the Orchestra: the basic human needs of creating community, being inspired."

Mari Carlson (1990-1992) agrees. "The more I became involved, the more it filled a place in my heart."

Holly Slocum (2001-2002) says, "With input from musicians, volunteers, board, and staff, WAMSO in 2002 completed a strategic plan to direct effective volunteer support in the coming century. Through their generous gifts of money, time, talent, and energy, WAMSO members remain committed to creative and passionate support of our renowned Orchestra."

—*P.H.N.*

Former presidents of the organization gathered in Orchestra Hall on the occasion of the 50th anniversary of WAMSO in 2000. By the time of the Minnesota Orchestra centennial season, two more WAMSO presidents, not pictured, would serve: Holly Slocum (2001-2002) and Barbara Burwell (2002-2003).

Front row, left to right: Nancy Moe, Kathy Cunningham, Mary Steinke, Sandy Coleman, Rosalynd Pflaum, Luella Goldberg, Ann Zelle, Betty Myers
Back row, left to right: Jolie Klapmeier, Linda Killmer, Judy Kishel, Jane Gregerson, Mary Schrock, Mari Carlson, Anne Miller, Judi Blomquist, Susan Platou

(continued from page 71)

Dayton's leadership was key in the great success of the New Dimensions Fund, a landmark initiative of the late 1960s. The Ford Foundation offered twelve orchestras each a two million dollar grant if they would match it with two million dollars of their own. "All the orchestras sooner or later met that match, but the Minnesota Orchestra far exceeded it," says Dayton. "We actually raised $12.5 million. That really said to the community that the Orchestra will always be here."

A deep believer in the importance of the Orchestra's relationship to the entire state, Dayton was highly instrumental not only in supporting concerts outside the metropolitan area, but in the board's decision to change the name from Minneapolis Symphony Orchestra to Minnesota Orchestra in 1968. In October 1970 a concert series was opened in St. Paul at I. A. O'Shaughnessy Auditorium; that series continues at the Ordway Center for the Performing Arts.

Kenneth and Judy Dayton are modest about their significant generosity to the Orchestra, but their commitment is well known, and they show their interest in varied areas of Orchestra development. They started a new hall fund while the Orchestra was still at Northrop Auditorium; the fund paid for acoustic studies of both Northrop Auditorium and the Lyceum Theater (then still standing on 11th Street) and kept the topic of building a new hall alive.

Says Judy, "I remember crawling all over this wonderful old building [the Lyceum] and visualizing what could happen . . . in the end, it came down . . . but I think the right thing did happen."

In 1973, the board decided to give the Orchestra an instrument of its own—to build a new hall. Dayton served on the building committee and worked with the architect and acoustician closely. He wrote a philosophy for the Hall, which opened in 1974, stating that it would serve audiences of the future and not express old-world elegance. "That's why you see no red velvet, no crystal chandeliers," he says.

When Dayton first joined the board, he remembers that "we used to borrow the plates from Westminster Church and pass them through Northrop Auditorium,

[taking a collection] to raise the last $25,000 of the annual Guaranty Fund. We would announce that if we couldn't raise it, the Orchestra would have to close. One of the things I vowed as president is that we would never do that again. After a few years we discontinued the practice, but that's how desperate it was then. I have no doubt in my mind that this community will rise to support all of the arts in the ways that are needed to keep them all first class. I know it's tough and it's going to be tougher, but I have no doubt that the leadership of the Orchestra, the other arts organizations, and the community is up for it.

"There is no great community that does not have a great orchestra. The greatest satisfaction of course is just to listen to it, and now to hear how great its reputation is. I don't think there was anything more thrilling for Judy and me than to hear [the Orchestra perform on tour in Vienna] and hear the crowd at the Musikverein go wild over the Minnesota Orchestra . . . they went absolutely wild, they called the Orchestra back and back and back, three encores, they just wouldn't let them go. That was a very high point in our musical life—to realize we do indeed have an orchestra that is recognized as one of the greatest in the world."

Judy and Kenneth Dayton backstage with Music Director Eiji Oue after the Orchestra's debut concert at Vienna's Musikverein

Guidelines for Orchestra Hall

ON MARCH 21, 1973, THE MINNESOTA ORCHESTRA board of directors approved a formal document written by board member Kenneth N. Dayton, "Design Philosophy for Orchestra Hall." The five guidelines of the document read, in part:

1. . . . The building should be an honest building, conveying a sense of dignity, simplicity, and eye-satisfying proportion.

2. . . . The building should enhance the total concert-going experience...and should help achieve that most important goal—excellence of acoustics.

3. . . . The building should help the music director achieve his mission and should honor those who have built this great Orchestra.

4. We have great respect for the men and women who play in this Orchestra—for their musicianship and for them as human beings. . . . [The building] should do everything possible to make their work rewarding and fulfilling.

5. . . . The location of the new hall makes it possible for the Orchestra to relate to the community far better than has ever been possible in the past. The building and site should help express this ideal relationship of the Orchestra to its community . . .

A Rare Privilege and Joy

JOHN COY

John Coy is the author of the award-winning picture books Night Driving, Strong to the Hoop, *and* Vroomaloom Zoom. *Both* Night Driving *and* Strong to the Hoop *have also been performed as plays. Coy wrote librettos for* All Around Sound *and* Patterns for Orchestra *in collaboration with composer Libby Larsen and elementary school students as part of the Minnesota Orchestra's Young People's Concerts and Adventures in Music for Families series. He also wrote and narrated* Copland Portrait *to celebrate the 100th birthday of Aaron Copland at Orchestra Hall. In addition to writing, Coy works as a visiting author in schools around the country.*

AN OCTOBER MORNING EARLY IN THE 21ST CENTURY. Strings of yellow school buses line the streets around Orchestra Hall for today's Young People's Concert. Students walk into the Hall talking and pointing at the cubes. Ushers scramble to get everybody seated, while teachers smile at their students' enthusiasm. Minnesota Orchestra musicians warm up onstage. When the conductor enters, the audience applauds, and the music begins. Students nod as they hear the pieces they have prepared for. Many tap their feet, and some conduct with their hands. They sit on the edge of their seats, mouths open in wonder.

Afterwards, they talk about how much they have enjoyed the experience. "The music was cool, even better than I thought it would be," one boy says. "I've never been to a concert before," says a girl. "I really liked the music," says another boy. "It was sometimes calm and sometimes wild. I can't wait to come back."

∾

The *Minneapolis Journal* of October 1, 1911 announced the news with large headlines: "Big Children's Concerts to Raise Musical Standards." "Smaller Guarantee Fund by Minneapolis Women an Example of Rare Public Spirit—Chicago and Other Large Cities with Permanent Orchestras Can Boast of No Similar Achievement." The article reported that "a band of public spirited Minneapolis women" had raised a $2,500 Guarantee Fund that surpassed expectations, and that the Young People's Symphony Concert Association had a roster of 123 charter members and a waiting list. Mrs. George Chase Christian was elected president, Frances Janney vice president, Mrs. C. C. Webber treasurer, and Ann Wells secretary of the fourteen-member board.

The Minneapolis Symphony Orchestra had performed for students at matinee concerts when on tour prior to 1911. In 1909, for example, the Orchestra had performed selections by Mendelssohn, Schumann, Moskowski, Mascagni, Delibes, Boccherini, Glazunov, Gounod, and Strauss for students in

Retired flutist Adele Lorraine, who was active in Kinder Konzerts, Adopt-A-School, and other educational programs, says, "Music is the way not only to communicate and be entertained, but it is a way to heal the human spirit and encourage cooperation." Lorraine frequently visited area classrooms, such as this one at Urban Arts in 1974.

locations as diverse as Duluth (Minnesota), Lincoln (Nebraska), and Joplin (Missouri). In June 1911, when the Orchestra returned to Duluth, Emil Oberhoffer, the music director of the Minneapolis Symphony, commented on his approach to programming. "I am making my programs a little stronger each year for the children. I think they can gradually take heavier numbers and this afternoon I have even put in part of one of Beethoven's symphonies."

That symphony was Beethoven's Fifth, and the *Duluth Herald* reported the reaction of the audience:

> Hundreds of children of all ages, some so small that they seemed lost in the big seats of the Lyceum, were enthusiastically delighted with the concert played by the Minneapolis Symphony Orchestra yesterday afternoon at the children's matinee.

Such matinee concerts for children, however, had not yet occurred in Minneapolis. Bringing the music of a great symphony orchestra to the young people of its own community was the goal that led to the formation of the Young People's Symphony Concert Association. Ann Wells, one of the founding members of YPSCA, had heard a concert for young people in New York City led by Walter Damrosch. She proposed a series of such concerts in the Orchestra's home. The response from women of the community was enthusiastic. Mrs. Christian even set up a meeting with Walter Damrosch to discuss the concerts.

They chose November 24, 1911, as the date for the first of five concerts. Oberhoffer agreed to select the program and provide explanatory remarks. Tickets priced at ten, fifteen, twenty-five, and 50 cents a seat went on sale November 18. The *Minneapolis Evening Tribune* reported the demand:

> An avalanche of school children, teachers, and principals descended upon the Cable Piano Company today at the sale of seats for the first of the children's symphony concerts to be given in the auditorium, and over 2,000 seats, which it had been calculated it would take three days to dispose of, were cleaned up in half an hour. The demand for seats was so much larger than was expected that only 10 of the 65 pub-

lic schools in the city could be provided with tickets. As many as 300 tickets went to a school. Mrs. Luella Ames, principal of the Harrison School, who was eleventh in line, and had stood at the ticket window two hours, was turned away.

It was quickly decided to present a duplicate concert so that more students could attend. Schools let out early on November 24 to allow students to come to the 3:45 concert. Some came in carriages, but most walked to the Minneapolis Auditorium on 11th Street. Inside, Oberhoffer presented a program on "The Construction of the Modern Orchestra" that was received enthusiastically. The *Minneapolis Daily News* reported:

> What a novel and thrilling sight was the eager mass of school children, marshalled by their teachers, packing the Auditorium to the last seat, following with alert ears and stareing [sic] eyes Mr. Oberhoffer's most interesting demonstrations of the four classes of orchestral instruments and fine examples of their special use, from his standard concert programs.

Among the selections were "Dance of the Toy Pipers" from *The Nutcracker* by Tchaikovsky, "Evenings Under the Trees" by Massenet, the minuet "Will o' the Wisp" by Berlioz, the Largo movement from the *New World* Symphony (condensed) by Dvořák, and Theme and Variations on the Austrian National Anthem by Haydn.

This initial Young People's Concert set the tone for what was to follow. The concerts were conceived, funded, and organized by women to present the Orchestra to the school children of the community.

In a letter to Mrs. Carlo Fisher, a member of the YPSCA board, Minneapolis Public Schools Supervisor T. P. Giddings expressed his gratitude:

> I wish you would convey to the ladies who are backing this movement my thanks and intense appreciation of their efforts to help the music work in the public schools. They have kindly placed at my disposal the greatest instrument possible for use in the musical training of children. It particularly pleases me to think that so large a number can go to these concerts for so small a sum.

SOME IN CARRIAGES, BUT MOST CHILDREN WALK TO CONCERT

WALKING TO THE CONCERT   IN STATE BUT NOT POPULAR

The very first Young People's Concert of the Orchestra in Minneapolis took place on November 24, 1911.

The pride and boosterism in this young city is illustrated in press accounts of the event. The *Minneapolis Morning Tribune* reported:

The concert was unique in annals of Minneapolis and practically so in the annals of the musical world. Damrosch, in New York, gave a series of children's concerts with his orchestra some time ago, but they were not planned so democratically as these.

These concerts were not quite as democratic as the *Tribune* implied. At the second concert, more than five hundred seats, priced at 50 cents, remained vacant on the main floor. Meanwhile, more than three thousand children were on a waiting list, because the ten-, fifteen-, and twenty-five-cent seats had been sold, and they could not afford the higher priced seats.

The demand for the concerts had been much greater than anyone anticipated. Of the 68 schools in Minneapolis, only 35 had tickets for the first two concerts. And due to the Orchestra contract and heavy schedule, it would be impossible to provide a duplicate concert each time. How would this new organization respond to these pressures?

The directors of the Young People's Symphony Concert Association released a statement on December 10, 1911:

The Y.P.S.C. Association aspires to a policy of the most inclusive character and the broadest usefulness, but such a policy is not to be ready made. In this task the association asks the patient cooperation of all who have welcomed their novel undertaking with enthusiasm and who desire to see it established as a permanent factor in the life of this community.

Attendance was to be limited to sixth-, seventh-, eighth-grade, and high school students for the rest of that year, and the block of 50-cent tickets would remain. The overflow from the first two concerts was to be accommodated at the second concert of the series. Oberhoffer, the young Bavarian-born conductor, had already announced the theme: "The Inception and Origin of the Symphony under Haydn," featuring three movements of the *Surprise* Symphony.

Oberhoffer was extremely effective in explaining the work of a symphony orchestra to children. The

The Junior Symphony Concerts

 IT is probably a just criticism that Americans are not as musical as older peoples. The Germans, the Scandinavians, the Italians are lovers and producers of music. Even their peasants have their great choruses and their beloved instruments. But in this country the masses of the people are comparatively uneducated in music.

It could hardly be otherwise. The arts are the last fruit of civilization. We are too young to have accomplished much in this line. People who are fighting Indians and putting down rebellions, who are building bridges and laying railroads have little time for the cultivation of the arts. We have not the musical heritage, traditions and environment of the older countries. We have not the great cathedrals, the great musical centers, the great artists.

But our pioneer period is past and America is awaking to her lack. In New York city Walter Damrosch is doing much to bring music to the very door of the people. We of the middle west are not without our musical prophet. What Mr. Damrosch is doing for New York, Mr. Oberhoffer is doing for Minneapolis. Since the establishment of the Symphony orchestra, Minneapolis has taken its place among the first musical centers of the country.

But it is not enough to provide the best music to delight those who are already music lovers. In order to place music on an enduring foundation in a community it is necessary to reach the young people.

There is nothing that promises more for the musical future of the city than the Junior Sumphony concerts soon to be established. If it were only to supplant less wholesome entertainments, the movement would be well worth while. But it aims at far more than this. The idea is to present the really great music in such a way as to appeal to young people, to awaken in them a taste for the best, and to stimulate them to achievements in musical lines. Merely bringing them together in a musical atmosphere means much. Popular enthusiasm tends to create popular standards. When the enthusiasm is roused often enough to become an habitual state, the standards are safely established.

The value of the concerts will be greatly enhanced by Mr. Oberhoffer's explanations, which will make the compositions played intelligible to all. Probably very few of the young people of Minneapolis will have individual music lessons from a great master. But here is an opportunity for every child in the city to be moved, inspired and stimulated by one who is a lover and a master of music.

Viewed purely from the practical standpoint such enterprises are gratifying. They mark a new place in the city's development. There is no surer sign of the prosperity and welfare of a people than such institutions as the Fine Arts Museum and the Symphony Concerts.

On August 20, 1911, the Sunday Tribune *expressed enthusiastic community support for the plan to bring symphonic music to young people.*

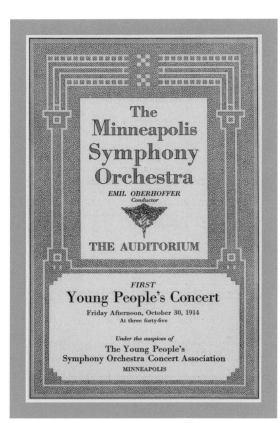

The Orchestra provided special program books in the early years of Young People's Concerts.

Minneapolis Evening Tribune reported after this concert:

> Mr. Oberhoffer gets so accurately and sympathetically the child point of view, that his verbal explanation of the origin, purpose, and construction of the highest form of musical composition must have been enlightening even to his youngest hearer.

One of the reasons for Oberhoffer's effectiveness was the thought and deliberation he put into this work, evident in a letter he wrote to Mrs. Carolyn McKnight Christian, president of the Young People's Symphony Concert Association, in 1921:

> From past experiences and my personal understanding of the child-mind, I have come to the conclusion that the essential aim of our concerts will ever be to clarify the meaning of orchestral masterpieces for them. In other words, direct their attention to the salient beauties or characteristic elements of a composition in necessarily short talks. To arouse interest, even curiosity in a composition means to hold their minds centered on the work in a half critical, half speculative state of expectancy, for if I claim for a composition certain excellencies, they will appraise them for themselves. This, "taking part in the concert," as it were, necessitates closest attention and will stimulate the one most needful factor for real understanding and consequent enjoyment of music —imagination.

Every person who has worked on Young People's Concerts since that time has strived to live up to the essential aim that Emil Oberhoffer expressed so clearly.

∽

One hundred years, a centennial, seems like a substantial amount of time. But when one talks with people like Virginia Jenness, who as a young girl went with her mother, Mrs. James B. Lindsay, to hear the Orchestra under Emil Oberhoffer, the connections with the early years seem close. In a 2002 interview she recalled that her father liked to go to the concerts featuring soloists. For the other concerts, she would often go with her mother. Young Virginia would wear one of her best dresses, and her mother would drive. Virginia Jenness now says, "Attending those concerts as a child led to a lifetime of orchestra going."

Burton Paulu is another Twin Cities resident who brings the early days of the Orchestra alive. Born in 1910, Paulu first heard the Orchestra in Aberdeen, South Dakota, in 1924 under the direction of Henri Verbrugghen, the Minneapolis Symphony Orchestra's second music director. The Orchestra played an afternoon concert for students in the high school gymnasium and an evening concert in the auditorium of the Northern State Teacher's College. "These details are impressed on my mind," says Paulu. "It was the first time I'd heard an orchestra, and for me these concerts were very important."

Paulu later studied music at the University of Minnesota and in 1929 began as a student announcer at WLB, the campus radio station. On May 2, 1938, WLB began broadcasting concerts of the Minneapolis Symphony Orchestra from Northrop Memorial Auditorium. Paulu, who also became a substitute trombonist for the Orchestra, served as manager of WLB (which later changed its name to KUOM) for 40 years. In this capacity he broadcast hundreds of concerts, including many of the Orchestra's Young People's Concerts, performed on live radio broadcasts.

"Northrop Auditorium would be filled," Paulu says, "and we had all these other students listening in their classrooms." In addition, a few days before the concerts, Dimitri Mitropoulos and, later, Antal Dorati previewed the works to be performed. "Teachers just loved these broadcasts," Paulu says. As part of his preparation, he worked closely with members of the Young People's Symphony Concert Association, whom he describes as "an able, dedicated, talented group of people."

Charlotte Karlen also remembers attending Young People's Concerts. In 1936, as Charlotte Greenfield, she attended John Hay Elementary School in North Minneapolis and went with her fifth-grade class to hear the Orchestra under Eugene Ormandy. "We sat in the very top of Northrop. I thought I'd died and gone to heaven listening to that glorious music. It was the most heavenly thing I'd experienced." Appreciation of music was a value Karlen learned from her family. "It didn't matter how rich or poor you were, there was still music

in the home," she says. "That Young People's Concert started a whole passion for symphonic music, and I've liked to sit in the balcony ever since." Karlen later became a volunteer and then worked for the Orchestra in marketing and development for seventeen years.

The numbers of students attending Young People's Concerts continued to grow. In 1938 Damrosch himself wrote in a letter to Mrs. Christian, "I do not think there is another city in the world that draws so huge an audience as you assemble at the Northrop Memorial Auditorium."

∾

On a bright day in 1941, Mary Ann Janisch walked with her third-grade classmates from Holy Spirit School in Saint Paul to catch the Randolph-Hazel Park streetcar. They were on their way to the concert hall of the Saint Paul Municipal Auditorium to hear the Minneapolis Symphony Orchestra. Mary Ann, like many of the students in her class, did not grow up in a concert-going family and had not had music lessons. Both her parents had an eighth-grade education and had gone to work at young ages on family farms.

Principal Oboe Rhadames Angelucci and student in University of Minnesota music studio

Music Director Antal Dorati and eight-year-old Stephen Pflaum study Paul Binstock's horn, backstage after a Young People's Concert at St. Paul Auditorium in 1949. As an adult, Stephen Pflaum became chairman of the Orchestra's board.

However, the Sisters of Saint Joseph of Carondelet at Holy Spirit School put a strong focus on music and the arts as an essential part of the curriculum. The students sang every day and learned to read music. Mary Ann was a member of the Children's Choir that sang the Requiem Mass in Gregorian chant at the 10:00 a.m. funerals.

At the concert, Mary Ann heard an oboe solo in a piece by Bizet. "It was the Pied Piper of my life. I was absolutely enchanted. The oboist was the great Rhadames Angelucci, the Minneapolis Symphony's principal, whose playing was musical seduction of a mighty kind."

The conductor was Dimitri Mitropoulos. "As anybody knows who ever heard or saw Mitropoulos conduct, the minute he walked onto the stage, there was such a high voltage charge. He brought that spiritual quality. He was riveting."

Mary Ann Janisch began her life-long passion for the Orchestra that day. At thirteen, she was given unused subscription tickets and took her parents to the Minneapolis Symphony for the first time. As a University of Minnesota freshman, she skipped the first twenty minutes of English class each day to listen to a fragment of the Orchestra's rehearsal through a crack in the locked lobby doors of Northrop Auditorium. Soon she discovered that Antal Dorati, now the music director, welcomed students to rehearsals. "He was so friendly, ebullient. He liked young people." She explained to her English professor that "nowhere else in America was there a great symphony orchestra smack in the middle of a campus." Her professor accepted Mary Ann's reason for arriving late. Before long, she went off to Columbia University as a Woodrow Wilson fellow to study musicology, met a young man in New York, and became Mary Ann Feldman.

That siren oboe sound led to a 60-year relationship with the Orchestra as a concertgoer, subscriber, 33-year program annotator and editor of *Showcase* magazine, public affairs associate director, teacher, musicologist, and historian. "Attending concerts by the Minneapolis Symphony Orchestra as a child changed my life," Feldman says. "It was like Alice in Wonderland falling through the hole. A new world opened up, one in which every instrument was like a new color and every piece was a new adventure."

On January 31, 1949, a significant date in the Orchestra's outreach activities, Orchestra supporter Rosalynd Pflaum led eight women in the founding of WAMSO, the Women's Association of the Minneapolis Symphony Orchestra. The purpose of WAMSO was "to stimulate interest and to encourage statewide support" of the Orchestra, and from the beginning, WAMSO focused on education. As one of the first projects, the volunteer association distributed unused tickets to college students. Another early project was to send performing ensembles of Orchestra members into schools. This accomplished two goals. First, it brought musicians to students in the more intimate school setting, and second, it provided musicians with some much-needed income in that era of the 36-week season.

Over the years, members of WAMSO developed a number of significant educational programs. In 1956 the organization held its first Young Artist Competition, in which talented young musicians compete for cash prizes and a chance to solo with the Orchestra. The program continues to the present day. As young violinists, three current members of the Orchestra—Pamela Arnstein, Sarah Kwak, and Frank Lee—were winners of these Young Artist Competitions.

In 1962 WAMSO became the sponsor for Young Audiences of Minnesota, a local chapter of the national organization dedicated to providing live performances in schools. In 30 years, hundreds of thousands of students were exposed to the arts through this program. In 1993 WAMSO provided seed money and administrative support to help Young Audiences become a separate organization. Mary Steinke, who coordinated the program for WAMSO for many years, says, "Young Audiences had grown up and was ready to go off on its own."

The WAMSO educational program that has generated the most attention, however, is Kinder Konzerts. These concerts for four- and five-year-olds began in 1978 after WAMSO member Ara Burwell returned from a meeting of the American Symphony Orchestra League with a new vision—that WAMSO could serve educational needs through a preschool concert program.

In October 1994 Yo-Yo Ma coached a young cellist in the WAMSO—Minnesota Orchestra Meet The Masters series.

WAMSO hired music educator Joanna Cortright to develop these concerts and serve as narrator. Cortright, who has an extensive background working with children in music, says, "Children of any age learn musical concepts as long as the teaching is grounded in age-appropriate vocabulary and strategies."

Kinder Konzerts provide kids with multiple musical experiences. In the Sound Factory, youngsters explore musical ideas and try out different instruments under the guidance of WAMSO volunteer docents. They take a tour of Orchestra Hall and sit on the stage for intimate concerts narrated by Cortright and performed by small groups of Minnesota Orchestra musicians. The music is composed especially for the Kinder Konzerts, and so far, WAMSO has commissioned fourteen new story compositions from composers such as Libby Larsen, Daniel Dorff, and Janika Vandervelde.

Orchestra Associate Principal Cello Janet Horvath says, "Kinder Konzerts are some of the best things we do." In 1989, Kinder Konzerts won a national award for excellence in education from the American Symphony Orchestra League. From 1978 to 2001, more than 90,000 four- and five-year-olds from Early Childhood Family Education, Head Start, day care centers, and parochial, public, and homeschools attended Kinder Konzerts. For most, this was their introduction to the symphony orchestra world.

Conductor Henry Charles Smith has played a significant role in introducing many young people to the world of classical music and this Orchestra. Smith, former principal trombonist of The Philadelphia Orchestra, came to the Twin Cities in 1971 to serve as assistant conductor of the Minnesota Orchestra under Music Director Stanislaw Skrowaczewski. In seventeen years, as associate conductor and then resident conductor, Smith led numerous Young People's Concerts. Many audience members remember his snapping of a dollar bill to demonstrate the acoustics at Orchestra Hall. Smith also tried to persuade school

Children at Kinder Konzerts performances sit close to the musicians (here, Elliot Fine), who talk with them about their instruments.

The Young People's Symphony Concert Association School Music Auditions winner, fourteen-year-old Jordan Hall, performed as violin soloist with the Orchestra at Young People's Concerts and Casual Classics Concerts (right, with conductor David Alan Miller) during the 2000-2001 season.

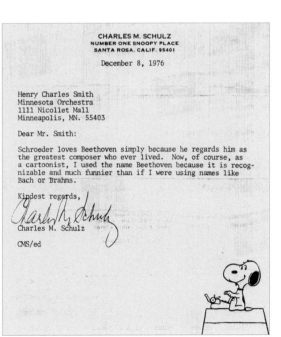

CHARLES M. SCHULZ
NUMBER ONE SNOOPY PLACE
SANTA ROSA, CALIF. 95401

December 8, 1976

Henry Charles Smith
Minnesota Orchestra
1111 Nicollet Mall
Minneapolis, MN. 55403

Dear Mr. Smith:

Schroeder loves Beethoven simply because he regards him as the greatest composer who ever lived. Now, of course, as a cartoonist, I used the name Beethoven because it is recognizable and much funnier than if I were using names like Bach or Brahms.

Kindest regards,

Charles M. Schulz

CMS/ed

boards not to cut music programs when faced with budget difficulties. "I'm a great believer in good public school music programs, because I came through one." Attending such meetings as a lone crusader wasn't easy, but early on, Smith recognized the importance of school music programs to the lives of the children and the future of the Orchestra.

Under Smith, the Minnesota Orchestra conducted numerous one-year residencies in urban high schools. Smith and other musicians visited these schools to work with the band, orchestra, and choir. He also talked in history classes about American music and in physics classes about the physics of music. He would invite an entire student body to Orchestra Hall for a concert for their high school. This would begin with the school alma mater, which Smith would orchestrate. "I still hear from students to whom it made an important difference," he says.

Smith also provided engaging commentary for Young People's Concerts that were broadcast live on public radio. He remembers introducing the programs by saying, "This concert is about hearing great music played by a great orchestra." Smith says there was pressure from teachers to include more visual elements to respond to students who were growing up with television, but that it was important to keep the focus on music. "Many of the concerts did involve a story with narrator, a mime, dancers, or projections. However, I always wanted to give kids an experience in which, when they got back on the bus, they would be thinking, first and foremost, about what they had *heard*."

As an example Smith offers a program he entitled "Why Schroeder Loves Beethoven." Smith wrote to cartoonist Charles Schulz to ask why the Schroeder character loved Beethoven. Schulz responded on Snoopy stationery (*left*), and Smith read his reply to students at an all-Beethoven concert.

Feldman, in charge of programming Young People's Concerts for the 1975-1976 season, along with her other duties, says she also felt the impact of television. "There was great pressure for the visual. How do we make it more like TV?" Feldman contrasts this with her concert expectations as a girl. "My generation was the last to grow up without television. Nobody ever said, 'We need visual stimulus. We need multimedia experiences.' The music-making was enough, especially music-making of the caliber that we got from this Orchestra."

After the move to the newly built Orchestra Hall in 1974, the Orchestra continued to attract large numbers of students to Young People's Concerts, and the Young People's Symphony Concert Association continued to provide extensive volunteer help, since the Orchestra had no staff person focused solely on educational matters. This changed in 1990, however, with the hiring of the Orchestra's first full time education/outreach administrator, Stephanie Lusco.

One of the programs developed in the early 1990s was Adopt-A-School, designed to introduce students to professional musicians outside the concert hall setting. Each year Minnesota Orchestra musicians, as well as musicians who perform as substitutes, make monthly visits to Twin Cities schools. The Adopt-A-School musicians plan the year's activities with partnering teachers and also invite other Orchestra members as guests to talk with students and to play for them. Students at nineteen schools (as of the 2001-2002 season) participate in Adopt-A-School programs, now under the direction of Orchestra staff member Mele Willis. The project culminates in children's visits to Orchestra Hall, as guests of their musician, to attend a Young People's Concert.

Horn player David Kamminga has been active in the Adopt-A-School program from its inception. Kamminga says that his colleague Manuel Laureano, principal trumpet, "told me many years ago that if you share your enthusiasm about the music with kids, they will get it—and he was right." For his Adopt-A-School students, Kamminga demonstrates the different horns he plays and brings in guest musicians, conductors, and librarians. The end of the 2001-2002 season found him working with students on writing a school song at Pullman Elementary School in St. Paul Park.

The musicians involved in Adopt-A-School design programs freely with their partner teachers and students. Violinist Pamela Shaffer has used this freedom to develop elaborate programs. In 1996 Shaffer and 105 students at the Field School in Minneapolis performed the Triumphal Scene from *Aida*. For the approaching centennial of Aaron Copland's birth, she worked with parents, teachers, and students to create a Copland celebration with scenery, costumes, and a choreographed hoe-down. In May 2002 her students created art works and performed Mussorgsky's *Pictures at an Exhibition*. Shaffer says, "I want the kids to feel successful." In discussing the impact of the program she says, "The rewards are really worth it. I've been more educated than the kids. Most of us would say we learned a lot in the program."

In the mid-1990s, as existing educational programs expanded and new ones developed under the direction of Gary Alan Wood, it became clear that the Orchestra needed additional educational staff. The Eugene Sit Grant from Sit Investment Associates, initiated in 1999, allowed the education and outreach programs to achieve a goal of three full-time staff members. Everyone involved agrees that enlarging the education staff has made an enormous difference. "The depth we are able to provide is night and

day from six years ago," says Robert Neu, Orchestra vice president and general manager. Historian Feldman, who has been paying close attention for 60 years, says, "Minnesota Orchestra Young People's Concerts have never been better. I feel very positive about the quality, the preparation, and the department that does it."

At a May 2002 Adopt-A-School performance, Violinist Pamela Shaffer's Field School students performed an original ballet to Mussorgsky's Pictures at an Exhibition *(The Ballet of Chicks in Their Shells).*

1 2

1. *The 2000-2001 Minnesota Music Educators Association All-State Orchestra performed side-by-side with members of the Minnesota Orchestra in an October 2000 concert under the direction of Conductor Laureate Stanislaw Skrowaczewski.* **2.** *Principal Pops Conductor Doc Severinsen and 2001 MMEA All-Stars Jazz Band in an Orchestra Hall workshop for jazz band educators* **3.** *Young People's Concert March 2002: Theatre de la Jeune Lune and Minnesota Orchestra in* Peter and the Wolf **4.** *Violinist Pamela Arnstein, here with students of Brookside Elementary, has been an active Adopt-A-School participant since 1998.* **5.** *WAMSO Sound Factory, a popular component of Kinder Konzerts*

87

Students now attend Young People's Concerts at Orchestra Hall from as far away as Austin, Willmar, Mora, St. Cloud, and Woodville, Wisconsin. In addition, ensembles from the Orchestra travel to different parts of the state for presentations and informal concerts as part of the Blandin Rural Residency program. People in Alexandria, Austin, Brainerd, Bemidji, Grand Marais, Perham, Willmar, and Worthington have connected with the Orchestra through this program. In other ongoing statewide efforts, the full Minnesota Orchestra performs as part of the Arts Across Minnesota program of the Minnesota State Arts Board. Fairmont, Worthington, and Hibbing have hosted Minnesota Orchestra concerts in recent years; these trips provide an echo of the extensive touring of the Orchestra's early years.

Sitting at his desk in Orchestra Hall in 2002, Director of Education and Outreach Jim Bartsch remembers coming to hear the Orchestra with his classmates from Homecroft School in Saint Paul. "I remember sitting in the balcony in Northrop Auditorium and hearing *Central Park in the Dark* by Ives and thinking it was really cool. "Henry Charles Smith was conducting and somebody shot a paper clip on stage. He said he'd stop the concert and empty the hall if that happened again." Smith was following a policy that had been developed in response to previous problems with students shooting paper clips with rubber bands. This had become so serious that some musicians were afraid of being injured.

In earlier years, Feldman remembers, unruly boys disrupted the concert by shooting spitballs from the balcony of Northrop Auditorium. No reports of paper clip or spitball problems have occurred recently, and long-time concertgoers say students at current Young People's Concerts are very attentive and respectful.

In looking back at Young People's Concerts, Bartsch says, "A little chunk of the history is in my lap right now. I am the steward of that for a while. It's a big responsibility." With a background as both a public school teacher and a professional musician, Bartsch has clear goals for Young People's Concerts. "I hope the kids have a great experience while they are here, and that *the music* is something they will remember. Kids are drawn to quality. We want the Orchestra to be the main focus. We also want this to be the beginning of their relationship with great music."

Recently, Bartsch has been thinking about Emil Oberhoffer's strategy of introducing children to "heavier numbers," such as a section of Beethoven's Fifth Symphony. In the fall of 2001, Bartsch chose the entire slow movement of Beethoven's Seventh Symphony for a Young People's Concert. "Kids said it was their favorite piece on the program, and when I go into schools, they ask when we are going to perform it again." Bartsch feels Oberhoffer's words resonate today as he balances the musical and visual focus of each concert. Like Oberhoffer, Bartsch benefits from the help of community volunteers—WAMSO and YPSCA. "There are a lot of people in this community who have a passion for connecting kids with great music."

As the Minnesota Orchestra celebrates the centennial of its founding, its education and outreach programs are more extensive than ever. More than 55,000 students attend Young People's Concerts each season at Orchestra Hall. With the single exception of one year during the Depression, these concerts have been performed continuously since 1911. The education staff creates and sends curriculum materials to schools in advance to prepare students for their concerts. Adventures in Music for Families—Sunday educational concerts attended by youngsters, their families, and friends—attract 15,000 adults and children annually.

Side-by-side rehearsals and concerts have begun to appear frequently on the Orchestra's schedule. Talented high school and college students participate in side-by-side sessions with the Orchestra, absorbing valuable lessons from professional musicians through working together on orchestral repertoire. Beginning in 2000, musicians from the University of Minnesota Symphony Orchestra have rehearsed annually onstage at Orchestra Hall alongside Minnesota Orchestra musicians conducted by Associate Conductor Giancarlo Guerrero. In April 2002, the combined orchestras performed Dvořák's Seventh Symphony and Shostakovich's First Symphony in a side-by-side concert before 1,700 people at Orchestra Hall.

Former Music Director Eiji Oue, too, often worked with young instrumentalists during his tenure, and in 2001, musicians of the Greater Twin Cities Youth Symphony

Minnesota Vikings great Carl Eller narrates Copland's Lincoln Portrait *at a 1976 Young People's Concert with Conductor Henry Charles Smith.*

and Minnesota Youth Symphony played in a side-by-side rehearsal and concert with the Minnesota Orchestra conducted by Oue. In the fall of 2000, Conductor Laureate Stanislaw Skrowaczewski conducted a side-by-side rehearsal and concert with the student members of the Minnesota Music Educators' Association All-State Orchestra. And, as part of his first full season, Music Director Designate Osmo Vänskä will conduct a side-by-side rehearsal with the All-State ensemble.

Two community orchestras of adult musicians, the Kenwood Chamber Orchestra and the Metropolitan Symphony Orchestra, have also played in side-by-side rehearsals. For Margaret Norling, a Kenwood bass player in her 80s, a side-by-side rehearsal under Associate Conductor Giancarlo Guerrero in May 2001 was her third such experience with the Orchestra. In 1934, as a

student at Roosevelt High School, she played under the direction of Eugene Ormandy. In 1939, as a member of the University of Minnesota Concert Band, she played the *1812* Overture under Dimitri Mitropoulos. "It was so exciting," she says. "He was so dynamic, so electrifying."

The Young People's Symphony Concert Association continues its work of more than 90 years by providing tickets and bus service for students from schools that would otherwise be unable to attend concerts. Volunteers visit Minneapolis and St. Paul schools to talk with students about the Orchestra and to prepare students for the concerts. YPSCA volunteers also work as ushers to greet students when they arrive at Orchestra Hall.

Rodney Nelson, who works as a YPSCA volunteer at Young People's Concerts, remembers that as a child he walked 28 blocks with his class from Sheridan School to

Minnesota Orchestra flutist Wendy Williams, center foreground, talks with University of Minnesota Symphony Orchestra flutists at a 2001 side-by-side rehearsal in Orchestra Hall.

Virtual Tour—Real Success

THE ORCHESTRA HAS CREATED A DIFFERENT, TECHNOLOGICALLY based form of education through a partnership with Mighty Media, Inc., an educational design company that has helped to develop virtual tours for the Orchestra's website. Through two Orchestra tours of Europe and one of Japan, students and adults on computers everywhere were able to follow the Orchestra's progress, see pictures, and write to musicians. During a six-week period surrounding the most recent tour, of Europe in 2000, more than 45,000 users joined the Orchestra in this way.

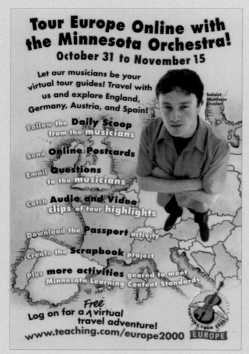

Virtual Tour postcard, Europe 2000, featuring violin soloist Matthew Trusler

Northrop Auditorium to attend Young People's Concerts. Later, as a teacher in the Minneapolis schools, Nelson took his students to these concerts. Now, as a retired teacher and YPSCA volunteer, he ushers a new generation of students to their seats in Orchestra Hall. YPSCA also sponsors annual School Music Auditions, which identify and reward talented young area musicians. Orchestra cellist Kari Jane Docter is a past winner of this competition.

WAMSO—Minnesota Orchestra Volunteer Association also maintains its strong educational focus. Its oldest educational program, the Young Artist Competition, continues to provide opportunities for aspiring young musicians to compete for prizes and scholarships. Kinder Konzerts reach more than 6,000 four- and five-year-olds each year, and the organization has commissioned a new work from composer Steve Heitzeg to celebrate the Kinder Konzerts 25th anniversary in 2002-2003. In the 1990s WAMSO also developed Gear Your Ear,© a program that offers a complete listening curriculum and state listening contest for fifth and sixth graders. It has proven enormously popular and successful. WAMSO also sponsors previews to Adventures in Music for Families Concerts for children and adults. Led by Joanna Cortright, these previews appeal to youngsters and their families by providing a context and exploring music through movement, stories, and pictures prior to Orchestra Hall concerts.

Young People's Concerts continue to put the music first, even while the Orchestra staff and musicians find ways of bringing in appropriate visual elements. Two

Millions of students have heard the Minnesota Orchestra since its founding in 1903.

recent concerts that were especially popular with audiences, staff, and musicians exemplify the quality of current YP programming. In October 2001 Jim Bartsch produced a Young People's Concert on opera, conducted by Assistant Conductor Scott Terrell, for fourth through sixth graders. The Orchestra hosted singers from Minnesota Opera, the Stillwater High School Choir, and the Wayzata High School Chorus, who performed selections from *La bohème*, *Samson and Delilah*, and *Carmen*. Students from the high school bands of Eden Prairie and Apple Valley marched down the aisles of Orchestra Hall in military tattoo ensembles playing Puccini's music for the Christmas Eve scene that occurs in the second act of *La bohème*. Though some teachers were initially unsure about their students' interest in opera, they were gratified by the response. "Some of the kids thought they wouldn't like it, but they loved it," Bartsch says. "We reached 10,000 kids who now think opera is okay." Julie Ayer, Minnesota Orchestra assistant principal second violinist, says, "The kids loved it. I spoke with many of them, and the enthusiasm was palpable."

YP concerts for younger children also put the focus on music. In a winter 2001 collaboration between the Orchestra and the Magic Circle Mime Company, two mimes provided a blend of the silly and the serious while the Orchestra, again under Terrell's direction, played music of Bach, von Suppé, Ives, and Grofé. Orchestra violinist Pamela Shaffer says the mimes were a "perfect collaboration, the kind that melds with the music rather than competes with it," and Cassie Allen, a teacher in

NotesAlive!®

FOLLOWING ITS INCEPTION IN 1996-1997, MINNESOTA Orchestra Visual Entertainment (MOVE) released three "StoryConcert" videos under the *NotesAlive!*® label, produced by E.B. Gill (later vice president and chief operating officer of the Orchestra) and Bruce Becker. Designed to weave together a symphony and a story to introduce young people to classical music, the animated videos received a total of 36 prestigious national awards, including a *Sesame Street Parents* Best Video of the Year and one of *TV Guide*'s Ten Best Kids' Videos citations. All videos featured music performed by the Minnesota Orchestra, two under Music Director Eiji Oue, and one under Associate Conductor William Eddins. The first MOVE video, *On the Day You Were Born*, received the American Library Association's 1996 Andrew Carnegie Medal for Excellence in Children's Video, the only video so honored that year.

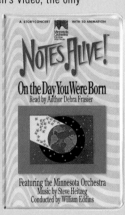

Based on Debra Frasier's award-winning book of the same title, *On the Day You Were Born* features music by composer Steve Heitzeg. The other two StoryConcert videos were *Dr. Seuss's My Many Colored Days*, with original music by Richard Einhorn and a narration by Holly Hunter, and *Nutcracker: The Untold Story*, with music from Tchaikovsky's *Nutcracker* ballet, and original story by Pamela Hill Nettleton with dancer James Sewell portraying the title character. *Dr. Seuss's My Many Colored Days* was also introduced in DVD format in January 2000.

Eden Prairie and Apple Valley high school band members performed Puccini in Orchestra Hall at October 2001 Young People's Concerts.

Young People's Concerts of January 2000 featured students from Ballet Arts Minnesota dancing to Aaron Copland's ballet Rodeo.

Jane Oxton, a teacher at Jefferson Elementary School in Saint Cloud, who has been bringing fifth graders to these concerts for fifteen years, agrees. "Preparation is the key. If we as teachers want the experience to pass through our students and not just over them, then they must be prepared." Oxton also cites the importance of a personal connection for the students. "One year one of the players, Ken Freed, made a school visit prior to the concert, and that made a real impact on the kids." Oxton says it's not always possible to predict how students will respond. "I remember one fifth grader who was autistic. She was very difficult to manage, and we almost didn't bring her along. It brought tears to see her spellbound by the music and the place. For one hour she was mesmerized and didn't so much as wiggle."

What does the future hold for education and outreach activities of the Minnesota Orchestra? Its first century was characterized by the active involvement of women volunteers in bringing classical music to the youth of a young city. An elite organization was opened up to the children of the community.

At the beginning of its second century, new challenges confront those involved in education and outreach activities. Visual stimulation continues to dominate young people's lives, with television, videos, movies, and electronic music delivered at high rates of speed. Commercials deliver narrative and emotional content in seconds, and children see thousands—even millions—of these. Composer Libby Larsen maintains that this has "changed the timing." Larsen points out that traditional symphonic work does not follow the conditioned timing of today's media. Great compositions of the past reflect the cultures in which they were produced, and creating additional compositions that incorporate this new timing will be one of the challenges for the future.

There is hope that with the increasing speed of visual and audio information, people will feel a need for experiences of deeper listening. Libby Larsen believes today's kids "are striving for moments to move inside themselves, to maintain a quiet, and dwell there." When this deeper listening occurs, new ways of seeing oneself and the world can emerge.

Cannon Falls, called it "one of the best concerts. All of our teachers and students enjoyed it."

Teachers, of course, are vital to the success of these concerts. They select an appropriate concert, prepare their students, collect money, and arrange transportation to Orchestra Hall. Prior to the concert, they receive a substantial curriculum packet (typically, 60 pages of materials) and compact discs. Beth Wallace, who has been bringing students from Pullman Elementary School in Saint Paul Park for nine years, believes preparation is vital. "I find that even if there isn't much visually going on, students can remain focused and maintain interest because they are listening with more understanding. That wouldn't happen if they weren't prepared."

The Orchestra's role in education is a challenge for the next century, and Minnesota Orchestra musicians will play a vital part. Cellist Janet Horvath says, "Our role has expanded to include a responsibility as educators." Violist Kenneth Freed agrees. "Using the same fervor you play with, you're going to have to communicate your passion for music with many different audiences."

Efforts to broaden the audience and increase the support for great orchestral music were a major focus of the Orchestra in its first century. These efforts were led by community-minded citizens and characterized by idealism and enthusiasm. Such people and such qualities will be essential in the Orchestra's second century to bring new young people and adults into Orchestra Hall.

In 1999, when Feldman stepped down from her position as editor of *Showcase* magazine, orchestral supporters established The Mary Ann Feldman Fund for Music Education. Feldman, who so clearly remembers going with her third-grade class to hear Dimitri Mitropoulos conduct the Orchestra, says: "What the music world needs today is listeners. We'd like to think that by third grade, every child will have regular adventures with our Orchestra and repeated experiences that bring them to the point where as young adults they know they must have music in their lives." What better way to acknowledge the sound of the oboe that became the Pied Piper of her life, than to provide a chance for other children to have such transforming experiences?

In his 1921 letter to Mrs. Carolyn McKnight Christian, Music Director Emil Oberhoffer expressed his views on presenting concerts for young people:

> I am fully conscious of the large responsibility of the part that the orchestra and myself have to bear in riveting and holding the attention of our Young People's audiences, and while I still consider it the hardest part of my season's work, *I regard it as a rare privilege and joy* to minister (in even a halting fashion) to the musical-aesthetic uplift of the coming generation. [Emphasis added.]

The Orchestra's challenge for its second century is no less than this rare privilege and joy.

WAMSO offers instrument "Sound Factories" as part of its award-winning Kinder Konzerts program. In 1982 this gleeful child experienced the thrill of setting a tamtam vibrating.

93

Recording and Broadcasting— Paths to the World

RICHARD FREED

Richard Freed has been a music critic for nearly 50 years, in both print and broadcast media (Saturday Review, The New York Times, Stereo Review, *etc.*), *focusing mainly on recordings. For sixteen years he was executive director of the Music Critics Association. He now is in his 27th year as annotator for the National Symphony Orchestra, having served 23 years with the Saint Louis Symphony Orchestra, ten years with The Philadelphia Orchestra, and shorter tenures with various other orchestras. Freed occasionally provides notes for Minnesota Orchestra concerts and has annotated some 400 recordings (among them historical series he programmed for the Smithsonian Collection). He has received two ASCAP Deems Taylor Awards and a Grammy for his concert and record notes.*

RECORDING AND BROADCASTING ARE probably the most specifically appropriate of an orchestra's communications efforts. While public relations and general promotion provide the impetus for such activity, recording can also produce significant historical documents, while preserving truly memorable performances. The Minnesota Orchestra's current activity continues a long and exemplary story of artistic, technical, and commercial interdependence on the most productive level. Few orchestras, in the United States or anywhere else, have made recording activity so significant a part of their history, and fewer still have played such a major role in the development of the recording industry itself, as the one whose centenary this book commemorates.

The Minneapolis Symphony Orchestra (MSO) began both broadcasting and recording early enough to qualify as a pioneer in both fields—somewhat earlier on radio than on records, if with more profound influence through recording. The first major orchestras to broadcast their concerts were American, but were not on the East Coast, as might have been assumed. The Detroit Symphony Orchestra started out on February 10, 1922 (less than two years after KDKA in Pittsburgh became the first radio station in the United States to launch regular operations), in a concert under its music director Ossip Gabrilowitsch, with the pianist Artur Schnabel as soloist, which Station WWJ beamed as far as Cuba.

Barely more than a year later, on March 2, 1923, the MSO made its radio debut, under the sponsorship of the L. S. Donaldson Company (a department store). Donaldson's laid two miles of cable to carry the sound from the microphones in the Auditorium to the studios of Station WLAG in the Oak Grove Hotel, from which the event, a regular Friday evening subscription concert, went out to numerous stations across the U.S. and Canada.

March 1923 found the Orchestra in the home stretch of a season without a music director. Emil Oberhoffer, its first conductor, had retired at the end of its nineteenth season, and the one that followed was given over entirely to guest conductors. The illustrious Bruno Walter was on the podium when the Orchestra went on the air for the first time. He had just come from Detroit, following his American debut with Walter Damrosch's New York Symphony Orchestra, and it was the first radio experience for him, as well as for the MSO. They broadcast together again twice that month, on March 9 and 23. In *Music and Maestros*, John K. Sherman's 1952 history of the MSO, Walter is quoted as remarking, "Imagine playing to an audience all across the continent, with thousands listening!"

Thousands were indeed listening, and more than 500 letters arrived in response to an offer of a $25 prize for the one from the most distant point reached by each broadcast. The *Minneapolis Journal* for March 18 quoted some of those letters, leading off with one from too close to home to qualify for the prize: A lumberjack in northern Wisconsin reported that an older man in his camp, who had never heard symphonic music before and seldom even spoke to his fellow workers, became so excited by the concert that he danced a jig and swallowed his tobacco. Somewhat less colorfully, two boys in Denver, who had built their own receiving set, stayed up late to hear the entire concert and wrote, "We didn't know there was such music." A banker in Birmingham, Alabama, expressed a similar response on the part of his family. A disabled Canadian war veteran in London, Ontario, who had had to give up his once active concert attendance, described the broadcast as "a godsend."

Following Walter's three broadcasts that March, the series was continued in April under the conductor Henri Verbrugghen, who had been named to become the Orchestra's music director in the fall. He not only continued and expanded the MSO's broadcast activity—in 1927 he began a series of concerts designed specifically for radio, with no audience allowed in the hall—but lost no time in making its first recordings. In those days, before the introduction of electrical recording (and indeed for some time after), record companies were for the most part concentrating on small pieces rather than

There was one especially nerve-racking [sic] afternoon on Northrop's stage in November 1946, when Artur Rubinstein and the Symphony played the Tschaikowsky B-flat minor concerto into recording microphones. The session was set for a Saturday —unfortunately the noisy and traffic-jammed Saturday on which Minnesota played Iowa in a football game at the university stadium . . . as the recording got under way it was discovered that the roar of airplanes over the football field was intruding into the concerto and spoiling side after side. Anguished pleas were relayed by telephone to Wold-Chamberlain Airport, base of the planes, and at length the pilots were called home.

—John K. Sherman, *Music and Maestros*

Verbrugghen Dons Earphones While Rehearsing Symphony For Radio Debut Tomorrow

On March 1, 1923, the Minneapolis Star *(above) and* Minneapolis Journal *(below) ran photos of preparations for the Orchestra's first radio broadcast, led by guest conductor Bruno Walter.*

JOURNAL   March 1, 1923

RADIO SET FOR SYMPHONY CONCERT

MINNEAPOLIS
JOURNAL PHOTO

COMPLICATED apparatus, costing more than $5,000, will be used to broadcast the Minneapolis Symphony orchestra concert Friday night by radio from the Auditorium and the

extended works, and, with very few exceptions, did their recording only in their own studios. Thus it was that at the end of Verbrugghen's first season (April 1924) a tour was extended to enable him and the Orchestra to record four items at the Brunswick studio in New York. The very first was an arrangement of the Maori folk tune *Waiata Poi*, which the conductor had picked up in the course of his previous post in Australia. Another was the best-known of Schubert's three *Marches militaires* (the only one to circulate in latter-day orchestral arrangements). In the following year Brunswick was able to switch over from the old acoustical method of recording to the new electrical one, and the pieces Verbrugghen and the MSO had recorded acoustically in New York were remade electrically in Brunswick's new Chicago studio.

While Verbrugghen's radio concerts continued until 1929, by which time they had grown to a series of twenty per season, he did very little recording, and what he did was limited to brief pieces, on the lighter side. His successor as music director, Eugene Ormandy, was to reverse that situation, without, however, neglecting radio. Ormandy came to Minneapolis as an experienced conductor of radio concerts; he was music director of the Columbia Broadcasting System at the time of his arrival and, in fact, conducted the MSO in a specially arranged live broadcast for CBS on the eve of his first formal concert with the Orchestra (and less than a week before his 32nd birthday).

At about the same point in each of the two following years Ormandy and the Orchestra were heard on nationwide "specials" for the National Broadcasting Company (NBC). On October 30, 1932, in the depth of the Depression (and a week before Franklin D. Roosevelt was elected President), they performed with singers from the Metropolitan Opera in a concert to announce the national Welfare and Relief Mobilization designed to meet some of the needs of that difficult time. A year later, NBC chose the MSO to give a two-hour concert to celebrate

the establishment of the network's new home, "Radio City," in New York's Rockefeller Center.

Midway between those two broadcasts, in April 1933, Ormandy began a series of eight one-hour radio concerts for regional circulation. Unlike his predecessor Verbrugghen, Ormandy invited a small audience, feeling its presence would "inspire" him and the Orchestra. In 1936, toward the end of his final season, they were heard nationally again on NBC, in a segment of the Sunday afternoon series *The Magic Key*.

Ormandy's most memorable activity, though, came halfway through his third season, when he seized an opportunity to make the MSO a force to be reckoned with in the world of recording. No one at the time could have foreseen the level on which he was to succeed, or the benefit to the recording industry itself as well as to the Orchestra's international recognition and the progress of his own career.

It is significant in this respect that Ormandy came to Minneapolis on the strength of his successful guest engagements with The Philadelphia Orchestra, which under Leopold Stokowski had begun recording for Victor in 1917. The Philadelphians continued over the years as that important label's house orchestra, not only undertaking major projects throughout the closing years of the acoustical era, but serving as a laboratory for the development of modern recording techniques made possible when the old horn was replaced by the electrical process. There was to be a sort of reciprocal phenomenon involving Ormandy and these two orchestras and their status in the area of recording. His success in Philadelphia led to his appointment in Minneapolis, and only five years later the impact of his recordings in Minneapolis (in addition, to be sure, to his continued guest engagements in Philadelphia) was a major factor in his becoming Stokowski's associate and, within two years, his successor as music director in Philadelphia.

Ormandy's background is given in some detail else-

When Henri Verbrugghen became music director of the Orchestra, members of his own string quartet followed him to the Twin Cities. Surrounding a microphone (center), the four prepare to perform on a radio broadcast: (left to right) Verbrugghen, second violinist Jenny Cullen, violist David E. Nichols, and cellist James Messeas. Cullen served as first female member of the Orchestra.

where in these pages; let it be noted here that his work with the Capitol Theater orchestra had brought him to the attention of the most powerful man in American music at that time, Arthur Judson, who was simultaneously manager of both the New York Philharmonic and The Philadelphia Orchestra, and of some of the country's most prominent conductors. Judson was also the founder of the Columbia Broadcasting System (CBS) and Columbia Concerts (today's Columbia Artists Management Inc.). It was Judson who put Ormandy on the radio, made him music director of CBS, got him his guest dates with the Philharmonic and the Philadelphians, and made sure the people in Minneapolis knew about him when Verbrugghen was incapacitated by the physical collapse that forced him to retire. (The half-hour broadcast in which Ormandy conducted the MSO the night before his first regular subscription concert with the Orchestra—and the day after he was given his contract as Verbrugghen's successor—was arranged on short notice to enable him to

fill his regular Thursday night commitment to CBS and its Eastern affiliates. Minneapolis Station WLB (the call letters later changed to KUOM) originated the broadcast and also put it on the air locally, since the city's CBS station, WCCO, was committed to other programming that evening.) Judson then continued to watch for further opportunities, which were not long in coming.

The Great Depression was rounding out its second year when Ormandy took up his duties in Minneapolis. Record sales had dropped dramatically, and there had been an enormous cutback in classical recording activity. While Brunswick in the mid-1920s had recorded the New York Philharmonic under Mengelberg and Toscanini, and the Minneapolis Symphony Orchestra under Verbrugghen, that label never became a major player in the classical arena; its parent company, the American Record Company, concentrated instead on developing new and inexpensive labels for circulating popular music.

The major classical labels were Victor and Columbia, and Victor was the indisputable leader. (Both of those companies today are under foreign ownership: RCA Victor is owned by the Munich-based Bertelsmann Music Group; Columbia has been renamed by its Japanese owner, Sony.) Columbia had done hardly any recording of American orchestras (its catalogue was filled with recordings from London, Amsterdam, Berlin, and Vienna under such conductors as Beecham, Walter, Mengelberg, and Weingartner). And, like Brunswick, it had been taken over by the American Record Company, which made little or no effort to make it more active. Victor (which also boasted numerous European orchestras from its own trans-Atlantic affiliate "His Master's Voice") had been recording, in addition to The Philadelphia Orchestra under Stokowski, the Boston Symphony under Koussevitzky, the New York Philharmonic under Mengelberg and Toscanini, the Chicago SO under Frederick Stock, the Saint Louis SO under Rudolph Ganz, the Detroit SO under Ossip Gabrilowitsch, the San Francisco SO under Alfred Hertz, and still others. By 1931, however, when Ormandy arrived in Minneapolis, only Stokowski and his Philadelphians were still actively recording.

Two years later, when sales began to recover a bit, Victor became cautiously serious about expanding its catalogue. At that point the ever watchful Judson discovered a clause in the MSO's contract with its musicians that gave management the right to use them for recording and broadcasting without additional payment. A word from him to Charles O'Connell, at that time music director for Victor and chief producer of that company's prestigious Red Seal classical line, was all that was needed. It may have helped that Edward Wallerstein, who had just been given overall responsibility for Victor's recording operations, had come to the company after starting out with Brunswick, the label on which the Orchestra had made its only previous recordings.

Ormandy proved to be an ideal conductor for recording. He had made a few records earlier in New York— as a violinist in solo pieces, as conductor of his own salon orchestra, and even with the Dorsey Brothers Concert

Elbert L. Carpenter, founder of the Orchestra, with Eugene Ormandy, music director from 1931 to 1936

Orchestra. That experience in the studios, combined with the precise timing requirements of his conducting on the radio and in a major movie theater, equipped him for making maximally efficient use of session and rehearsal time. O'Connell put those skills to prodigious use on nine days of virtually nonstop activity in January 1934 and eleven days a year later. The results, remarkable enough for the sheer quantity of usable material produced in so short a time, put the MSO and its conductor on the map, because the recordings proved to be genuinely outstanding both musically and sonically, and imaginative in respect to repertoire. (The original labels, incidentally, while identifying the RCA Victor Company, Inc., in small print, bore the name "Victrola"; this reverted to "Victor" later in the 1930s, and was changed to "RCA Victor" in or about 1942.)

The Twin Cities community was enormously supportive when the 1934 sessions were announced. Newspapers carried stories of various activities having been moved to different locations or simply set aside in order to assure silence in the area of Northrop Auditorium for the period in which O'Connell and his crew were at work there with Ormandy and *his* crew. Ormandy himself was not only superbly prepared, but had the good judgment to leave the technical issues to the production team and to co-operate with his producer fully. He was receptive to O'Connell's repertoire suggestions and more than agreeable to the idea that an American orchestra ought to record American music— and other music of its own time.

In the 1934 sessions Ormandy and the Orchestra recorded Rachmaninoff's big Second Symphony, Schumann's Fourth, some Percy Grainger settings, ballet music by Delibes, Mozart German Dances, and pieces by Dvořák, Smetana, Ravel, and Enescu. The Orchestra's splendid strings were shown off in the premiere recording of Schoenberg's *Transfigured Night*, a set of Kreisler pieces, Mozart's *Eine kleine Nachtmusik*, the *Andante cantabile* from Tchaikovsky's D-major Quartet, and an unbelievably elegant account of Drigo's once popular *Valse bluette*. Premiere recordings, in addition to the Schoenberg, were those of John Alden Carpenter's *Adventures in a Perambulator*, Charles Tomlinson Griffes's *Pleasure-Dome of Kubla Khan*, and two works quite new at the time: the Polka and Fugue

In 1934 the Victor recording company turned Northrop Auditorium into an elaborate studio for the Orchestra and Conductor Eugene Ormandy.

Early Air Waves

"TYPICAL OF GEORGE AND NELSON DAYTON'S APPROACH TO THE program of maintaining simultaneously the prestige of the store and of the community itself was the plan to put the Minneapolis Symphony Orchestra on the air as part of the silver anniversary celebration. These two institutions had made their debuts at approximately the same moment and now that each was celebrating its 25th anniversary it seemed appropriate for them to join forces. . . . Having experimented with two privately sponsored concerts, George Dayton had traveled to New York to hear the reception and been delighted with the result. In the following year he arranged for a much more ambitious program: six concerts to be broadcast over station WCCO, one a month between Thanksgiving Eve, 1927, and April, 1928. As Elbert Carpenter pointed out, this was the most elaborate, as well as the most expensive, program of radio concerts undertaken up to that time by any orchestra except the New York Symphony [later, Philharmonic]."
—*James Gray*, You Can Get It At Dayton's, *privately published, Minneapolis, 1962*

from Weinberger's opera *Schwanda the Bagpiper* and the suite from Kodály's *Háry János*. And the works named here do not constitute a complete list.

The 1935 sessions (January 5-16) were still more ambitious. Among the titles were Beethoven's Fourth Symphony, Sibelius's First, and the first American recordings of symphonies by Bruckner (No. 7) and Mahler (No. 2). Ormandy's was the first electrical recording of the Mahler, taken down "live" in a Sunday afternoon concert, with a patch or two the following day. Another "first" was a work commissioned by Victor specifically for recording on the two sides of a 12-inch 78-r.p.m. disc: Roy Harris's "American Overture," *When Johnny Comes Marching Home.* In his memoir, *The Other Side of the Record,* O'Connell, whose idea it was to commission

the Harris piece, recalled the extraordinary circumstances involved in recording it:

> Harris's music did not arrive in Minneapolis until the morning of the last day of recording; thus neither conductor nor orchestra had time to give it much study. Ormandy was in a rage—one of the few occasions when I have known him completely to give way to anger. However, even before he had finished breakfast he had his head in Harris's score, and an hour later he had the score in his head. A perilous fifteen minutes before recording time he declared he knew *Johnny,* then ripped the score in half and threw it on the floor. We went roaring to the Northrup [*sic!*] Auditorium where the orchestra waited, and twenty

minutes later that overture was on wax. Ormandy had rehearsed, corrected, conducted, and recorded the piece after learning and memorizing it, in detail, in something less than two hours. He corrected mistakes in the orchestral parts—from memory!—and Harris, who was present with a score in his hand, checked and found Gene correct. This was the most startling stunt of musical assimilation and memory I have ever known.

There were premiere recordings, too, of Eugene Zádor's Hungarian Caprice (whose scoring gives solo prominence to the *tárogató*, a Hungarian rustic clarinet, on this occasion played by Ray Fitch, who was not in the Orchestra's wind section but was a double bassist— he joined the MSO in 1925, became principal bass in 1938, retired in 1970), Honegger's Concertino (with the Minneapolis pianist Eunice Norton), and Arnold Zemachson's Chorale and Fugue for organ and orchestra. Among Ormandy's best-sellers were a set of waltzes and overtures by Johann and Josef Strauss, the *Rosenkavalier* waltzes of the "other Strauss," Enescu's Romanian Rhapsody No. 1, and pieces by Gounod, Brahms, and Wolf-Ferrari. Beethoven's *Leonore* Overture No. 3 and a Bach transcription by Lucien Cailliet were recorded but never released. Even without them it was quite a harvest. All told, Victor issued a total of 54 titles performed on 169 sides by the MSO under Ormandy, and revived some of them on LP and 45 in the 1950s.

Although the musicians, according to the terms of their contract, received no payment for the first year's sessions, in the second year (1935) O'Connell, mindful of their splendid commitment and the fine results obtained, persuaded Victor to come up with a token payment of $2,500—for *all* of them, not *each* of them— and Ormandy provided a matching amount out of his own pocket. He received no fee or royalties for either year's sessions—though of course they made his name and led to his 44-year tenure with Philadelphia, throughout which he continued to surpass virtually all of his colleagues in the productivity of his recording sessions.

In the meantime, Ormandy's Minneapolis recordings, issued promptly in Europe as well as the United States, not only enjoyed healthy sales, but were played on the radio everywhere. North American tours, as early as the Oberhoffer years, and radio broadcasts had made the MSO well known throughout our own continent; the recordings, thanks largely to their being heard on the radio throughout Europe, gave Ormandy and the Orchestra international celebrity status. O'Connell reported in his book that as of November 1, 1944, when he left RCA Victor, the company had paid a total of $163,362.58 in royalties to the MSO—and its records continued to sell and to be heard often on the radio.

Apart from the personal benefits to Ormandy, the success of his MSO recordings on an unexpectedly grand scale encouraged Victor to undertake what O'Connell described as a "renaissance of recording." The Victor team did not return to Minneapolis in Ormandy's final season (the union had by then taken action to eliminate the possibility of recording without paying the musicians for the sessions), but the company did return to Koussevitzky in Boston and to Toscanini in New York and Victor also began new relationships with Howard Hanson and his Eastman-Rochester Orchestra, the pianist and conductor José Iturbi and the Rochester Philharmonic, Eugene Goossens and the Cincinnati SO, and Hans Kindler and the National SO in Washington, as well as Arthur Fiedler and the Boston Pops, who were to become one of the most constant and durable of all classical recording entities. Within a few years the San Francisco SO (now under Monteux) and the Saint Louis SO (now under Golschmann) would return, and Fabien Sevitzky, who had made a few recordings with his Philadelphia Sinfonietta, would come on board with the Indianapolis SO. In the meantime, Stokowski continued recording in Philadelphia till the end of 1940, Ormandy was at it even more busily, and when Toscanini left the Philharmonic, the National Broadcasting Company, another arm of RCA, formed the NBC Symphony Orchestra, with which he proceeded to record the bulk of his repertoire and conduct broadcast concerts until his retirement in 1954.

At about the same time Toscanini began recording with his new orchestra, Columbia Records also began to bestir its corporate self. Edward Wallerstein, who had been the top executive of RCA Victor Records, persuaded William S. Paley, the legendary head of the Columbia Broadcasting System (CBS), to acquire the eponymous

Advertising from the Orchestra's program book, January 1937

record company and engage him to revitalize it, with an emphasis on classical recording in America, which that label had never demonstrated before. The Columbia Broadcasting Symphony, formed for radio concerts under the capable and imaginative Howard Barlow, was one of the first American orchestras on the new Columbia Masterworks label. Victor had not been keen on recording the Philharmonic after Toscanini left; Columbia took it on and recorded it with Bruno Walter and Igor Stravinsky as well as the Maestro's successor, John Barbirolli. The company began recording also with Stock in Chicago, and with three of the great conductors of the twentieth century who had not been identified with recording before: Artur Rodzinski with The Cleveland Orchestra, Fritz Reiner with the Pittsburgh SO—and Dimitri Mitropoulos in Minneapolis.

Wallerstein, who had vetoed the idea of a third visit to Minneapolis for Victor, signed the MSO for Columbia two years after the start of Mitropoulos's tenure. The Greek conductor's personality and his conducting style were utterly different from Ormandy's—charismatic, fiery, more concerned with intensity and passion, perhaps, than with subtlety and polish—but the Orchestra his predecessor had brought to its peak was flexible enough to respond fully to his demands. Together they produced some memorable recordings. Mitropoulos and the MSO recorded a clutch of basic repertory pieces— symphonies by Schumann (No. 2), Tchaikovsky (Nos. 2 and 4), Franck, Beethoven (the *Pastoral*), Borodin (No. 2), Mendelssohn (the *Scottish*); overtures by Beethoven, Weber, Glazunov; Brahms's Haydn Variations—and the Orchestra's first recordings with internationally recognized soloists.

Curiously, though Ormandy earned a reputation as one of the finest-ever collaborators in concerto performances, the Honegger Concertino with a pianist of mainly local celebrity was his only Minneapolis recording of a concerted work of any dimensions. Among Mitropoulos's early efforts were Busoni's arrangement of Liszt's Spanish Rhapsody, with the pianist Egon Petri, and a vastly admired account of Chopin's E-minor Concerto with Edward Kilényi (Jr.); there was also a Dvořák Cello Concerto with Gregor Piatigorsky, which, however, was never issued. (Columbia re-recorded Piatigorsky in that work with Ormandy.)

Where Ormandy had made the first American recordings of Mahler and Bruckner symphonies, Mitropoulos made the first ever of Mahler's First. It was a knockout, a listening experience that brought Mahler to thousands of listeners for the first time and made true believers of them—possibly in that respect the most important recording the Orchestra made on 78s. It also, of course, solidified and expanded upon the status Ormandy had won for the Orchestra in his earlier recordings.

A timely economic advantage worked to the benefit of Mitropoulos's Mahler First. When Ormandy had made his live recording of the Second, in 1935, the Depression was still at or near its peak and, even though Victor had thoughtfully put that recording on its lower-priced $1.50 Red Seal discs instead of the top $2.00 series in which all the other Ormandy/MSO were issued, the eleven-disc set still came to a hefty $17 (including the album itself), which in those days was a pretty steep proposition; relatively few shops actually stocked the set. By the time Mitropoulos's Mahler First was issued, on only six records, the price of all Columbia Masterworks and all RCA Victor Red Seal 12-inch discs had been reduced to one dollar, which meant the Mahler First was available at about one-third of the price of the Second—and of course the work's dimensions made it more approachable on the part of listeners accustomed to, say, Tchaikovsky symphonies of similar length. In any event, it was, and remains, quite a landmark. It had an extended life on LP, and nearly 60 years after its initial release that unforgettable performance was restored to circulation on CD in Sony's regrettably short-lived "Masterworks Heritage" series, to be acknowledged yet again as one of the most compelling accounts of that now familiar work ever committed to recording.

Mitropoulos's repertoire interests proved to be as broad as Ormandy's. He recorded Elie Siegmeister's *Ozark Set*, Ravel's *Tombeau de Couperin*, Massenet's *Scènes alsaciennes*, Dukas's famous scherzo *The Sorcerer's Apprentice*, Vaughan Williams's Tallis Fantasia, Rachmaninoff's *Isle of the Dead*, Bach transcriptions by himself, and others.

During World War II the notorious "Petrillo ban" brought a two-year hiatus to recording in our country; Mitropoulos and the MSO resumed their work for Columbia when the ban was lifted, but after a year or so

SATURDAY, JANUARY 13, 1934

Symphony Will Make 25 Phonograph Recordings

Victor Engineers Say Ormandy, Orchestra Popularity Justifies Work

With 1,500 pounds of wax and 30 trunks full of phonographic recording equipment, recording directors and engineers arrived in Minneapolis today from Camden, N. J., to make the first records of the Minneapolis Symphony orchestra in eight years.

Twenty-five compositions will be recorded on wax next week in Northrop auditorium and will be issued to music lovers throughout the country during the year.

Ormandy Popular

Symph—— or—

said Charles O'Connell, in charge of recording for the Victor company.

"We feel the expense of bringing our equipment out here amply justified by the large following Mr. Ormandy has created here and in the east, and the popularity of your orchestra gained on its tours and through its radio broadcasts."

To Test Acoustics

Engineers will spend all day Monday testing the acustics of Northrop auditorium and setting up equipment for a crowded week of recording. Among the compositions scheduled for recording are the "Rumanian Rhapsody" by Enesco, the Fourth Schumann symphony, Griffes' "Pleasure Dome of Kublai Khan," Schienberg's

R——

As a perambulating civic advertisement, the Minneapolis Symphony is probably unique of its kind in the U.S. In addition to being the only traveling symphony in the country, it is one of only three or four major orchestras regularly heard over the air and one of only two which are regularly making phonograph records.

—Editorial boast midst the Depression (*Minneapolis Star*, January 21, 1935)

The St. Paul Pioneer Press *ran this photo of Vincent J. Liebler, recording director for Columbia Records, taken during a session with Mitropoulos and the Orchestra in 1940.*

they left that label for the one that had given the Orchestra its status. For RCA Victor Mitropoulos remade some of the titles Ormandy had recorded on that label —Rachmaninoff's Second Symphony, the Weinberger Polka and Fugue—and added Morton Gould's *Minstrel Show*, Schumann's *Rhenish* Symphony, and a fiery performance of the Tchaikovsky Concerto in B-flat minor with Artur Rubinstein.

Antal Dorati, who succeeded Mitropoulos in 1949, was the first music director of the MSO whose reputation had preceded him in the form of recordings. He had begun recording chiefly ballet music with the big London orchestras in the late 1930s, while on tour with the Ballet Russe, but had also by then established a broader reputation in the U.S. after making his debut with the National SO in Washington in a Beethoven program in 1937. He made a recording or two for American Decca with the Ballet Theatre Orchestra, and several for RCA Victor with the Dallas Symphony, whose podium he held briefly just prior to his appointment in Minneapolis. It was Dorati's destiny to take the MSO into the era of high fidelity and stereo, which he did brilliantly and abundantly, adding several certifiable landmarks to the Orchestra's discography.

Dorati at first continued with RCA, which had just ended its stubborn hold-out against the LP (developed and introduced by Columbia) in favor of its own 45-r.p.m. format, and was beginning to refer in its labeling to "high fidelity" and "New Orthophonic Sound." (The labels

on Ormandy's 78s had carried the legend "Orthophonic Recording.") Victor gave Dorati a handsome sonic frame in the first American recording of the Dvořák Violin Concerto, with Nathan Milstein, and a stylish coupling of Mozart's *Paris* Symphony (No. 31 in D) with Bartók's Divertimento for Strings, the latter subsequently recoupled with the first of Dorati's two MSO remakes of another Ormandy favorite, the *Háry János* Suite. He also recorded his own ballet suite *Helen of Troy*, adapted from music of Offenbach. But the period with Victor was brief, and it was on the newly important Mercury label that Dorati made recording history with the Orchestra, enhancing its status along with that of sound recording itself as an important medium for the circulation and enjoyment of classical music on a global level.

Mercury, a sort of upstart label that entered the classical marketplace with LP reissues of 78s and radio tapes from Europe, made a striking breakthrough into the era of "high fidelity" with its 1951 recording of the Mussorgsky/Ravel *Pictures at an Exhibition*, with the Chicago Symphony Orchestra under Rafael Kubelík, in sound so unprecedentedly vivid that Howard Taubman, reviewing it in *The New York Times*, used a phrase the label adopted as heading for its subsequent releases: "Living Presence." Howard Hanson was engaged to record American music with his Eastman-Rochester Orchestra, and Frederick Fennell's Eastman Wind Ensemble (which observed its 50th anniversary in 2002)

February 25, 1947: three images from a recording session with RCA engineers and Music Director Dimitri Mitropoulos (center of middle photo)

Dimitri Mitropoulos with Columbia Records producer "Pappy" Theroux, backstage at Northrop Auditorium

astounded listeners with the richness of its repertory and the brilliance of its performances. The Detroit SO, under the venerable but vigorous Paul Paray, was presented in a broad repertoire.

But it was Dorati's Minneapolis SO that became the label's flagship orchestra, starting just as the LP decisively replaced 78s as the standard medium for recorded music and exploiting each successive advance in the art of sound recording with blockbuster "sonic showpieces" that retain legendary status even now. More than a few of them, in fact, created new excitement in the last dozen years when the company reissued them on CD in demonstration-class remastering from the original master tapes undertaken under the supervision of Wilma Cozart Fine, who had produced most of the original recordings.

In 22 visits between February 1952 and April 1960, ranging from two to five days of sessions (and one session in Carnegie Hall), the Mercury team recorded dozens of impressive LPs. Some of the pieces taped monophonically in the early sessions were remade a few years later in stereo; one of these, Dorati's famous 1958 remake of Tchaikovsky's *1812* Overture, with the MSO augmented by the University of Minnesota Brass Band, a 1775 French cannon taped at West Point, and the bells of the Laura Spelman Rockefeller Memorial Carillon at New York's Riverside Church, set sales records when it was first issued—and now enjoys similar popularity in the stunning CD reissue, which includes Deems Taylor's spoken commentary from the original LP.

Dorati was a phenomenally active recording artist, and he covered a vast repertoire in Minneapolis, including

Two representatives of Radio Free Europe interviewed Music Director Antal Dorati (center) during the Orchestra's 1957 Mideast tour.

The Orchestra's Mercury recording of
Tchaikovsky's 1812 Overture, conducted by
Antal Dorati, earned a Gold Record for
sales of more than a million copies within
four years of its initial release.

*Recording session with Music Director Stanislaw Skrowaczewski (foreground) and Dennis Rooney,
Richard M. Cisek, Henry Charles Smith, and D. Michael Shields*

Beethoven, Brahms, and Tchaikovsky symphonies, Stravinsky and Copland ballets, pathbreaking complete versions of the three Tchaikovsky ballets, and, among other ballet scores, the Offenbach/Rosenthal *Gaîté Parisienne*, complete *Daphnis et Chloé* and *Coppélia*, and Dorati's own *Graduation Ball* (on music of the Strauss family). There were several works of Respighi (the then unfamiliar *Roman Festivals* and *Church Windows* as well as the well known *Pines* and *Fountains*) in which the Mercury engineers achieved new levels of realism. Among the American material were Gunther Schuller's *Seven Studies on Themes of Paul Klee* (a work Dorati and the MSO commissioned and introduced) and the premiere recording of Copland's Third Symphony.

Especially noteworthy were the authoritative performances of works by Bartók and Kodály, who had been among Dorati's teachers in Budapest. Among these were the MSO's third recording (and its second under Dorati) of the *Háry János* Suite, a compelling account of Bartók's big Violin Concerto No. 2 with Yehudi Menuhin (the

second of the three recordings of the work by Menuhin and Dorati, whose Dallas version for RCA Victor was the first one on records), and the same composer's seldom heard Second Suite for orchestra. That premiere stereophonic *1812* earned a Gold Record for sales of more than a million copies within four years of its initial release; combined sales of all of the MSO recordings under Dorati, which exceeded two million by 1963, brought in another Gold Record.

Under Stanislaw Skrowaczewski, who succeeded Dorati in 1960, the MSO continued to record for Mercury, but only briefly, in three sets of sessions (March and November 1961, April 1962). While relatively few in number, the Skrowaczewski recordings for Mercury brought further distinction to the Orchestra's discography, with a powerful Shostakovich Fifth Symphony, a noble Schubert C major, the Suites Nos. 1 and 2 from Prokofiev's ballet *Romeo and Juliet*, and the Schumann Piano Concerto with Byron Janis (who had done the Rachmaninoff Second with Dorati). These now

Viennese Sommerfest Artistic Director Leonard Slatkin (second from left) works with recording engineer Marc Aubort (left) and producer Joanna Nickrenz, with Steven Vining, director of artists and repertoire for Pro Arte Records, Minneapolis, looking on.

circulate on CD. Later in the 1960s Mercury terminated its Living Presence series and the Minneapolis Symphony Orchestra changed its name.

In 1973 the Saint Louis Symphony Orchestra signed a new contract with its musicians that called for a certain minimum guaranteed payment to them for "electronic services." George H. de Mendelssohn-Bartholdy, the founder of Vox Productions, recognized the opportunity thus provided and not only signed the Missourians, but used their contract as a model for several other American orchestras with which he proceeded to record. Mendelssohn turned to Cincinnati, Atlanta, and most conspicuously Minneapolis, where he was the first to record the Minnesota Orchestra under its new name, and with Skrowaczewski made not only recordings of individual works, but several "integral" or related sets of music by various composers. Skrowaczewski remade his Prokofiev for Vox, remade the Stravinsky works Dorati had done, recorded a half-dozen of Bartók's major works and all of Beethoven's overtures (with some additional

stage music), did a pair of Mozart piano concertos with Walter Klien, and a vastly admired set of Ravel's orchestral works. All of these were originally recorded quadraphonically, and the original four-channel tapes were subsequently remastered for exceptional transfers to cassettes on the In Sync label and Vox's own currently circulating CDs.

(Most of the Orchestra's stereophonic recordings are circulating on CD now, from the respective originating labels; many of the Ormandy and Mitropoulos recordings from the 78-r.p.m. era have reappeared on CDs issued by various "historical" labels.)

During the productive period with Vox, Skrowaczewski and the Orchestra also made the premiere recording of the Penderecki Violin Concerto, with Isaac Stern, for Columbia (now on a Sony Classical CD), and there was a Desto recording (eventually re-issued on a Phoenix CD) of Skrowaczewski's own English Horn Concerto (with Thomas Stacy) and two works by William Mayer. Years later Skrowaczewski would be the first

Philip Brunelle rehearses the Orchestra with narrator Garrison Keillor at the microphone in preparation for recording on the Highbridge label.

Music Director Edo de Waart, onstage with the Orchestra, checks in with the recording booth backstage at Orchestra Hall.

former music director to record with the Orchestra. In the meantime, there were a few recordings under conductors who never held the music director title: Leonard Slatkin, during his years as artistic director of the Orchestra's summer concerts, recorded suites from Tchaikovsky's *Swan Lake* and *The Nutcracker* and overtures by Johann Strauss and Franz von Suppé for Pro Arte. Philip Brunelle, the resourceful director of the Plymouth Music Series (now VocalEssence), conducted the Orchestra in a Garrison Keillor piece on Highbridge.

Neville Marriner (not yet Sir Neville), who had amassed an enormous discography with the Academy of St Martin-in-the-Fields and big orchestras in London and Amsterdam when he succeeded Skrowaczewski, made few recordings in his seven seasons as music director, but made them on five different labels. For Philips he did the last three symphonies of Dvořák; for EMI, a disc of works by Copland and another devoted to Britten; for Nonesuch, music by the Orchestra's composers-in-residence at the time, Libby Larsen and Stephen Paulus; for CBS (Sony) Haydn and Vieuxtemps violin concertos with Cho-Liang Lin; and for Telarc a Wagner collection.

Edo de Waart had recorded quite a bit in Holland and then in San Francisco before his arrival as Marriner's successor. He and the MO also made one CD for Telarc: Glazunov's *Scènes de ballet* and the same composer's real ballet score *The Seasons*. They recorded violin concertos by Brahms and Bruch with Nadja Salerno-Sonnenberg for EMI, and Charles Wuorinen's *Genesis* with the Minnesota Chorale for Koch. Most of the de Waart recordings, though, were for EMI's affiliate Virgin Classics: a Gershwin collection (with Garrick Ohlsson in the *Rhapsody in Blue*), Mahler's First Symphony, and three CDs of Richard Strauss, including *Sinfonia domestica*, *An Alpine Symphony*, and two of the early works for winds, as well as the more familiar tone poems.

Eiji Oue, who succeeded de Waart in 1995 and stepped down as music director in 2002, had no history of recording when he arrived. However, in all seven of those seasons, Oue made recordings with the Orchestra that were impressive enough to generate a new kind of excitement possible only in the age of "high-end" audio.

Oue came at a propitious time in that respect. The Orchestra had just signed with the audiophile label

Concertmaster Jorja Fleezanis and Music Director Eiji Oue confer during a Reference Recordings session in Orchestra Hall.

Eiji Oue, surrounded by Reference Recordings producer, engineer, and Orchestra musicians, listens to a session playback in the recording booth.

Reference Recordings, which had won extraordinary recognition for the vivid realism of its orchestral recordings made with the HDCD (High Definition Compatible Digital) process. Keith Johnson, the company's chief engineer (a legend among his colleagues, and co-inventor of HDCD), has been the engineer for all the Reference sessions. He and his producer, J. Tamblyn Henderson, Jr., found Orchestra Hall to be a near-ideal venue, and the Minnesota Orchestra recordings they have issued have been enthusiastically received on the part of critics, the listening public, and audio writers. Oue is the conductor on fourteen of these; his *Pines of Rome* and Copland Third Symphony (two of the big works Dorati recorded nearly 50 years ago) have won exceptionally strong recommendations from virtually every critic who reviewed them. There are similarly striking CDs devoted to Rachmaninoff (the *Symphonic Dances*, etc.), Mahler (*Das Lied von der Erde*, with the mezzo Michelle DeYoung and the tenor Jon Villars), Strauss, Stravinsky, Ravel, Bernstein, and the Orchestra's composer laureate, Dominick Argento, as well as several collections of shorter pieces.

During Oue's tenure Stanislaw Skrowaczewski, who now holds the title conductor laureate, also recorded with the Orchestra for Reference. His authoritative Bruckner Ninth soared to the top of numerous lists and brought Keith Johnson a Grammy nomination (as did three of the Oue CDs); both Skrowaczewski himself and Reference Recordings received the 1998 Golden Note Award from the respected audio magazine *The Absolute Sound*. In the Orchestra's centennial season Skrowaczewski is recording his own Concerto for Orchestra and the new Concerto for the Left Hand he composed for the pianist Gary Graffman (with Graffman as soloist). In the same season, the British conductor Paul Goodwin is conducting the world premiere of John Tavener's *Ikon of Eros*, a concerted work commissioned by the Orchestra for its concertmaster, Jorja Fleezanis, and will record that work and Messiaen's *Et exspecto resurrectionem mortuorem*, also for Reference.

The Orchestra's tenth music director, Osmo Vänskä, who begins his tenure in the fall of 2003, first came to international notice through his recordings, chiefly the dozens he has made of music by Sibelius and other

*In the 1952-1953 season, WCCO-TV televised nine hour-long Orchestra performances from the University of Minnesota's
Northrop Auditorium (left and above) in honor of the Orchestra's 50th anniversary.*

Finnish composers with his Lahti Symphony Orchestra on the BIS label, but also in a broader repertory with the BBC Scottish Symphony Orchestra on BIS, Hyperion, and other labels. He will be continuing the Minnesota Orchestra's productive and significant recording activity in a broad repertoire when he takes up his duties in the Orchestra's 101st season.

While the Orchestra's achievements in the area of recording established its international reputation and have helped to sustain it for nearly 70 years, broadcasting, which came into the picture a bit earlier, has also contin-

ued to be a significant part of its activity. The Minnesota Orchestra's presence on radio has received greater and more consistent emphasis over the years and now enjoys a unique status among orchestras on this continent.

As already noted, both Henri Verbrugghen and his successor Eugene Ormandy (whose route to the Minneapolis podium began with his radio work in New York) actually broadcast with the Orchestra before taking up their duties as its music director. Both continued broadcasting throughout their tenures, and all the subsequent music directors as well as numerous guest conductors conducted the Orchestra on the air—some in the regular subscription concerts, some in "radio only" presentations, without an audience. For nearly 50 years it was a fairly sporadic undertaking. At various times the broadcasts were circulated locally, statewide, regionally, or throughout the U.S. and Canada. In the Dorati era the MSO made its first appearances on television. Radio was used also as an effective medium in the Orchestra's educational efforts, in programs designed for broadcast in local area schools.

One of Dimitri Mitropoulos's special broadcasts, toward the end of his second season in Minneapolis, went out nationally on CBS at an odd hour: midnight to 1 a.m. on March 12, 1939, in honor of the coronation of Eugenio Pacelli as Pope Pius XII, which was broadcast live from Rome immediately following that concert.

Mitropoulos had begun conducting for radio the previous fall. From 1938 to 1942 he and the Orchestra gave Sunday morning concerts originated by WLB (later KUOM) and going eventually to a total of eleven regional outlets, under the rubric "Make Minnesota More Musical." The concerts ran from one to two hours and usually presented music from the lighter part of the symphonic repertoire. The MSO's manager at the time, Arthur J. Gaines, and one of its cellists, Carlo Fischer, introduced the music and invited listeners to contribute to the support of the series. During the late 1930s the NBC affiliate radio station KSTP originated some MSO broadcasts, and in the 1946-1947 season there was an appearance on NBC's Saturday afternoon series *Orchestras of the Nation*.

In 1949, the year Mitropoulos passed the baton to Antal Dorati, both conductors appeared with Toscanini's NBC Symphony Orchestra. In that same transitional year, the University of Minnesota's KUOM put the MSO's Young People's Concerts on the air. Heard as on-air hosts at various times were Arnold Walker, WCCO's Bob De Haven, and KUOM's own Burton Paulu, all of whom would figure in the Orchestra's subsequent activities. The final concert of Dorati's first season, on April 16, 1950, was the first MSO performance presented on television, and the TV debut for the conductor as well. Two years later there was a series of six hour-long concerts on WTCN-TV; it was headed *Music to Look At*, and included film clips and slides of material related to the pieces performed.

In October 1952 the University of Minnesota received a grant of $8,900 from the Ford Foundation

MPR host Eric Friesen interviews composer John Corigliano about his Symphony No. 1, as Music Director Edo de Waart looks on.

In 1997 Music Director Eiji Oue spoke with on-air host Mark Sheldon for an "At Home with the Minnesota Orchestra" radio program geared for Twin Cities nursing homes and broadcast from Mt. Olivet Careview before an audience of residents.

for Adult Education, to support ten one-hour concerts by the MSO. WCCO radio matched the grant with "in-kind" services, and the Minneapolis Musicians Association was also a sponsor. In the same year the Orchestra began recording concerts for Voice of America.

Burton Paulu, at KUOM, was determined to put the MSO on the air on a more regular basis, and in 1955 he began recording classical subscription, Young People's, and Twilight Concerts for delayed broadcast in the summer. In 1957 his team returned for another such series, and again in the 1960s recorded material for two summers. He and his associate Arnold Walker, who was announcer for these broadcasts, were dyed-in-the-wool music-lovers who had grown up with the MSO and formed strong ties with it. Paulu, now in his nineties, sat in with the Orchestra in summer concerts and on other occasions when an extra trombone or baritone horn was

needed; he recalls playing in the Bruckner Seventh under Ormandy before he began his radio career. Once he did begin, he was serious enough about his craft to earn a doctorate in mass media from New York University and to receive Fulbright fellowships for studies of broadcasting practices in various European countries, which he documented in five books.

The next appearance of the Orchestra on radio was in 1964, when KUOM and KQRS (a local FM station) began taping concerts for delayed broadcast to the Upper Midwest, with proceeds going to the Orchestra's Pension Fund. These continued till 1967, and then there was a quiet period, except for three live concerts broadcast by WCCO radio in 1969.

In 1971, however, the Orchestra (by then renamed Minnesota Orchestra) took on a far more substantial radio presence than it had ever had before, and which it main-

Award-winning MPR broadcaster Brian Newhouse interviews Associate Conductor Giancarlo Guerrero.

tains now, after more than 30 years. Arthur Hoehn, MPR's music producer, had been recording occasional concerts in O'Shaughnessy Auditorium and at the Benedicta Arts Center in the late 1960s and early 1970s. With the support and encouragement of former Governor Elmer L. Andersen and the H.B. Fuller Company, MPR initiated the live Friday night concert series heard across the state of Minnesota and, by 1981, across the nation.

Dennis Rooney served as the series' first host and producer, followed by Don Manildi from 1982 to 1986. Brian Newhouse was host/producer from 1986 to 1992, succeeded by Eric Friesen (1992-95), Silvester Vicic (1995), and Mark Sheldon (1995-98). In 1998, Brian Newhouse returned to the host's chair of the weekly broadcasts. Newhouse's broadcasts have won several awards (see sidebar) and strengthened a long tradition of Minnesota Orchestra broadcasts at a time when orchestras across the country have been losing their radio presence. As of September 2002, the national broadcasts, distributed by Public Radio International, are now heard on more than 135 stations from New York to New Mexico.

The continuity and thoughtful expansion of the activity begun so modestly back in the 1920s add up to something more than an impressive set of calling cards. From the onset, the Minnesota Orchestra earned a reputation—across the continent with its broadcasts, across the world with its recordings—for distinguished (and frequently definitive) performances of significant music, and for imaginative and appropriate exploitation of electronic advances in its service. The Orchestra enters its second century now with a full awareness of its past accomplishments, and with both the resources and the commitment to surpass them.

Invaluable help in assembling background for this chapter was provided by Leslie Czechowski (archivist for the Orchestra's collection at the University of Minnesota); Paul Gunther (the Orchestra's principal librarian); Dennis Rooney, Burton Paulu, Arnold Walker, and Brian Newhouse, all of whom have figured so significantly in the Orchestra's broadcast activity; and Mary Ann Feldman, who now is the Orchestra's historian, following her many years as its program annotator and lecturer. By no means incidentally, these sources represent four generations of individuals whose admiration, affection, and enthusiasm for the Orchestra have contributed substantially to its achievements over the years and the recognition it enjoys today.

This Evening's Program . . .

MICHAEL STEINBERG

Michael Steinberg has achieved international renown in a distinguished career devoted to writing and speaking about symphonic music. A Minneapolis resident, he appears frequently with orchestras in other cities— the Boston Symphony, San Francisco Symphony, and New York Philharmonic among them—as lecturer and program annotator. He has served in the same capacities for the Minnesota Orchestra, in addition to having headed the Orchestra's Sommerfest as artistic adviser and artistic director from 1989 to 1992.

Steinberg is a frequent commentator on National Public Radio programs such as Morning Edition, All Things Considered, *and* Performance Today, *and his program notes have been widely praised for both musical authority and readability. Oxford Press has published two collections of his annotations,* The Symphony: A Listener's Guide (1995) *and* The Concerto: A Listener's Guide (1998). *A third book in the series, on repertoire for chorus and symphony orchestra, is scheduled for publication during the coming year.*

HAVING LIVED MOST OF MY LIFE in urban centers of long-established and solid classical music activity, I am awestruck when I think about what Emil Oberhoffer had to do when he became the first conductor of the Minneapolis Symphony Orchestra in 1903. There had of course been orchestral music here before. Various homegrown enterprises, most of them nobler in intention than truly effective in execution, included a series of concerts directed by Frank Danz, Jr., who would become the new orchestra's "concertmeister" for its first five years. The Theodore Thomas Orchestra, whose marathon pioneering tours were so crucial in establishing an orchestral culture in America, visited Minneapolis twice—in 1883 and again two years later. On the third of its 1883 concerts, Thomas made musical history in a small way by giving the first complete performance of the Beethoven Fifth west of the Mississippi. And in 1890, the young but already eminent Boston Symphony under the great Arthur Nikisch made Minneapolis one of its tour stops, but, alas, in an impossible hall and, it seems, on an "off" night. What was missing here was a steady diet of concerts by an orchestra of fixed personnel and reasonable quality.

At 36, the German-born and -trained Emil Oberhoffer (except for 32-year-old Eugene Ormandy, the youngest of the Orchestra's music directors at the time of appointment) was the right man for the job: a well-schooled musician, a strong conductor, an imposing podium personality, good at organization, and full of energy. Moreover, he had lived in the Twin Cities for six years, garnering visibility and respect as the conductor of several choral organizations and as a member of the University of Minnesota music faculty.

Nothing in an orchestra's life is more important than the question: What shall we play? Oberhoffer needed to create programs that would make audiences want to come to concerts *and to come back*, that would get the public acquainted with a canon of core repertory, that would keep them informed about what was new in the musical world. The programs needed to be stimulating to him and to his

Orchestra without overtaxing players who had some way to go before being forged into a unified and confident ensemble. Also, with just 28 strings in its first season—today the Minnesota Orchestra has a larger number of violins alone—the ensemble was not yet in a position to ideally realize the sumptuous sound and rhetoric of most Romantic music.

The audience, too, was a bit different from the Minnesota Orchestra's audience today. It contained a higher percentage of musically literate listeners—men and women, that is, who could read music and had some skill at playing or singing. These people had the inestimable advantage of having learned their classics, not by hearing them on the radio or on recordings, but by doing their best to decipher them at home as piano duets, enthusiastically thumped out with parents, children, siblings, teachers, sweethearts, and friends. On the other hand, if their musical experience was often deeper, it was also narrower, in that listeners in 2003, if they so choose, can have access to a range of music far wider than that

which they could ever encounter in a lifetime of playing the piano or going to concerts.

For his first concert with the brand-new Minneapolis Symphony (November 5, 1903), Oberhoffer, with due regard for the not-quite-certain entity that constituted the Orchestra before him and the audience behind him, stepped out carefully. For high-end classics, he offered Wagner's *Meistersinger* Prelude, Schubert's *Unfinished* Symphony, *Les Préludes* of Liszt, and the *William Tell* Overture (not yet relegated to "pops" status). A *Serenata* by Moszkowski and the zippy *Aragonaise* from the ballet music in Massenet's *Le Cid* represented the muse of lighter things and for some listeners undoubtedly provided relief from the stress of heavier fare.

Of course there had to be a soloist: Then, as now, famous names sold tickets. That role was to have been filled by Anton van Rooy, the leading Wagner baritone of his day, but as things turned out, the new Orchestra's innocent management got an early lesson in one of the prime hazards of the profession: artist cancellations. One week

In this early photo of the Orchestra and founding conductor Emil Oberhoffer, musicians are seated below a flat backdrop that, according to John K. Sherman, was known colloquially as "E.L. Carpenter's pine forest," after 40-year Board President Elbert L. Carpenter.

The Choral Component

THE MINNESOTA ORCHESTRA HAD ITS ORIGIN A CENTURY AGO in the desire of conductor Emil Oberhoffer to provide The Philharmonic Club of Minneapolis with the best possible orchestra for its concerts. Under Oberhoffer's leadership, The Philharmonic Club specialized in the great works of the symphonic choral repertoire and until the founding of the Minneapolis Symphony Orchestra had used a revolving body of free-lance musicians for its performances. With the concert of November 5, 1903 (program cover below), the Minneapolis Symphony became the dominant musical organization, performing not only for the Philharmonic series, but providing its own concert series. The Orchestra has continued to present important choral works in the symphonic repertoire with such valued choral partners as the Dale Warland Singers (Dale Warland, music director), Metropolitan Boys Choir and Metropolitan Choralaires (Beatrice Hasselmann, music director), Minnesota Chorale (Kathy Saltzman Romey, artistic director), and Vocalessence (formerly the Plymouth Music Series chorus, Philip Brunelle, artistic director). In addition, the Orchestra has invited many of the area's fine college and university choruses, as well as community and church choirs, to perform under the leadership of music directors and guest conductors, providing audiences and choruses alike with unforgettable concert experiences.

The first program book

before the concert, van Rooy pulled out, explaining that he was needed for rehearsals at the Metropolitan Opera. (A hundred years later, a jet plane would have made it easy for him to slip the Minneapolis date in between his rehearsals for the Met's first *Parsifal*.)

In the event, van Rooy's replacement was an even more famous singer, the excellent and stunningly expensive Marcella Sembrich. She sang "Ah, fors'è lui" and "Sempre libera" from *La traviata*; with Oberhoffer at the piano, she obliged with a group of songs by Schumann, Thomas Arne, and Richard Strauss (whose *Ständchen* was an endearing novelty by a composer widely regarded as a dangerous modernist); and she ended the evening with *Voices of Spring* by Johann Strauss, sung in Italian. Audiences enjoyed the diversion of solo groups without orchestra (no doubt the Orchestra did, too), and we find those into the 1920s, from piano and violin soloists as well as from singers.

Singers were hugely important in the life of orchestras a century ago. Three of the eight concerts of the Orchestra's first season had vocal soloists. Today, we tend to engage singers only when there is a symphonic vocal work to be done, whether large like Mahler's *Song of the Earth* or relatively modest in scale like Ravel's *Shéhérazade*. Then, singers were engaged for their own sakes and that of their box-office draw, and they brought their party pieces—most often opera arias but occasionally well-loved songs such as "Danny Deever," "Where My Caravan Has Rested," or "Home, Sweet Home."

I don't know what van Rooy had planned to sing, but I am sure he would have offered at least one monologue from his Wagnerian repertoire. The Minneapolis Symphony's inaugural season included less Wagner than would appear in subsequent seasons, but in the programs of those early years one is constantly aware of "der Meister's" immense popularity. More seasons than not featured an all-Wagner evening (one of which made room for an aria from Tchaikovsky's *Eugene Onegin*), some of them with such Wagnerian eminences as David Bispham, Julia Claussen, Olive Fremstadt, and Johanna Gadski. America's entry into World War I put a damper on that, and Wagner never regained such steady dominance in programs here—or elsewhere.

Other Wagner repertoire in the first season, aside from the *Meistersinger* Prelude on the opening concert,

included a single song, "Träume," sung by Fremstadt. Was it because of the diciness of the Orchestra that the greatest Wagnerian soprano of her time chose Verdi and Grieg plus a number from *Carmen* for her first orchestral appearance in her home state? Audiences also heard the *Tannhäuser* Overture ("by special request," according to the program book) and the Good Friday music from *Parsifal*. In addition, there was a "symphonic transcription" of *Lohengrin* by the French opera composer Gabriel Dupont featuring, the program note tells us, "clever contrapuntal devices of his own."

Oberhoffer introduced two symphonies in his first season, Dvořák's *From the New World* and Goldmark's *Rustic Wedding*. Both composers were still alive, and it is worth remembering that only ten years had passed since the premiere of the *New World*. That great work and Goldmark's delightful Symphony may be comfort food for us, but, while both pieces were generally well received here, the Dvořák put some people off with its folksiness (especially since it involved folks from the wrong side of the tracks), while the Goldmark struck Caryl B. Storrs, the critic of the Minneapolis *Tribune*, and later one of the orchestra's best program annotators, as "fantastic, bizarre, and ultra-modern." Other building blocks laid down in the slow gathering of a repertoire included two Beethoven symphonies, No. 2 (but without its first movement) and the *Pastoral*.

Looking through those programs, we also see that program order was thought of quite differently a century ago. Today we plan programs so that they move toward a climax, most often provided by a big symphony. For us, the *New World* is a program closer, but in that first season as well as in several thereafter, it appeared early in the program. What felt right was to have the center of gravity placed early in the evening, and most often, concerts ended with something lighter, such as an overture. The idea was to send the audience home cheerful but not necessarily exalted. And not only might we find the Tchaikovsky Fifth in the first half, but it could well be followed by a single French opera aria before proceeding to the intermission.

Mozart got a hearing when Ruby Cutter Savage sang the Queen of the Night arias from *Il flauto magico*, whose Overture was also played. Like the title in the program, the singing was in Italian, the language neither of the opera, the singer, nor the audience. In general, though, linguistic bias leaned toward German. Thus we also find arias from *Figaros Hochzeit*, and the first season included one of the waltzes from Tchaikovsky's *Dornröschen*, (*Sleeping Beauty*, mistranslated as *Cinderella*). Nor, for that matter, was anyone at home enough with Shakespeare to recognize "pomp and circumstance" as a phrase from *Othello*: The title in the program note (probably Oberhoffer's own) is described as "curious."

Choral music *seems* to be absent, but in fact Oberhoffer was still in charge of the Philharmonic Club's chorus, and the Minneapolis Symphony Orchestra took part in those concerts. The works sung in the 1903-04 season were the indispensable *Messiah* and *Elijah*, plus Saint-Saëns's *Samson and Delilah*, and *Paradise Lost* by the now nearly forgotten Théodore Dubois. Is there, I wonder, any living person who has heard that work?

In his second season, Oberhoffer still moved cautiously, adding two Mozart symphonies, No. 39 and the *Jupiter*, and the Beethoven No. 1, but also repeating the *Unfinished*, the *New World*, and the *Rustic Wedding* from the previous year. We see a lot of such repetition in the early years: Mozart 39 and the *New World* would come back in the third season as well, the Dvořák being a steady presence for several years to come, showing up in eleven of Oberhoffer's nineteen seasons.

The first, uncharitable thought might be that Oberhoffer was lazy about learning new scores, but nothing we know about him suggests indolence. I tend now to think that these repetitions, aside from their value at the box office, were part of his regimen of orchestral training. Bringing pieces back firmed them up in the players' lips and hands, and the rising quality of performance both boosted confidence in the Orchestra and gave the musicians a clear standard to which to aspire. And, as every conductor knows, to program something the orchestra knows is to buy time for the preparation of something unfamiliar and difficult.

∾

Other indispensable items introduced in the early years were César Franck's Symphony in D minor, first performed in 1905-06 and reappearing eleven times in the Oberhoffer years; the Tchaikovsky (then "Tschaikowsky")

Fifth, introduced 1906-07, returning eight times; and above all the Tchaikovsky *Pathétique*, introduced 1907-08, and after that absent in only one of Oberhoffer's seasons.

Seasons grew longer, and by the end of its first decade the Orchestra had attained both the size and the quality that made it equal to the demands of its repertoire. Oberhoffer expanded it to encompass all the Beethoven symphonies (the Fifth, with twelve performances in nineteen seasons, being especially popular), the Schubert *Great* C-major, Schumann (though the *Rhenish* did not appear until Ormandy conducted it in 1935!), and Brahms, with plenty of performances to get audiences used to a composer still considered "difficult" and excessively intellectual.

Bach was another "difficult" composer, and the 1907 program note for a little set of orchestral transcriptions by J. J. Abert states that the purpose of the performance was to counter Bach's reputation as "a dry mathematician." Oberhoffer ventured the Brandenburg Concerto No. 3 in 1907-08, but aside from that, all the Bach was hyphenated, one of the items being the (to us) curious suite assembled and orchestrated—"skillfully modernized . . . with exquisite taste," the program note assured the audience—by Oberhoffer's opposite number at the New York Philharmonic, Gustav Mahler. (Mahler's own music would not be heard here until Oberhoffer brought the Fourth Symphony in 1921-22.) In the Bach-Mahler Suite, the "clavicembulam"—the early program books are rich in typos—was played on a modern piano, the original instument being "too faint."

In due course, Richard Strauss entered the picture: the Wind Serenade and *Death and Transfiguration* in 1907-08, followed by *Don Juan*, *Aus Italien*, *An Alpine Symphony* (only thirteen months after its premiere in Berlin), and, very daringly, the shocking final scene of *Salome*. Debussy was another new name. The program note for *Fêtes* in 1909-10 informed the audience that Strauss, Reger, Elgar, and Debussy "represent the most advanced school of modern music," going on to observe that Debussy's "melodies are always novel and bizarre and often sound harsh to ears not yet accustomed to the peculiar scale employed." (By way of assurance to a possibly apprehensive audience, the note on a serenade by the 24-year-old Hungarian composer Leo Weiner referred to "this wholesome little modern work.") But Debussy's

Emil Oberhoffer's musical successes in Minneapolis brought him widespread attention. Here he graces the cover of the important national journal Musical Courier.

Afternoon of a Faun was so well liked in 1913-14 that Oberhoffer repeated it later that same season.

Ravel had to wait a bit longer, with *Mother Goose* and the *Rapsodie espagnole* making cautious appearances late in Oberhoffer's tenure. There were many hearings of Sibelius's *Finlandia* and *Valse triste*, and the Symphony No. 1 became one of Oberhoffer's warhorses. Some Stravinsky was heard: *Fireworks* in 1916-17, the program note citing a testimonial from a London pyrotechnist, and a suite from *The Firebird* came along five years later.

A still unfamiliar figure from an earlier time, Anton Bruckner, got a hearing when his Seventh Symphony was played in 1907, though it would not be repeated for another 24 years. Its composer was described as one whose "honest heart [is] the home of longings his uncultivated mind was not fully able to express" but who was "great as Epictetus, Aesop, and Burns were great." (Catch a 21st-century editor allowing a reference to Epictetus in a program note!) And what, I wonder, did the 1917 audience make of Percy Grainger's *In a Nutshell*, a suite including movements titled "Arrival Platform Humlet" and "Gum-Suckers March," and using such novel instruments as the marimbaphone?

Always, looking at old programs, one looks with wonder and perhaps a touch of melancholia at the music that has vanished from the scene. Sometimes the composers are well known, at least by reputation: Louis Spohr, whose *Gesangscene* for violin and orchestra makes a couple of appearances*; Joseph Joachim Raff, whose symphony *In the Forest* got an outing in 1905-06; Anton Rubinstein, whose piano concertos were played here by such giants as Josef Lhévinne and Josef Hofmann, one of them as a party-crasher on a Schumann centennial program; and George Whitefield Chadwick, five of whose works Oberhoffer programmed.

And what about Henry Hadley's *The Culprit Fay* and his symphony *North, South, East, West*; the symphonies of Arthur Hinton; and Edgar Stillman Kelley's *New England* Symphony, each of whose movements is headed by a quotation from the *Mayflower*'s log-book? Or the

Festival March and Hymn to Liberty by Hugo Kaun, a German composer who taught in Milwaukee for fourteen years and who was hailed in the program book as "easily in the front rank of living composers of the saner school"? And who remembers E. R. Kroeger, whose *Lalla Rookh* had enjoyed a triumph at the Saint Louis World's Fair; Georg Schumann, whose *Liebesfrühling* Overture Oberhoffer gave six times; or Karl Bleyle, just 28 when his piquantly named but in fact religiously themed *Flagellants' Procession* was played.

One work that intrigues is a *pasticcio* by six Russian composers, each contributing one variation on a folk tune. We readily recognize the names of Rimsky-Korsakov, Glazunov, and probably Liadov, but Artzibushev, Nicolai Sokolov (not the one who would become The Cleveland Orchestra's first conductor), and Wihtol are more esoteric.

One piece that really got my attention was Paul Scheinpflug's Overture to a Shakespeare Comedy—*The Merry Wives of Windsor*, according to the program note. Scheinpflug was a highly regarded opera conductor in Germany whose career went on into the 1930s. Reading through the program books, I came to think of his *Lustspiel Overtüre nach Shakespeare* as "the overture that would not die": Oberhoffer ended programs with it nine times in seven seasons, and even his successors Verbrugghen, Ormandy, and Mitropoulos brought it back.** I would be curious to know the secret of its appeal, but unfortunately there is now no score of it in the Twin Cities.

Two other men we think of primarily as conductors had works played: Frederick Stock, long of the Chicago Symphony, whose Symphonic Waltz was described as "just like *The Blue Danube*," and Victor de Sabata of La Scala, whose symphonic poem *Juventus* (now the name of an Italian soccer team, the word itself meaning "youth") Oberhoffer introduced in 1921. Of one thing I am confident: someone in 2102 going through the programs of

---

* On one of these occasions, in 1924, this was played by Béla Bartók's former sweetheart Stefi Geyer, for whom he had written his long-suppressed Violin Concerto No. 1. Bartók himself does not appear on Minneapolis Symphony programs until 1943!

** Sometimes the repetition of a work within a season came on the Sunday afternoon Popular Concerts. These were not at all what we think of as pops concerts. They were a bit lighter than the main subscription programs, but, for example, the Busoni Violin Concerto (played by Szigeti) had its only performance by the Orchestra at one of those Popular Sunday matinées. Think, too, of the reference in *The Mikado* to "Bach interwoven/With Spohr and Beethoven/At classical Monday Pops."

Henri Verbrugghen

Commissions and Premieres

DEDICATED TO THE MUSIC OF ITS OWN TIME, THE MINNESOTA ORCHESTRA HAS commissioned and/or premiered more than 175 works since its founding. Following, a very abbreviated list showcases a handful of the compositions the Orchestra has contributed to the symphonic repertoire.

Aaron **Copland**	Statements (two movements, Jingo and Prophetic) (1936)
Paul **Hindemith**	Symphony in E-flat (1941)
Bela **Bartók**	Viola Concerto (1949)
David **Diamond**	*Rounds* for String Orchestra (1944)
Ernst **Křenek**	Piano Concerto No. 3 (1946)
Walter **Piston**	Symphony No. 4 (1951)
Harald **Saeverud**	Minnesota Symphony (1958)
Gunther **Schuller**	*Seven Studies on Themes of Paul Klee* (1959)
Roger **Sessions**	Symphony No. 4 (1960)
Dominick **Argento**	*Casa Guidi* (1983)
Alan **Hovhaness**	Symphony No. 29 (1977)
Stephen **Paulus**	Concerto for Orchestra (1983)
Libby **Larsen**	Symphony No. 1: *Water Music* (1985)
Stanislaw **Skrowaczewski**	Concerto for Orchestra (1986)
Steven **Stucky**	*Dreamwaltzes* (1986)
Edgar **Meyer**	Bass Concerto (1993)
John **Adams**	Violin Concerto (1994)
Steve **Heitzeg**	*On the Day You Were Born* (1995)
Aaron Jay **Kernis**	*Lament and Prayer* (1996)
Christopher **Rouse**	*Kabir Padavali* (1998)
John **Corigliano**	Phantasmagoria on "*The Ghosts of Versailles*" (2000)
Einojuhani **Rautavaara**	Concerto for Harp and Orchestra (2000)
John **Harbison**	*Partita* (2001)
Osvaldo **Golijov**	Three Songs for Soprano and Orchestra (2002)

Friday, December 3, 1926, the Orchestra performed with the St. Olaf Lutheran Choir in a special concert. The choir's renowned conductor, composer Dr. F. Melius Christiansen, met with the Orchestra's music director, Henri Verbrugghen.

1950 to 2000 will look at some of the names and reputations of our time with equal wonderment.

After the abrupt end of Oberhoffer's tenure, 1922-23 was a season of guests. One of its events was the first Wagner evening in several years. That was led by the man who would be the Orchestra's next conductor, Henri Verbrugghen, who, drawing on repertory he had learned while concertmaster in Glasgow, introduced two notable English works, Elgar's *Enigma* Variations (announced in 1916 but not performed) and Vaughan Williams's *London* Symphony. There was also that rarity, a symphony by Haydn, of which the program note condescendingly said that it "now appeals to us of today through [its] minutiae and archaic beauties, their general sense of simplicity and fragrant romance."

In his first season, Verbrugghen introduced a second Haydn symphony, led another Wagner evening, brought back the *London* Symphony, and introduced Strauss's *Ein Heldenleben*, Roussel's *The Spider's Feast*, the Brahms Alto Rhapsody, a new symphony by Daniel Gregory Mason, the much-enjoyed *Through the Looking-Glass* by Deems Taylor, and an immensely popular bit of hokum, Ernest Schelling's *A Victory Ball* after the poem by Alfred Noyes. He also brought a three-piano concerto by Bach.

Verbrugghen—and the management—made what turned out to be a colossal mistake, which was to devote six consecutive subscription concerts entirely to Beethoven, including all the symphonies, three of the piano concertos (No. 2 had to wait a few more decades for its first hearing in Minneapolis), and the Violin Concerto with Verbrugghen himself as a nervous soloist. It was a jolt to discover that there can be too much of a good thing.

Notable additions to the Orchestra's repertoire in the Verbrugghen years included two more Brandenburg concertos; more Haydn; Strauss's *Don Quixote* and *Also sprach Zarathustra*; Holst's *The Planets*; Honegger's portrait of a locomotive, *Pacific 231*; Respighi's beautiful *Concerto gregoriano*, *Pines of Rome*, and *Roman Festivals* (Oberhoffer had performed *The Fountains of Rome* in his last season); Brahms's 45-year-old Piano Concerto No. 2; the *Nordic* Symphony by a new figure on the American scene, Howard Hanson; Ravel's *La Valse* and *Bolero*; another Vaughan Williams symphony, the *Pastoral*, and his Fantasia on a Theme of Thomas Tallis; Scriabin's

Poem of Ecstasy; Gershwin's *An American in Paris*; and the Ravel orchestration of Mussorgsky's *Pictures at an Exhibition*; the Violin Concerto of Mario Castelnuovo-Tedesco, the debut vehicle for a virtuoso whose name was misspelled "Heifitz"; and—hold your hats—Schoenberg's *Transfigured Night*, liked so well that it was repeated in the same season.

In 1929 a new and alarming-looking name appeared: Szostakowicz, a 23-year-old in Leningrad, who had stunned the musical world with a brilliant First Symphony he had offered as a conservatory graduation exercise when he was nineteen. Why his name was spelled in the Polish manner I cannot tell; perhaps it looked less threateningly Bolshevik than a Russian-looking transliteration. (For a time he appeared in a German spelling as Schostakowitsch.)

Verbrugghen risked another Bruckner symphony, the *Romantic*, which made up the first half of a program that continued with arias by Verdi and Bellini, separated by Chabrier's *España*. He also introduced the idea that there were Tchaikovsky symphonies other than nos. 4, 5, and 6, when he brought No. 2, the *Little Russian*, in 1929.

A name new to all but scholars was that of Antonio Vivaldi. Among the normal quota of oddities one stands out: a prize-winning "completion" of the Schubert *Unfinished* Symphony by the Swedish composer Kurt Atterberg. Still conspicuously rare were the now ubiquitous Mozart piano concertos: Oberhoffer had introduced two during his last season, with Alfredo Casella and Harold Bauer as no doubt interesting soloists, but pickings were slim for a long time. Ironically, the most-played Mozart concertos were two spurious ones for violin, the E-flat, K. 268, and the so-called *Adelaide*. All in all, the Verbrugghen years must have been an adventure-filled ride.

The story goes that the 58-year-old Verbrugghen suffered a physical collapse while rehearsing *Ein Heldenleben* for the opening of the 1931-32 season. Suddenly he was gone, and his assistant, Paul Lemay, took on Strauss's virtuosic self-portrait. To the rescue on November 13, 1931, came a Hungarian violinist and conductor who was just about to celebrate his 32nd birthday: Jenö Blau, who had changed his name to the more elegant and less Jewish-sounding Eugene Ormandy when a job at New York's Capitol Theater and engagements with the

New York Philharmonic at the Lewissohn Stadium and The Philadelphia Orchestra at Robin Hood Dell seemed to hold promise of a real conducting career.

Oberhoffer's years had been ones of building an orchestra, an institution, and a repertoire virtually from scratch, and he succeeded remarkably. Verbrugghen had a solid platform on which to continue the good work, and even if he was a less grounded musician than Oberhoffer, the Orchestra continued on its path of quest and growth.

But the overwhelming fact of life in the Ormandy years was the Great Depression—even the program advertisements by the First National Group of Banks referred to "these lean years"—which was economically and humanly devastating to the Orchestra and its players. The governors of the Orchestra had made the right choice in plucking the young unknown concertmaster and part-time conductor from the pit of the Capitol.

Ormandy: fiery but safe, energetic about making his presence and that of the Orchestra felt in the community, confident, adept at self-promotion, and without a single modest cell in his body. It was just the formula for that moment.

What we do not find in the Ormandy years is an explosion of notably interesting repertory. It was not the time for it. What was needed was above all comfort food that would draw an audience to the hall and give it reassurance at a very scary moment in history. Ormandy's Minneapolis programs give a skewed picture of him. He was not by nature a missionary like his successor, Dimitri Mitropoulos, nor was he an interpreter whose level of investigation ran deep, but as his half-century of Philadelphia Orchestra programs show, he *was* a good citizen who easily did his share in nurturing new, unfamiliar, and American music.

Ormandy's most celebrated achievement during his tenure in Minneapolis was the performance in 1934 of the Mahler Symphony No. 2, which yielded the first American recording of that work—and, remember, that was a time when programming Mahler was a risk and his fans were isolated cranks. Along with the tried and true—even Schelling's *Victory Ball* came back, and of course that Scheinpflug overture that had been such a favorite of Oberhoffer's—Ormandy revived and recorded Schoenberg's *Transfigured Night*, played Schoenberg's

By the time of Ormandy's appointment, which began officially with the season of 1932-33, we had entered the modern age, with programs shaped and patterned according to expectations familiar to us.

Grainger Visits Ormandy

MINNEAPOLIS
JOURNAL PHOTO

PERCY GRAINGER, NOT-
ED pianist-compose—

Pianist Percy Grainger was the "assisting artist"
on the Orchestra's concert of March 22, 1936,
when Music Director Eugene Ormandy conducted
three of Grainger's own compositions—
two for piano and orchestra, one for harmonium
and orchestra, and all featuring the composer
at the keyboard.

Bach transcriptions as well as his own (Eugene Goossens also weighed in with transcriptions of movements from the French Suites), led a Verdi Requiem in memory of Oberhoffer, and introduced Debussy's *Iberia*, the Sibelius Fifth Symphony, the *Water Music* in Handel's own orchestration, Mahler's *Songs of a Wayfarer* (with Nelson Eddy), and Schumann's *Rhenish* Symphony and he gave a partial premiere of the *Statements* by that dangerous young man Aaron Copland. Rachmaninoff's *Isle of the Dead* and Second Piano Concerto had been popular since the Oberhoffer days, but Ormandy added the Third Piano Concerto with Horowitz in his local debut and the brand-new Rhapsody on a Theme of Paganini with the great man himself, Rachmaninoff, at the piano.

∾

The 1936-37 season brought someone new and amazing to the podium, Dimitri Mitropoulos, who seemed forever fired up by absolutely otherworldly forces. This was the season that preceded his official appointment, but in just two weeks on the podium he made himself vividly and forcefully known. What made the most stunning impression was his performance of Respighi's Toccata for Piano and Orchestra, in which he doubled as piano soloist and conductor. Later, both here and elsewhere, Mitropoulos repeated that tour de force with concertos by Ravel, Křenek, Aubert, Malipiero, Milhaud, Schubert-Liszt, and Prokofiev (whose Concerto No. 3 came to be one of his most requested party pieces). *Life* magazine even ran a feature about Mitropoulos and his Steinway with the plexiglass lid through which he could see the Orchestra and be seen. Mitropoulos also put in a bid as a transcriber of Bach organ music, thrilling audiences with a larger-than-life version of the G-minor Fantasia and Fugue and later with the B-minor Prelude and Fugue as well.

The Mitropoulos years in Minneapolis have become part of legend, not only for the volcanic force of the best of his performances, but also for his passion for the new and unfamiliar. He had been a composer of serious ambition until his middle twenties, and although he stopped pursuing that activity, he always thought like a composer and ever believed that his most serious obligation—and this was truly a point of deep morality for him—was to the living composer and, more largely,

to the execution of tasks that others were unwilling or unable to take on.

Mitropoulos had been crucially formed by his years of study in Berlin, and he had a special sympathy for the German and Austrian Expressionists, most notably Schoenberg and his students Anton Webern and Alban Berg. During Mitropoulos's years with the Minneapolis Symphony, audiences heard Schoenberg's Violin Concerto and the orchestral transcription of the String Quartet No. 2; Webern's Passacaglia (his name given as Anton von Weber); and Berg's Violin Concerto, parts of the opera *Wozzeck*, and movements from the Lyric Suite in the string orchestra version.

An invaluable ally for Mitropoulos was his new concertmaster, Louis Krasner, who had commissioned the Berg Concerto and given its first several dozen performances and who had also given the first performance of the Schoenberg Concerto. Krasner also played the Violin Concerto of Roger Sessions, and in defending such repertory rather than going for guaranteed success concertos, he set a noble example nobly followed by his successors in the concertmaster's chair—Rafael Druian, Isidor Saslav, Norman Carol, Lea Foli, and Jorja Fleezanis.

Among the new music Mitropoulos added to the Minneapolis Symphony's repertoire we can find Mahler's Symphony No. 1, yielding a notable recording from which many in my generation first learned that work; Rachmaninoff's Piano Concerto No. 1 (with Rachmaninoff as soloist) and Symphony No. 3; the Fourth, Sixth, and Seventh symphonies and the Violin Concerto of Sibelius; and Copland's Dance Symphony. The extraordinary list continues with Hindemith's *Mathis der Maler* and Symphony in E-flat (a world premiere); Walton's Viola and Violin concertos and *Portsmouth Point* Overture; Liszt's *Totentanz* (with Rachmaninoff); the recently unearthed Schumann Violin Concerto; the Dvořák Violin Concerto; and Paul Scheinpflug's irrepressible Shakespeare Overture. Further, Mitropoulos conducted Barber's Adagio for Strings, Cello Concerto, and *Knoxville, Summer of 1915*; the Fifth, *Leningrad*, and Ninth symphonies of Shostakovich as well as his Piano Concerto No. 1; Strauss's *Symphonia domestica*; the fierce Vaughan Williams Symphony No. 4; Dvořák's Symphony No. 8 (then still known as No. 4) and Piano

Dimitri Mitropoulos

On January 29, 1937, Dimitri Mitropoulos in his MSO debut concert "turned the normally phlegmatic Minneapolis audience into an excited mob," as his biographer William R. Trotter has written. Mitropoulos programmed Beethoven's *Leonore* Overture No. 2 and Second Symphony and his own arrangement of Bach's Organ Fantasia and Fugue in G minor. Most provocatively, he played and conducted simultaneously the Toccata for Piano and Orchestra by Respighi. Eyewitness John K. Sherman reported: "Mitropoulos...conducted the orchestra like a man possessed....With the first downbeat he started punching the air barehanded, unleashing a weird repertoire of frenzied gestures.... It was as if the music were an electric current that passed through his body to make it jerk and vibrate.... The impression was that of a leader pulling tone from ninety instruments by almost physical coercion, by exhortation and pleading and command....It was especially memorable because the sound that went with it was intensely compelling, music so full of blood, muscle, and nerves as to seem alive and sentient, and bearing unmistakable overtone of great thought and aspiring spirit."

Concerto; Mahler's *Song of the Earth*; Prokofiev's *Lieutenant Kije*; the symphonies in C of Bizet and Dukas; and Elgar's Violin Concerto (with Heifetz, whose playing of the work the composer had hated).

Mitropoulos and the Orchestra also peformed the Bartók Violin Concerto (that composer's first appearance on these programs, in 1943) and Dance Suite; the complete Debussy Nocturnes; the Second Symphony of a recent arrival in the United States, Bohuslav Martinů; David Diamond's Rounds for String Orchestra (which Mitropoulos commissioned), Mendelssohn's *Reformation* Symphony (a belated gift from a Greek Orthodox conductor to a Lutheran community); the Symphony No. 3 of Arnold Bax; the *Sinfonia da Requiem* and *Young Person's Guide to the Orchestra* of the just emerging Benjamin Britten; the Reger Piano Concerto (a performance Rudolf Serkin remembered for the rest of his life as the most joyous and satisfying concerto experience of his long career); and Prokofiev's Symphony No. 5, Piano Concerto No. 1, and Violin Concerto No. 2.

One novelty that caused distress in 1946-47 was the Symphony No. 1 by Artur Schnabel, revered as a great exponent of the German and Viennese piano classics (he was the piano soloist in Beethoven's Concerto No. 4 on the same occasion), but less gratifying to most as the composer of dense and dissonant "modern" music.

Mitropoulos also had a special fondness for the hyphen, and he programmed many fascinating transcriptions: his own, not only of Bach organ music, but of string quartets by Beethoven, Grieg, and César Franck; one by Nicolas Nabokov of part of Bach's then virtually unknown *Goldberg* Variations; Felix Weingartner's orchestral arrrangement of Beethoven's *Art of Fugue* and the *Hammerklavier* Sonata; Max Reger's beautiful setting of a Bach chorale-prelude; Vittorio Gui's orchestration of Franck's Prelude, Aria, and Finale; and the brilliant transcription of Smetana's *From My Life* quartet by Mitropoulos's Cleveland colleague, George Szell.

In 1938-39, Mitropoulos offered music by some of his Greek countrymen—Kalomiris, Sclavos, and the remarkable Skalkottas (one of his contemporaries in the Berlin circle around Busoni). He featured Twin Cities figures such as the eminent Ernst Křenek, then teaching at Hamline, and James Aliferis, and he was ever ready to promote the gifted young such as Ross Lee Finney,

Morton Gould, and Oscar Levant. Stravinsky was not a composer for whose music Mitropoulos had great sympathy, but he made sure to get the composer, newly arrived in America, to come and conduct in Minneapolis. His programs included the first performances here of *Card Game* and the Suite from *The Fairy's Kiss*, as well as suites from *Petrushka* and the inevitable *Firebird*.

At his last concert (he never returned as guest conductor), Mitropoulos spoke to the audience: "The inexorable laws of destiny tell me that I must follow my duty and not my heart's desire, that I must climb the mountain. . . . If you, the audience, have been hurt by my playing modern compositions [*laughter*], don't keep it in mind." He had fulfilled his own sense of mission to the best of his ability, and he went on to bloody himself, trying to do the same thing in the harsher, meaner world of New York. His Minneapolis audience had grown vastly in the inspiring company of this great man, but reading through his moving correspondence with his friend Katy Katsoyanis gives a sobering picture of the closely guarded sacrifices he practiced during his tenure with the Orchestra.

Mitropoulos's successor, Antal Dorati, was a businesslike figure by comparison, which makes it too easy to underestimate his achievements with the Minneapolis Symphony, particularly with respect to repertoire. (He was also as testy as Mitropoulos had been near-saintly.) Unlike Mitropoulos, Dorati was an active composer. He had studied with Leo Weiner (of the "wholesome little modern" Serenade Oberhoffer had played in 1908 and 1909) and Kodály and he regarded Bartók as his mentor. Dorati, too, saw the performance of recent and new music as central to his responsibilities. And for all of Mitropoulos's pioneering, Dorati found that there was plenty for him to do by way of widening his audience's experience, and particularly in the matter of Bartók and Stravinsky, two masters not at the center of Mitropoulos's universe.

In his first season, Dorati introduced the Barber Violin Concerto; Bartók's Divertimento for Strings, Viola Concerto (in its world premiere as worked out by Tibor Serly from Bartók's sketches), and the Concerto for Orchestra (hard to imagine that in response to this brilliant and likable work a member of the board reportedly waved his handkerchief in surrender); the Sea Interludes from Britten's opera *Peter Grimes*; Hindemith's

In December 1940 Igor Stravinsky conducted the Orchestra in a concert of his own works, an event that John K. Sherman described as "one of the historic evenings in Symphony annals." He returned once more in 1966 (above), at the age of 83.

In *Ovation,* THE 75TH ANNIVERSARY HISTORY OF THE
Orchestra, author Barbara Flanagan quoted Antal
Dorati's remarks about his tenure (1949-1960) in
Minneapolis:

"To lead the Minnesota Orchestra was a great
opportunity, a tremendous challenge," he wrote.
"In Minneapolis, I became the successor—I never
was anybody's 'successor' before—of one of the
most exciting orchestra conductors of all time.
I have chosen the word 'exciting' for its precise
meaning—Dimitri Mitropoulos. I was, at least in
the beginning, very conscious of this fact. It stimulated me not to emulate him. To the contrary, the
comparison was inevitable. I didn't make it. Life
made it for me. . . . There was a lot for me to think
over and to do when I took over the fine, experienced Minnesota group. It had extremely gifted,
splendid artists among its members. There was no
need for many changes in personnel, apart from
the routine turnover which was not large. Minnesota
exercised a certain fascination upon us musicians.
. . . One came willingly, in spite of the severe winters,
the rather short concert seasons (in those days)
and the not-too-opulent salaries. The call to join
the Minnesota Orchestra was like getting a badge
of honor."

Antal Dorati

Rehearsal by the Minneapolis symphony for the premiere of the late Bela Bartok's Concerto for Viola continued yesterday. William Primrose (left), will be the guest violist and Antal Dorati (right) will conduct the orchestra at 8:30 p.m. tomorrow in Northrop auditorium. Dorati first met Bartok when he was still a student at the Budapest conservatory. He helped Bartok to assemble material for his now famous collection of Hungarian folk tunes.

THE MINNESOTA DAILY   Thursday, December 1, 1949

On December 2, 1949, violist William Primrose
performed the world premiere of Bartók's Concerto
for Viola and Orchestra with the Orchestra and
its music director, Antal Dorati.

The Minneapolis Star *of November 26, 1959*
ran a photo of Concertmaster Rafael Druian
rehearsing with the Orchestra and
Music Director Antal Dorati for the violinist's
final solo performance in his eleven-year
tenure as concertmaster.

Symphonic Metamorphosis on Themes of Weber; Mahler's Symphony No. 3 and *Kindertotenlieder* (the latter with Marian Anderson, who also sang a Bach cantata, a first for Minneapolis Symphony programs); Messiaen's *L'Ascension*; William Schuman's Symphony No. 3; Vaughan Williams's *Dona nobis pacem*; and—most exciting of all—Stravinsky's *Rite of Spring*, 37 years after its turbulent premiere. And for dessert, Dorati offered a concert performance of Wagner's *Tristan*.

On a roll, and with the splendid recording contract with Mercury that did so much to spread the name and fame of the Minneapolis Symphony Orchestra, Dorati went on to bring—or encouraged guests to program— Bartók's Music for Strings, Percussion, and Celesta, as well as *Bluebeard's Castle* and *Miraculous Mandarin*; Prokofiev's *Scythian* Suite, Symphony No. 7, Piano Concerto No. 2, and Violin Concerto No. 1; the Song of the Wood-Dove from Schoenberg's *Gurre-Lieder*; Beethoven's *Missa solemnis*; Debussy's *Jeux*; complete Strauss *Salome* and *Elektra*; Bruckner's Symphony No. 9; Copland's Symphony No. 3; the symphony based on Berg's opera *Lulu*; the first complete performance anywhere of Ives's *Holiday* Symphony; Puccini's *Suor Angelica*; Tchaikovsky's complete *Nutcracker* ballet score; Stravinsky's Symphony of Psalms and *Persephone*; the complete Ravel *Daphnis and Chloe*; the Vaughan Williams *Sinfonia antartica*; the Berlioz Requiem, complete *Romeo and Juliet*, and *L'Enfance du Christ*; Roger Sessions's Symphony No. 4 (a commissioned work), the Webern Six Pieces for Orchestra, Gunther Schuller's *Seven Studies on Themes of Paul Klee* (another Orchestra commission); and William Schuman's Violin Concerto. Which—trust me—is a very incomplete list indeed.

Dorati also introduced several works of his own, including a symphony, a cello concerto, and an oratorio, and he and his guest conductors gave plenty of representation to many American or American-based composers such as Bloch, Menotti, Piston, Helm, Hovhaness, Dello Joio, Mohaupt, Sessions, Mennin, Riegger, Fetler, Aliferis, Cowell, Creston, Martinů, Toch, and Thomson.

I can't resist mentioning the most bizarre programming idea in the Orchestra's history, which came up on Dorati's watch: playing Mendelssohn's *Italian* Symphony in honor of the tenth anniversary of the founding of the State of Israel.

The choice of Stanislaw Skrowaczewski to succeed Dorati ensured the continuation of what Mitropoulos had begun and Dorati so effectively continued, strong commitment to the idea that there was life and music beyond Brahms, Tchaikovsky, and Dvořák. Skrowaczewski is a composer of high rank—in fact, at the time of his appointment he was better known as a composer than as a conductor —and he is a musician with a passion for exploration and adventure. And like Mitropoulos, he is not by temperament drawn to the easy ride.

Skrowaczewski's first season, 1960-61, gave some idea of what lay in store when programs included the Concerted Piece for Tape Recorder and Orchestra by Otto Luening and Vladimir Ussachevsky, a Concerto for Jazz Quartet by Gunther Schuller (with the Modern Jazz Quartet as the four-headed soloist), and, most startling of all, Henry Brant's *Antiphony I*, in which five groups of instrumentalists were stationed in widely separated locations in Northrop Auditorium, each playing music quite unrelated to that of the others in color, texture, rhythm, and style.

Further works new to the Orchestra (which during the Skrowaczewski era was re-named the Minnesota Orchestra) included Stravinsky's Symphony in C (brought by guest conductor Colin Davis), Elliott Carter's *Holiday* Overture, *And the Fallen Petals* by Chou Wen-Chung, and Honegger's Symphony No. 2. The sudden death of Mitropoulos on the podium of La Scala in 1960 was commemorated in a performance of the Mozart Requiem.

Over the nineteen years of his tenure, Skrowaczewski and his guest conductors introduced, among many works, Schoenberg's Five Pieces for Orchestra, *Music to Accompany a Film Scene*, *A Survivor from Warsaw*, and the complete *Gurre-Lieder*; Stravinsky's Symphony in Three Movements, Symphonies of Wind Instruments, *Pulcinella*, *Agon*, and *Canticum Sacrum*; Martinů's Concerto for Double String Orchestra; Frank Martin's *Petite Symphonie*

Concertante; the Szymanowski *Stabat Mater*; the Barber Piano Concerto; Copland's Piano and Clarinet concertos; the Britten *War Requiem* and Symphony for Cello and Orchestra; many Shostakovich symphonies and concertos; the Ives Symphony No. 4; Webern's Five Pieces for Orchestra and *Das Augenlicht*; Berg's Three Pieces for Orchestra; Bernstein's *On the Waterfront* and *Age of Anxiety*; symphonies by Mennin, Schuman, Piston, Prokofiev, Nielsen, Walton, and Vaughan Williams; concertos by Bartók; Edgard Varèse's *Arcana*; Elliott Carter's Variations for Orchestra; pieces by Messiaen and Carl Ruggles; Ligeti's *Atmosphères* (recently become a film star in *2001: A Space Odyssey*); and Orff's *Carmina burana*. This list, too, is very incomplete.

Skrowaczewski was reticent about conducting his own music, but he was an eager champion of his Polish compatriots, then doing some of the most exciting new work in Europe. Lutoslawski, Penderecki (whose *Threnody for the Victims of Hiroshima* and *Saint Luke Passion* made especially strong impressions), Baird, Palester, Karlowicz, Panufnik, and Gorecki were all represented. More or less local composers got hearings too, among them Dominick Argento (later the Orchestra's laureate composer), Libby Larsen (newly prominent in the musical community), Paul Fetler, Marga Richter (a MacPhail alumna), John J. Becker, and Gene Gutchë. Opera was explored as well, and audiences heard either complete performances or large chunks of *Fidelio*, *Tannhäuser*, *Tristan und Isolde* (an occasion graced by the work of a distinguished guest program annotator, the composer Dominick Argento), *Salome*, Ravel's *L'Enfant et les sortilèges*, and Alban Berg's *Wozzeck*.

Skrowaczewski also filled gaps in older repertoire by performing, for example, Bach's B-minor Mass; Mozart's Mass in C minor; several Haydn symphonies; Berlioz's *Damnation of Faust*; the less familiar, earlier symphonies of Schubert, Dvořák, and Tchaikovsky; several of the Bruckner and Mahler symphonies (the former a special passion of Skrowaczewski's); the Fauré Requiem; and a number of Richard Strauss pieces, among them *Le Bourgeois Gentilhomme*, *Metamorphosen*, the Horn Concerto No. 2, and the Four Last Songs, the last three of these works not so far removed in date but bringing the aroma of a vanished time.

At this point the climate changed. In addition to being driven by their deep moral commitment to defend the new, the difficult, and the sometimes disturbing, Mitropoulos, Dorati, and Skrowaczewski were entirely at home in the music of the twentieth century. For Neville Marriner, who became music director in 1979, after having made the Academy of St Martin-in-the-Fields into one of the world's most renowned ensembles, and Klaus Tennstedt, the orchestra's beloved principal guest conductor from 1979-1982, true home and ownership were elsewhere.

Still, in his seven seasons here, Marriner brought some welcome scores from England, among them Britten's Serenade for Tenor, Horn, and Strings and *Les Illuminations*; Michael Tippett's Concerto for Double String Orchestra, Triple Concerto, and the Holocaust oratorio *A Child of Our Time*; the Vaughan Williams *Sea Symphony*; *Tintagel* by Arnold Bax; William Walton's Cello Concerto and a sequence drawn from his music for Olivier's *Henry V* film; and a suite put together by Peter Maxwell Davies from Sandy Wilson's delicious pseudo-1920s musical comedy, *The Boy Friend*.

Haydn's great *Wind-Band* Mass was another of Marriner's superb gifts to the community, as were the performances of some hitherto unplayed Mozart piano concertos. Another Nielsen symphony, *The Inextinguishable*, entered the repertoire, as did Rachmaninoff's cantata *The Bells*. Skrowaczewski, who had continued to live at his home in Wayzata, appeared as guest conductor, bringing more Bruckner, the long-suppressed Shostakovich Symphony No. 4, and Lutoslawski's Concerto for Oboe and Harp, and now that he was no longer music director, he even programmed some music of his own.

Under Marriner, Dominick Argento's settings of letters by Elizabeth Barrett Browning, *Casa Guidi*, were introduced, and audiences became acquainted with another Minneapolis composer, Steven Paulus. What is probably most vividly remembered from those years—so I gather from subscribers and players with long memories — are Tennstedt's impassioned and luminous performances of Beethoven, Bruckner, and Mahler symphonies.

Music Director Stanislaw Skrowaczewski frequently programmed music by his Polish compatriot Krzysztof Penderecki (right). At Orchestra Hall in the 1977-1978 season, the Orchestra performed the American premiere of Penderecki's Violin Concerto with soloist Isaac Stern, for whom the work was written. They subsequently performed the work in Carnegie Hall and recorded it for Columbia Records.

1. *In 1983 Dominick Argento and Music Director Neville Marriner conferred before the first performances of* Casa Guidi, *a song cycle for mezzo and orchestra commissioned by the Minnesota Orchestra and written for Frederica Von Stade, who sang the premiere. She and the Orchestra later recorded the work under Music Director Eiji Oui for a Reference Recording CD.* **2.** *In October 2000 Principal Harp Kathy Kienzle performed the world premiere of Einojuhani Rautavaara's Concerto for Harp and Orchestra, written for her under a Minnesota Orchestra Centennial Commission. Conductor was Osmo Vänskä, who later the same season was named music director designate.* **3.** *Composer Libby Larsen applauds the Orchestra and First Associate Concertmaster Sarah Kwak after the premier performance of Larsen's String Symphony, a Centennial Commission written for the 1997–1998 season.*

Vänskä   *Kienzle*   *Rautavaara*

126

I am so grateful to have had the opportunity to perform two world premieres of important new concertos for harp with the Minnesota Orchestra. To work with legendary flutist James Galway in the Liebermann Concerto in 1995 was a great thrill—and then to come to know the great Finnish composer Einojuhani Rautavaara and work with him on the premiere of his new concerto in 2000 was one of the top experiences of my musical career.

—Principal Harp Kathy Kienzle, Bertha Boynton Bean Chair

4. *Associate Conductor (1992-1997) William Eddins led student flutists and the Orchestra in John Corigliano's* Pied Piper *Suite at a Young People's Concert in April 1996.* **5.** *In January 1994 Concertmaster Jorja Fleezanis performed the world premiere of the John Adams Violin Concerto, written for her under a commission from the Minnesota Orchestra.* **6.** *Senator Eugene McCarthy joined the Orchestra in 1975 for a performance of Aaron Copland's* Lincoln Portrait *conducted by the composer himself. The piano rehearsal took place onstage at Orchestra Hall.*

Principal Guest Conductor (1983-1986) Charles Dutoit followed Tennstedt. Longtime member of the violin section (1955-1967, 1970-1999) Henry Gregorian has said in an interview, "I think that all the music directors I've worked with over the years were very good . . . but it was something else to play under the famous visitors."

Two long-time Minnesota Orchestra program annotators, Donald Ferguson and Mary Ann Feldman, stood together in 1972, the year Ferguson celebrated his 90th birthday. He had provided distinguished program notes for 30 years (1930-1960). Feldman followed in his footsteps, writing program notes for 33 years while also serving as program book editor, educator, and member of the public relations and artistic staff. In 1999 she graduated to the position of Orchestra historian.

Revered Principal Guest Conductor (1979-1982) Klaus Tennstedt commanded everyone's respect. Co-Principal Clarinet Joseph Longo: "We were on the edge of our seats when we played for him. I've never seen that kind of excitement, in the players and in the audiences. And he was a nice fellow, a real Mensch."

Edo de Waart (music director 1986-1995), another twentieth-century "natural," expanded the repertoire with music by John Adams (*Shaker Loops*, which he had presented when he was a guest conductor, *Harmonium*, *Harmonielehre*, *El Dorado*, and the Violin Concerto, written for concertmaster Jorja Fleezanis), Schoenberg (Variations for Orchestra), Bernd Alois Zimmermann, Alexander von Zemlinsky, Messiaen (*Chronochromie*), Charles Wuorinen, Leon Kirchner, Janáček (the *Glagolitic* Mass), and Martinů.

De Waart also brought back—or got guest conductors to bring back—important works that deserved a new hearing. These included some classics such as Robert Schumann's Violin Concerto and Berlioz's *Damnation of Faust, Romeo and Juliet*, and Requiem (the first memorably delivered by Valery Gergiev, the other two equally so by Roger Norrington). Fresh repertoire also included more recent works such as the Berg Three Pieces, the Berio *Sinfonia*, Schoenberg's Five Pieces for

Orchestra, the Sessions Symphony No. 4 and his Violin Concerto, Lutoslawski's *Venetian Games*, and Walter Piston's Symphony No. 4.

Opera being a special love of de Waart's, he ended his tenure with performances of Verdi's *Otello*, having previously done *Falstaff* and much of *Rosenkavalier*. Most people would agree that his most memorable achievements, along with sprucing up the Orchestra technically, were his concert performances of Mussorgsky's *Boris Godunov* and, most especially, those of Wagner's *Rheingold*. De Waart arrived at a time of economic hardship for the Orchestra, and all in all more conservatism in planning was called for than he would ideally have chosen.

Eiji Oue, who took over in 1995, focused on the "big statement" repertoire of Mahler, early Stravinsky, and Shostakovich. The nurturing of new music was a top priority for Asadour Santourian, director of artistic planning, who assumed many programming responsibilities in the first five Oue years. During this time the Orchestra

acquired a new music advisor, the composer Aaron Jay Kernis. Very crucially, their joint planning included a number of commissions from composers as stylistically diverse as John Corigliano, Marc-André Dalbavie, John Harbison, Kernis himself, Einojuhani Rautavaara, Kurt Schwertsik, Osvaldo Golijov, and Sir John Tavener. Vice President and General Manager Robert R. Neu continued on this path when he assumed responsibility for artistic direction in 2000.

The musical scene has changed incredibly in the last few decades, and change seems still to be accelerating. With the rise in attention given to opera and dance,

chamber music, and what is compendiously classified as "early music," symphony orchestras are no longer the uncontested residents at the top of the heap as they still were at the twentieth century's mid-point. One hears much about a symphony orchestra's need to reflect, to reconsider, to re-invent itself in matters both core and peripheral. Repertoire will be central in this agenda, and the challenge that Music Director Designate Osmo Vänskä faces is perhaps no less demanding—and no less stimulating—than the one that Emil Oberhoffer had to deal with when he first sat down with a pile of blank paper and a heap of sharpened pencils to plan the season of 1903-04.

In April 2000 soprano Renée Fleming sang the world premiere of Aaron Jay Kernis's Valentines, Song Cycle for Soprano and Orchestra, *a Centennial Commission written for her. Fleming and the composer, who serves as new music advisor for the Minnesota Orchestra, accepted audience and Orchestra applause onstage at Orchestra Hall.*

Sounds of Summer

BRIAN NEWHOUSE

Brian Newhouse hosts Minnesota Public Radio's live broadcasts of the Minnesota Orchestra, Friday nights at 8 p.m. He also hosts the Orchestra's national broadcasts, currently carried on more than 135 public radio stations. A native of Illinois, Newhouse came to Minnesota Public Radio in 1983. A decade later he moved to Cologne to serve as a broadcaster at Radio Deutsche Welle, German State Radio. Happily returning stateside, he and his family make their home in St. Paul.

YOU KNOW THE COLOR the sky takes just before a tornado forms, that swirl of black, green, and dust? This was the color hanging over Minneapolis the first time I crossed the Mississippi from St. Paul. It was a sticky July evening in 1983, and I was brand new at Minnesota Public Radio, just up from small-town Illinois. There lay the big city and my first job, announcing the opening night broadcast of the Minnesota Orchestra's summer series, Sommerfest. Complete with tornado warnings.

I pulled into the Orchestra Hall parking ramp as a storm of Biblical ferocity broke. Rain beat the downtown for a half-hour while I sat in the car listening for that telltale roar of an oncoming train that tornado survivors recount.

Thankfully, the twister never dropped, and the storm moved off. I walked out of the parking ramp as the sun poked through the last shred of cloud and the air cleared. A bird under the eaves, probably surprised still to be alive, began to chirp. Then came the sound of voices as people stepped onto the street, emerging from skyscrapers as if from farmhouse storm cellars. We began heading to the Hall, jumping over the rainwater that rivered down sidewalks, or we hopped puddles that dotted the street. That's the sound I remember now, running water and laughter or profanity, as we all succeeded or failed at the jump.

But sound isn't the main memory of that evening. Somewhere in the deluge, one of Orchestra Hall's fresh-air vents had been ripped off. Rainwater had funneled onto the lobby carpet. On top of that, here came wet shoe soles by the hundreds. The carpet, I learned later, had been newly laid that afternoon. The smell of water-logged new carpet blossomed in my face as I opened the stage door.

The carpet was quickly replaced. But twenty years later the faintest hint of that smell still resides in the Orchestra Hall brickwork. Or is it just in my memory? Regardless, a tiny whiff of it seems to rise every Friday night when I open the same stage door and make my way to the broadcast booth to announce the live subscription concerts on MPR.

I love that smell. Deep in January, it reaches back into my brain and suggests July. It says music and tornadoes. It says anything can happen here in summer.

For three weeks in July the Hall and Peavey Plaza were simply the place to be. This 1983 scene of families enjoying music on the Plaza has been repeated over and over through the years. The Minnesota Orchestra has staged Sommerfest, Musicfest, Music on the Marktplatz, and Marshall Field's 24-hour Day of Music as contributions to pleasurable summer life at Orchestra Hall.

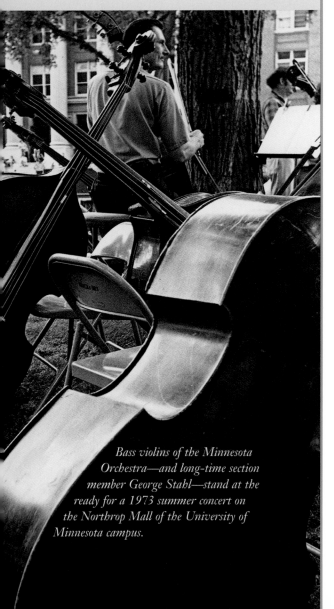

Bass violins of the Minnesota Orchestra—and long-time section member George Stahl—stand at the ready for a 1973 summer concert on the Northrop Mall of the University of Minnesota campus.

~

"You can't enjoy Beethoven with rain coursing down your neck."

—James Bliss, president, Civic Music League,
March 19, 1923, *Minneapolis Journal*

The mix of symphony and summer has always been volatile and tenuous.

"Minneapolis likes music. If the Symphony Orchestra can be held together through the summer, and its music brought to the general public, then every person at all interested in music will support it." Hal C. Paris, president of the Minneapolis Rotary Club, was saying more than he knew on March 19, 1923. These remarks of Mr. Paris showed up in the *Minneapolis Journal* a day after the Orchestra announced grand new summer plans.

Details of those plans in a moment, but first, note that phrase: *"If* the Symphony Orchestra can be held together. . ."

Nowadays, members of the Minnesota Orchestra have what many of the rest of us have always enjoyed: a 52-week paycheck. For decades, though, Orchestra players enjoyed no such luxury. Across the country, orchestras disbanded in the spring and reconstituted themselves in the fall. To find out how summer orchestral seasons even came about, it's essential to look into the specifics of an orchestra player's June-through-August life.

The first season of the Minneapolis Symphony Orchestra, 1903-1904, was six weeks long, augmented by another four weeks of *Messiah* performances and collaborations with a variety of local musical organizations. By 1911-1912 the MSO's season had grown to 23 weeks, mid-October to late March. At the end of that season, as in dozens of others, an extensive tour began that effectively extended the season with nightly concerts for weeks, often through May. After that, though, after getting off the train and collapsing at home for a few days, how did a player keep life and limb together?

In a word, any way he could. (Yes, he. All-male orchestras then.) Though many players taught, others sold water softeners, Fuller brushes, and used cars, or they stocked grocery shelves, stock-brokered, pumped gas, peddled door-to-door insurance, on and on. By the time the men got back together in the fall, most of their chops were shot. Predictably, fall seasons suffered.

To Mr. Paris's 1923 remark. By then, the benefits of holding the Orchestra together through the summer were more than apparent—at least they were apparent to the Orchestra and its management. Now they needed to make their case to ". . . every person at all interested in music." In a city where nothing like a summer orchestral season had ever existed, the community needed to be convinced. With huge fanfare the March 18, 1923 *Journal* headline declared:

"Minneapolis, the summer music capital of the nation."

E. L. Carpenter, then president of the orchestral association, said: "A great many of the Minneapolis Symphony Orchestra players are members of the park bands in the summer. But naturally they lose their identity. It is my dream to have them play summer symphonic concerts as a group under their regular conductor."

Carpenter's dream was grand: a new building seating *seven thousand* and nestled between Lakes Harriet and Calhoun. Theodore Wirth, superintendent of Minneapolis parks, got busy fleshing out the plan. The age of cars was upon our grandfathers, and the building was to be located, said Wirth, "far enough from the highway to avoid noise from passing autos." W. F. Webster, Minneapolis schools superintendent, suggested an open-air design which, Wirth's idea notwithstanding, would allow people to drive their Model Ts as close to the auditorium as possible, park, and enjoy the concert with the windows down.

The projected cost was staggering, nearly $100,000. Orchestra officials asked the city to pay for it. The *Journal* entries about this glorious proposal end with the triumphantly hopeful, "Details should be completed this year to have everything ready for 1924."

Ah, the best-laid plans . . .

No mention of breaking ground for the new building shows up in the 1924 *Journal*, nor in 1925, nor in any of the Park Board's annual reports through the rest of the 1920s. Then came the Great Depression of the 1930s. The dream faded into oblivion.

Minneapolis had found what nearly every other city with a symphony orchestra knew or would come to know:

Were people clamoring for summer orchestral music, that hall would've been built. But Minnesota summers are short, and the lake cabin calls, so there is little public demand for it—unless something extraordinary is created to generate demand.

It may not have been extraordinary, but a paying gig did arise in the late 1930s for some MSO musicians. In 1937, St. Paul began what became a beloved tradition involving light classics. For six weeks every summer through the 1950s, the St. Paul Pops Concerts took up residence at the St. Paul Auditorium. If you're used to the pristine acoustic and rapt audience attention at modern-day Orchestra Hall concerts, consider this: musicians playing on the Auditorium stage in front of which was spread a large ice rink. As the players struck up a Strauss waltz, audience members laced up skates and headed out onto the ice. Patrons who preferred *terra firma* could chat and munch popcorn in the stands. The building was cool, the music was nice, and that made the St. Paul Pops a great escape, especially in the days before home air conditioning. One longtime fan remembers it as *the* summer entertainment for Twin Cities families. For a few dozen out-of-work MSO musicians, it was *the* summer paycheck.

For other players, though, most seasons until the mid-1960s looked dispiritingly like that of 1911: concerts beginning in October and ending with the spring tour. Summers, they were on their own.

"I've never seen so many well-dressed poor men in my life."

—Entertainer Danny Kaye,
to the MSO at a pension-benefit concert

Violinist Joseph Roche joined the MSO in 1959, young, single, fresh out of the New England Conservatory. For him, the $105 he got each week was just enough to live on. "But my motto was 'Have violin will travel.'" That meant, come summer, Roche hit the road. He remembers his first MSO season ending with a recording of a Rachmaninoff piano concerto with Byron Janis at Northrop Auditorium on the University of Minnesota campus. As soon as the recording light turned off, Roche hopped in his car

parked outside Northrop and drove straight to Boston to make the first rehearsal of Arthur Fiedler and the Pops. Roche played for Fiedler every night for the next ten weeks, then got on the road again, this time to the Chautauqua Festival in New York. He spent the next several weeks in that orchestra and then headed back to Minneapolis.

"I made it work by staying mobile," he says. "Besides, I'd been a poor student in Boston. I knew how to live off that kind of money. For others, though, if they had a family, there was no way to make it."

Music under the Stars: An Evening of Gershwin at the Metropolitan Stadium. In August 1958 Paul Whiteman conducted the Orchestra with soloists soprano Helen Rice and baritone Arnold Walker. Musicians visible: pianist Buddy Lueed and cellists Eddy Blitz and Bob Jamieson

Violinist Kirke Walker had a wife and indeed did find it harder to make ends meet, particularly in the job he held in Indiana just before he joined the MSO in 1966. When the Indianapolis Symphony took off, Walker eked out a living working in a bakery for several summers. Other summers he picked up trash in local parks. Then he started a house-painting company. It all ended when the Indianapolis Symphony players went out on strike for better conditions. Walker lost his job and wrote

More than Meets the Ear

THE PAST 40 YEARS HAVE SEEN A DRAMATIC TRANSFORMATION IN THE LIVES of symphony orchestra musicians, both on and off the stage. In 1960 the average professional symphony player earned less than $5,000 per year, far below the income of other professions.

Few major orchestras in the early 1960s provided a summer season, with the exception of the Boston Symphony's Summer Pops. The period of employment ranged from 28 to 32 weeks, which meant the musicians were obligated to find other work during the off-season—and still maintain their high standards of performance.

Some musicians traveled to summer venues in various parts of the country; others stayed home and worked at such jobs as clerk, handyman, cab driver, factory worker, or door-to-door salesman. Scrambling for part-time employment was a demoralizing financial burden on musicians who had studied and worked most of their lives to have a professional career in music.

Music directors at that time had total control over the hiring and firing of musicians. Lacking support from their union, the American Federation of Musicians, players had no say in their employment contracts or, for that matter, in workplace decisions—artistic or otherwise.

The establishment in 1962 of the orchestra players networking organization ICSOM (International Conference of Symphony and Opera Musicians) slowly transformed the profession. ICSOM was not immediately welcomed by the AFM, and the early road was a rocky one. According to ICSOM's first legal counsel, the renowned labor lawyer Philip Sipser, "ICSOM fought a three-front battle all the time: against the AFM, locals, and management. And they lived to tell about it. Their story is unique in labor history."

Every aspect of the American symphonic music world has benefited from these labor struggles. Committees and legal counsel now represent musicians at every stage of labor negotiations. They increasingly participate in workplace dialogue on matters that affect them.

In 2002, most of the 50 ICSOM member orchestras, including the Minnesota Orchestra, enjoy full-time salaries, benefit packages, and job protections. The AFM today recognizes ICSOM as a vital partner and force for change.

—*Julie Ayer, assistant principal second violin,*
Minnesota Orchestra

On a summer day in 1982, Minnesota Orchestra musicians gathered on Peavey Plaza, re-named the Marktplatz for Viennese Sommerfest: (from left) Assistant Principal Second Violin Julie Ayer, Assistant Principal Bass William Schrickel, violinist Emily Basinger, violist John Tartaglia.

a violinist-friend in the MSO to inquire about Minneapolis openings.

"He called me one night," says Walker, "and said the MSO was looking for a fiddle player, and he asked me to drive up and audition right then. I'd been painting houses all summer. My hands were shot. I stalled him for ten days so I could crash-practice. But I finally made the audition and got in."

MSO players had one edge over their colleagues in many other markets: unemployment insurance. Though they describe the trip to the unemployment office as humiliating, MSO players of the early 1960s were able to collect $50 a week during the summer—half their regular salary—and try to survive on it.

"I never had to collect unemployment," says Roche, "because I got paid for my jobs in Boston and Chautauqua. But one time I went to the unemployment office. I'll never forget it. I was afraid someone would see me and think I was unemployed. But then I recognized all kinds of people, Vikings players, some of the principals of our Orchestra. . . . It was what they had to do to survive."

Part-time work with few benefits—this was a professional orchestra player's lot in America for most of the twentieth century.

A new organizational force came on the scene in 1962: the International Conference of Symphony and Opera Musicians (ICSOM). This U.S./Canadian networking organization began exerting pressure on orchestra managements across the continent to expand seasons. ICSOM's point was valid: Good labor conditions benefited the players, which in turn benefited the music and ultimately the audience. The so-called Big Five orchestras (New York, Philadelphia, Cleveland, Boston, Chicago) were the first to respond, lengthening their player contracts; then a ripple effect spread to markets like Minneapolis.

In 1965, Judson Bemis, MSO president, called a weekend-long meeting at the Lowell Inn in Stillwater. Richard M. Cisek, then general manager of the Orchestra and later its president, describes that summer meeting as a turning point for the Orchestra.

"Our players had to scratch and scrape every summer. So the Stillwater meeting was about the organization's musical integrity. We in management were collaborators with the players, and we had the same ends in mind: Our musicians had to rely on us for full-time work."

During the weekend, Bemis, Cisek, and their team put together a long-term plan committing the institution to a 52-week season. Cisek says, "The players, of course, wanted it to happen immediately. The truth is, when we came out of that meeting we had no idea of where or how soon we'd get the resources."

A major opportunity presented itself not long afterward through the Ford Foundation. The Foundation was awarding American orchestras challenge grants to expand their seasons. The grants in most cases were one-to-one matches, i.e. an individual orchestra raised $2 million and Ford granted $2 million. Cisek and his team asked Ford for a 5-to-1 match totaling $10 million. The Orchestra ultimately exceeded its goal, for a total of $12.5 million, which in turn became the underpinning for year-round music-making in Minneapolis. After decades of seasons locked at 26 or 27 weeks, the musicians' contracts now began expanding. In 1965, the season grew to 36 weeks. In 1969, it leaped to 45 weeks.

But as grand as $12.5 million sounds, not even that was enough to pay the full freight of expanding seasons. Richard Cisek: "Our staff had to continually stretch their imaginations to the utmost to find economically productive ways to use the Orchestra."

∾

"I have this vivid memory of David Hyslop, who was then assistant manager, running around the Orchestra outside Northrop with a can of bug spray trying to keep the mosquitoes from driving the players nuts. I can still hear David say, 'Do you suppose [former MSO executive] Boris Sokoloff got his start this way?'"

—Henry Charles Smith,
former Minnesota Orchestra resident conductor,
on outdoor concerts of the early 1970s

Most of the attempts to create "economically productive" summer venues centered round the newly named Minnesota Orchestra's grand old home on the University of Minnesota campus, Northrop Auditorium—which in the 1960s had been enhanced with air-conditioning.

The University of Minnesota's Northrop Auditorium served as the Minnesota Orchestra's concert hall home from 1930 to 1974. In the late 1960s and early 1970s the Orchestra played outdoor summer concerts in front of the Auditorium on Northrop Mall.

Inside Northrop Auditorium, programs like Music 60 (created in 1966) showcased the Orchestra in imaginative lecture-demonstrations. Family Summer Twilight Concerts were short programs of only about an hour and a quarter, priced at $1.00 for adults, 50 cents for children. Outside Northrop, the Mall provided another venue: The Orchestra often set up shop on the grass and performed, mosquitoes and all. Away from Northrop, Symphony for the Cities kept the Orchestra outside with a series (still in existence) of free early-summer concerts at metro-area parks.

For all of the imagination and energy poured into summer orchestra programming, the Orchestra still hadn't hit a home run economically. Richard Cisek: "We learned that most of the serious music lovers seemed to want a vacation after the winter season. We had to find another audience to support an expanding season." Cisek sent then-assistant manager David Hyslop (later, president) on a reconnaissance trip to learn how other orchestras who'd lengthened their seasons were drawing summer audiences. Hyslop saw what a hit Arthur Fiedler's

Boston Pops concerts were proving to be, and the idea was transported to Minnesota. In 1969, the Orchestra started "Summer Pops Jubilee" in the Minneapolis Auditorium. The Auditorium was swanked up with tables and chairs, food and beverages (including alcohol) were served, and as many as three thousand Minnesotans flocked to hear the Orchestra play Mancini and Nero four nights a week, the music mingling with the clink of ice in tall glasses.

The Pops proved to be great box office, but there was another side to that coin. Having cut their teeth on Mahler, Strauss, and Mozart in the nation's top conservatories, Orchestra players often found the repetitiveness of Pops heavy sledding. Others outside the Orchestra agreed and challenged the organization to do more. Peter Altman, the *Minneapolis Star* critic, summed up the whole problem in 1969 when he wrote: "The Minnesota Orchestra has a critical problem: what should it do in the summer? So far the orchestra, which from fall to spring consistently presents adventurous, lively programming representative of a wide variety of important musical trends and appealing to a wide range of popular tastes, has failed to come up with a summer format that is both artistically valid and commercially viable."

Altman posed an answer to the summer problem— one that had striking echoes of 1923. "The answer to the crisis, judging from the experience of other cities and other orchestras, is an outdoor concert center. At places like Tanglewood, Saratoga, Blossom, and Meadow Brook, as many as 50,000 people often are attracted for a weekend of concerts. And these concerts maintain the musical standards of the orchestras . . ." Altman even posed potential venues: "For scenic and recreational appeal the best sites for our Tanglewood would be in the St. Croix valley . . . or south along the Mississippi, near Winona and La Crosse, where Chicago and Milwaukee vacationers could get to it."

(The lure of an outdoor summer home for the Orchestra reasserted itself in the mid-1990s when the organization explored the option of building a 19,000-seat outdoor amphitheater in Brooklyn Park. The project was halted in 2001 by dramatically increased development costs.)

In 1923 the word was Outdoors. In 1969 the word was Outdoors. Everyone pointed Outdoors. Which made the success of what was to come all the more unlikely.

Since 1969 the Orchestra has brought free outdoor summer concerts, a series known as "Symphony for the Cities," to communities of all sizes in, and well beyond, the metropolitan area. In 1982 an audience gathered at the Old Mill in Terrace, Minnesota.

> **"The idea of an American symphony orchestra doing a summer season of such musical substance, and inside the Hall rather than outdoors in a park or other venue, was virtually unheard of."**
>
> —Pianist Jeffrey Siegel

The completion of Orchestra Hall in 1974 changed everything. The organization threw open its doors and imagination. "For the first time, the Orchestra had its own home," Cisek says. "We could do anything we wanted there, at any time."

Pops concerts were presented in the Orchestra Hall auditorium, with the audience seated on a removable platform built over the Orchestra Hall main floor seats. And in 1975 a 31-year-old conductor named Leonard Slatkin came to Minneapolis with a break-the-mold summer idea that put that platform to another use: Rug Concerts.

For the Rug Concerts, the Pops tables were cleared and the platform covered in rugs of Plywood Minnesota. "Bring your own pillow and lounge to new music by Penderecki, Slatkin and Foss," enticed the 1975 summer season brochure. "There'll also be 'Music of Chance,' an on-the-spot creation of a completely new work. After the excitement, relax with Rachmaninoff's Symphony No. 2."

That was the format for each Rug Concert: new music paired with classics.

"Sonic Explorations: Varèse, Xenakis, then Brahms Symphony No. 1"

"Electronic Magic: Erb, Ligeti, for orchestra and 100 metronomes, then Shostakovich Symphony No. 5"

"It was sit on a rug, sit on a friend," laughs Henry Charles Smith when he recalls those concerts. The audience was young, the hair was long, and the whole thing was loose and very 1970s. But those concerts were also frequently only half-full—and this at a time when the winter subscription concerts (counting turned-back tickets) often pulled in 102% capacity.

The dilemma of drawing a summer audience indoors for good music continued, and in 1978 financial pressure intensified as the Minnesota Orchestra players got their first 52-week season.

If the Stillwater weekend was a turning point of the 1960s, another pivot in the Orchestra's history was planted on a late October afternoon in 1979. Slatkin, then principal guest conductor, had outlined a number of imaginative French concerts for the following summer, and a team from the Orchestra's marketing and artistic departments met to dream up ways to sell them.

Mary Ann Feldman, the Minnesota Orchestra's long-time concert annotator and editor of the program book, *Showcase*, was present and remembers a sense of gloom as the team looked over the concert plans.

"Leonard's programs were beautiful but they were too esoteric. French music wouldn't grab our audience. Our people loved our new hall, but they were just not going to come inside during summer." Staffers around the table tried to re-shape the programs but eventually gave in to the dark October mood.

Audiences enjoyed the long-running Cabaret Pops from tables set up on platforms over the Orchestra Hall main-floor seats. Food and beverages complemented the ambience created by a wide range of musical programs featuring the Orchestra and renowned guests.

Principal Guest Conductor Leonard Slatkin introduced an innovative series of Rug Concerts in the 1970s. Sitting, lounging, and sprawling, music lovers relaxed as Slatkin provided commentary from the stage and conducted the Orchestra in wide-ranging symphonic repertoire. Platforms erected over the auditorium seats provided the base, and audience members supplied pillows and cushions.

Then Feldman had an inspiration. The spring before, she'd toured Vienna with her friend soprano Benita Valente. The two roamed the woods where Schubert had walked, drank wine in what had been Beethoven's summer home, visited the hall where Bruckner lectured students (such as Mahler) in counterpoint, and ate at Brahms's favorite café. That fall she was delivering a lecture series at Orchestra Hall called "The Great Composers and Vienna."

"Why not a Vienna festival?" Feldman posed to her colleagues that fall afternoon. The idea instantly caught. With an umbrella like Vienna, the city of greatest significance to Western music, practically anything could be staged underneath it. Program ideas tumbled out around Mozart, Beethoven, the Strauss family, Schoenberg, and others. Karen Koepp, from the Orchestra's marketing department, came up with the title: "Viennese Sommerfest."

"Karen's title unlocked the vision," Feldman wrote in a 1999 *Showcase* article. "Suddenly, the grimly empty Peavey Plaza outside, steeled for winter, was populated in our minds with Sommerfest throngs—people drawn to the Orchestra's music-making by the lure of a lively city square. They would eat, drink, visit, and dance in what we soon dubbed our little corner of Vienna. Downtown Minneapolis would never be the same in the summertime."

∽

"You never thought of saying 'no' to anything he proposed."

—Pianist John Browning,
on conductor Leonard Slatkin

When the Sommerfest idea was phoned to Slatkin he ran with it. Programming ideas of his own immediately spilled out. And Feldman, famous in orchestral circles for her vivid musical imagination, started what she called a decade-long game of "Can you top this?" She'd pose a programming idea to Slatkin and inevitably hear him say "Yes, that's good, but how about. . ." Feldman: "You gave Leonard Slatkin a tenth of an inch, and he came back with a yardstick or a whole mile."

Sommerfest opened on July 17, 1980, with a Strauss waltz. Then, from the Orchestra Hall podium, Slatkin did the unthinkable: He turned and talked to the audience. He welcomed everyone and spoke about the program that evening, "A Gala Vienna New Year." In a blink a new audience was captured by Slatkin's warmth. Sommerfest was underway.

The Orchestra finally had a summer hit on its hands. For three weeks in July (and later, four) the Hall and Peavey Plaza were simply the place to be. The Plaza was renamed the Marktplatz, and quickly nicknamed the Platz. It swarmed with people buying brats and beer at the vendor stands while others took a break from the sun by ducking under the red-and-white table umbrellas for an ice cream cone. An endless stream of ensembles kept oom-pah, barbershop, mariachi, jazz, klezmer, you name it, wafting over the best people-watching spot in the entire city.

Gemütlichkeit on the Platz, *Geschwindigkeit* in the Hall. For the musicians, it was all about speed. Tuesdays through Saturdays, Sommerfest concerts were stacked one on top of another. An 8 p.m. concert was followed the next day by an 11 a.m. concert. Another concert at 8 that night, then the next evening a 6 p.m. chamber program, followed by an 8 p.m. concert. For the players who only a few years earlier had champed at the Pops bit, or before that had dreaded the summer unemployment line —many found themselves remembering the old adage "Be careful what you wish for."

Co-Principal Oboist Basil Reeve: "Now we could get our teeth sunk into some real repertoire, but the challenge was finding adequate rehearsal time to prepare it. Leonard Slatkin was an absolute master at working fast, though, like no one I'd ever seen before."

How did Slatkin do it? Reeve had been a Juilliard student at the same time as Slatkin and says, "He and James Levine both studied under Jean Morel at Juilliard and learned this incredible stick technique. If you look at the very end of his baton, that's where all the information is that the players need. Not all conductors have that. Slatkin also has a way of speaking extremely clearly about what he expects. He can do it during the first read-through. For instance, he'll say to the oboes while the orchestra is playing, 'Next time at the repeat, play it softer. . .' and he does this without stopping. He's not experimenting on the job."

As part of Sommerfest fun, Artistic Director Leonard Slatkin had a fondness for marathons and other extravagant musical events. In 1989 composer Peter Schickele (P.D.Q. Bach's alter ego) contributed a work for ten Steinways, a concert that will live in stage manager memories for its logistical challenges. Audience and performers (John Browning, Emanuel Ax, and Leonard Slatkin in foreground) applauded Schickele enthusiastically.

Sommerfest

RATWURST

1 2
3

1. *Opening night festivities of 1983 Viennese Sommerfest included Artistic Director Leonard Slatkin leading the Orchestra in music for dancing on Peavey Plaza. For years music lovers looked forward to their annual summer opportunity to waltz with the Minnesota Orchestra.* **2.** *Every summer the Orchestra utilizes adjacent Peavey Plaza as outdoor setting for exceptional regional talent. The Plaza showcase features instrumentalists, singers, and dancers (like this dirndl-clad Austrian lady) performing music of the entire world.* **3.** *In 1980 bass Marius Rintzler, conductor Leonard Slatkin, sopranos Arlene Saunders and Benita Valente, pianist Walter Klien, and mezzo D'Anna Fortunato enjoyed eating on the Marktplatz, happily unaware that photographer Mary Ann Feldman had neglected to include the "B" that would properly identify their food.* **4.** *In the 1970s, Principal Guest Conductor Leonard Slatkin introduced a popular series of Rug Concerts at Orchestra Hall. Music lovers could sit close to the musical action— in this case, Slatkin playing a toy piano. The spirit of these concerts lived on in Viennese Sommerfest, which began in 1980.*

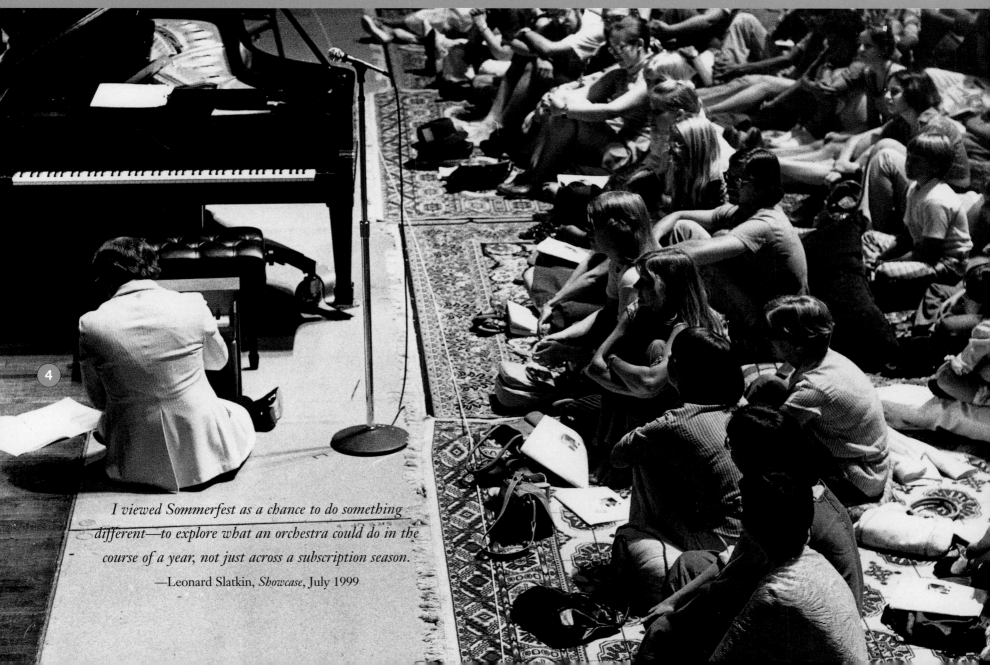

4

I viewed Sommerfest as a chance to do something different—to explore what an orchestra could do in the course of a year, not just across a subscription season.

—Leonard Slatkin, *Showcase*, July 1999

"I have nothing but the happiest memories
of all the years I spent there. . . . We did
a Beethoven Seventh on literally five
minutes of rehearsal that was just talking,
and that night we went out and did,
I think, the best Beethoven Seventh that
I've ever had the opportunity to conduct.
A lot of our performances were like that—
on the edge of your seat. The Orchestra
always came through. It was the most
exciting time that I can remember."

—From a videotaped interview with
Leonard Slatkin, December 2001

"The 1980s were the Sommerfest glory years,
as Slatkin, the Orchestra, and a roster of
great guest artists filled the Hall with chamber
concerts and orchestral programs. . . . Great concerts
in the Hall, great atmosphere on the Platz. . . .
You never knew what would happen next."
In 1983 Viennese Sommerfest Music Director
Leonard Slatkin opened the festivities with
a stroll through an Austrian arbor to the
applause of opening night music lovers.

The 1980s were the Sommerfest glory years, as Slatkin, the Orchestra, and a roster of great guest artists filled the Hall with chamber concerts and orchestral programs. The National Endowment for the Arts gave Sommerfest the highest summer festival award for years running, bettering the grants to Tanglewood, Ravinia, Hollywood Bowl, and others.

One of the most remarkable Sommerfest concerts in any Orchestra musician's memory is the Beethoven Seventh Symphony of 1989. Since it's a relatively familiar work and time was scarce, the Seventh got a paltry five minutes rehearsal. Feldman says, "I ducked my head in his office right before the concert and asked Leonard if he was worried. He said, 'I trust this Orchestra, and if they trust me, everything's going to be fine.'"

Violinist Pamela Arnstein: "That night Leonard was on fire. He obviously loved the work and knew it perfectly. The Orchestra too caught fire—combining our love for Leonard and his trust in us. It was magic!"

Great concerts in the Hall, great atmosphere on the Platz. One other element made Sommerfest a hit. Zaniness. Things like a visiting elephant, or the ten-piano extravaganza complete with a performance of *Ride of the Valkyries* during which women (one wearing sunglasses) decked out in 46D breastplates ran down the aisles, spears in hand. You never knew what would happen next.

Mary Ann Feldman (the one in sunglasses) gives the credit for Sommerfest's success to Leonard Slatkin's unflagging imagination and energy, plus his open-door leadership style. "He would take ideas from marketing, artistic, the stage hands, and put it all together. There isn't a corporation in the world that couldn't benefit from watching that teamwork."

After a decade, Slatkin's career took him to other ventures, and in 1990 Sommerfest tapped the renowned musicologist and writer Michael Steinberg to take the helm. This was supposed to be a one-year interim post, but Steinberg (a non-conductor) programmed concerts with such a flair that his tenure lasted three years. Highlights included chamber concerts with, for instance, ingenious pairings of pieces by Janáček and Beethoven, the "Candlelight Recital" series, and Steinberg's own matchless onstage hosting of the concerts.

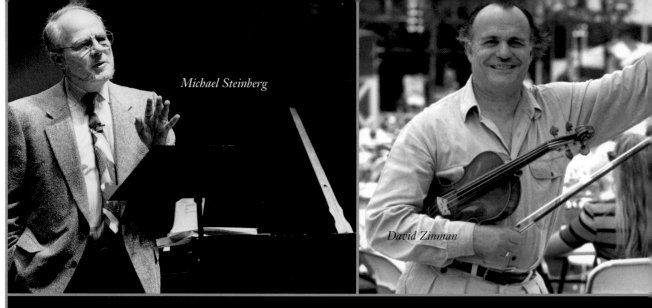

Michael Steinberg

David Zinman

Jeffrey Tate and Rodney Gilfry

SOMMERFEST ARTISTIC DIRECTORS who followed Leonard Slatkin (1980-1989): Michael Steinberg (1990-1992), David Zinman (1993-1996), and Jeffrey Tate (1997-2000). The three photos capture some of their special contributions: Michael Steinberg, who hosted many concerts with witty commentary and depth of musical knowledge; American conductor David Zinman, who occasionally performed as violinist as well; and English conductor Jeffrey Tate, who brought opera to Orchestra Hall in semi-staged concert performances (here, *Falstaff*, with baritone Rodney Gilfry as Ford).

David Zinman arrived in 1993 and charmed audiences by conducting Strauss waltzes as the composer himself had done 150 years earlier: violin under chin and bow in hand. Zinman led Sommerfest for three years, and several festival veterans remember his first-season performance of Bernstein's *Candide* as an all-time highlight. Zinman racked up artistic successes each year, but two of his concerts really stand out. For comic appeal nothing will ever top the Tchaikovsky Concerto No. 1 at which Garrick Ohlsson's piano bench exploded and spilled hydraulic fluid onstage. Ohlsson didn't bat an eye—until his bow, when he chirped to the audience that this was his first experience with an incontinent piano bench. And in his final season Zinman turned 60 with a birthday concert that took the cake. Nineteen composers—count 'em: 19—wrote birthday scores for Zinman. Each piece was short and sweet, but performed back-to-back, they made a memorable gift.

When English conductor Jeffrey Tate took over as Sommerfest's principal conductor in 1997, he brought a stellar reputation as a conductor of singers. Long a Sommerfest tradition, the closing-night opera performances became special attractions under Tate. His affinity for Richard Strauss made 1999 (the 50th anniversary of Strauss's death), a standout season, particularly his conducting of Strauss's *Ariadne auf Naxos*.

Slatkin, Steinberg, Zinman, and Tate each brought unique vision to the Minnesota Orchestra's summer season, and with each director Sommerfest evolved. By 2001 that evolution produced a new name and format.

Music*fest* opened on July 13, 2001 with a 24-hour splash of non-stop music in and around Orchestra Hall, all free and open to the public. The Marshall Field's Day of Music allowed patrons to go where most mere mortals have never ventured: onstage, backstage—even into the Holy of Holies, the basement rehearsal room, where standing-room-only jazz sessions stretched into the small hours. On Peavey Plaza, Japanese percussionists turned drum-playing into a full-body sport. The sounds of gospel, folk, brass band, all caromed off the buildings around 11th and Nicollet and—oh, did I mention the Orchestra's spitfire reading of Saint-Saëns's Piano Concerto No. 2 with Christopher O'Riley? More than 10,000 people trooped through Orchestra Hall that day, and—as nice as it would be to have a scenic concert venue between Lakes

Harriet and Calhoun or on the St. Croix—that mob seriously tested (as had Sommerfest) the conventional wisdom that Minnesotans simply won't come indoors in the summer to hear good music.

Music*fest* continued for four weeks at a whirlwind pace familiar to summer patrons, but instead of a season-long Vienna theme, the focus shifted each week: to France, Spain, America, then Russia. Each week also featured a new conductor who led the Orchestra and chatted with audiences from the podium. That delightful spirit of "why not?" was still alive and well. A few audience eyebrows were raised when harmonica player Robert Bonfiglio walked onstage, but his soulful Villa-Lobos Harmonica Concerto won the audience over; then he knocked them dead with Delta blues improv.

Sommerfest and Music*fest* seem, to me, like sisters. They bear strong family resemblance yet differ one from another. Sommerfest was the first to prove It Can Be Done, while Music*fest* has already showed her own success: Ten thousand people on opening day is enough to make any orchestra green with envy.

Yet success can also be measured in ways that have little to do with numbers. A personal story to close:

When I made that first drive into stormy Minneapolis in 1983, I was single. In 2001, I came to the Marshall Field's Day of Music with my wife and two daughters, and we wended through the Hall taking in food and performances left and right. We stopped in the lobby, where a group of high school volunteers offered little kids the chance to play classical instruments. Our Claire, 4, tried a few, then quickly wanted to get out onto the Plaza to see those amazing Japanese drummers. But Ellie, 2, was handed a violin and with only the slightest guidance tucked it under her chin as if she knew exactly where it belonged. She held the bow naturally and moved it across the strings.

That moment—how I wish I'd had the camera. The look on her face was one of such delight, even of ease. I watched her face and wondered, Is this where it starts, where a musician is born? I know, I know: She may be tone-deaf, never again hold a fiddle under her chin, and most likely never remember that scene. But what if? What if those few minutes somehow fixed themselves in her brain and one day she announces that she wants to learn the violin? That would be nice.

In July 2001 the Minnesota Orchestra entered a partnership with Marshall Field's to present a 24-hour music marathon at Orchestra Hall. The success of the first Marshall Field's Day of Music led to an even larger second annual event in July 2002. In 24 hours, three hundred instrumentalists and singers on five stages in Orchestra Hall and on Peavey Plaza attracted more than 12,000 music lovers for outstanding performances of a wide range of music. Here, Global Drums enchanted the 2001 crowd.

This young snare drummer is one of thousands of children who have tried out orchestral instruments courtesy of the Sound Factories presented by WAMSO—Minnesota Orchestra Volunteer Association.

Whether that ever happens or not, though, is secondary to this: For one moment in a little girl's life the world stopped, and an everyday miracle occurred—she learned that she can make music.

It happened because of this hundred-year-old Orchestra. It happened in summer. It happened to my little girl. The look on her face that moment will stay with me, residing somewhere near the memory of that storm-slogged carpet. Both tell me that anything can happen here in summer.

and furthermore…

Marcella Sembrich,
the first guest of honor

RICHARD EVIDON

Minneapolis-born writer and musicologist Richard Evidon was formerly on the London editorial staff of the New Grove Dictionary of Music and Musicians *and has written music criticism for* The Times *(London),* Musical Times, St. Paul Pioneer Press, *and the* Star Tribune. *For nearly two decades he was English editor and editorial manager of Deutsche Grammophon in Hamburg, Germany. Now a freelance writer, translator, and editorial consultant, he divides his time between Minneapolis and Lake Sylvia, Minnesota.*

Guests of Honor
Chronicling a Century of Illustrious Visitors

THE ROSTER OF CELEBRATED MUSICIANS who have performed with the Minnesota Orchestra throughout its first century is extraordinary by any standard and reflects the time-honored cultivation of fine music in the Twin Cities. Onto its stage and podium the Orchestra has welcomed the cream of the music world's soloists and conductors. The following—highly selective—survey of the greats and the near-greats who came to Minneapolis to perform with the Orchestra (their debut or first mention is marked by capital letters) substantiates this claim. An exhaustive list would fill this book.

The Oberhoffer Era (1903-22)

I (through 1913)

On November 5, 1903, the Minneapolis Symphony Orchestra made its debut under Emil Oberhoffer at the International Auditorium. Obviously such a grand occasion called for a "big" soloist, and, reflecting the tastes of the time, it clearly had to be a vocal soloist. Although her asking fee of $1,800 (equivalent today to around $36,000) was more than three times what the Orchestra's backers had been prepared to spend, the honor went to MARCELLA SEMBRICH. The Polish-born star of the Metropolitan Opera in New York, one of the greatest and best-loved sopranos in opera history, was no stranger to local audiences—she had already appeared in recital in Minneapolis a year earlier. As John K. Sherman relates in *Music and Maestros* (1952), his invaluable history of the Orchestra's first half-century, Sembrich's appearance "drew attention away from the fledgling orchestra's liabilities. But she had kind words for the ensemble and its conductor in a later press interview."

That first season also saw the homecoming of another leading Metropolitan star: OLIVE FREMSTAD, born in Stockholm but raised in Minneapolis. This celebrated artist, who sang frequently under Toscanini and would be the Isolde in Mahler's legendary *Tristan und Isolde* performances at the Met in 1908, offered arias from two of her most famous roles—the Seguidilla from *Carmen* and Eboli's "O don fatale" from *Don Carlo*.

Of course there were instrumentalists among the first season's six soloists, and some important ones at that. The English Paderewski protégé pianist HAROLD BAUER had been performing in this country only for a couple of years when he appeared with the Orchestra; he was followed, the next month, by French violinist JACQUES THIBAUD, famous as the chamber music partner of Pablo Casals, Alfred Cortot, and Harold Bauer.

The first decade of Oberhoffer's nineteen-year tenure was afforded a patina of glamour by a parade of internationally celebrated prima donnas, whose home base was generally the Met in New York. Sembrich returned in

November 1909, the superb German Wagner-Verdi soprano JOHANNA GADSKI also came twice during those years, and another Metropolitan Wagnerian, the American LILLIAN NORDICA (Bayreuth's first Elsa in *Lohengrin* in 1894, coached by the composer's widow, Cosima), came to the Orchestra in November 1908, near the end of her career. One more Wagner singer from the Met, the great mezzo/contralto ERNESTINE SCHUMANN-HEINK, stopped in Minneapolis in November 1909 to sing orchestrated Schubert songs, and the following season, DAME NELLIE MELBA (who lent her celebrated name to both a peach dessert and a crisp form of toast) came to sing with the Orchestra.

Among the first decade of pianists, the highly regarded American FANNIE BLOOMFIELD ZEISLER, a pupil of the legendary Leschetizky in Vienna, made her debut in November 1906. She would return to the Orchestra several more times in the coming decades, including an appearance at the age of 61 in 1925, her 50th anniversary as a concert pianist. Harold Bauer also returned, in December 1911, to give the first Minneapolis performance of Schumann's Piano Concerto, and would become a regular soloist with the Orchestra until the early 1930s.

A handful of other keyboard giants made their MSO debuts in the early years. The Leschetizky pupil KATHARINE GOODSON, another outstanding English pianist, came in February 1909 and would return several times before her final appearance in January 1930. The Venezuelan pianist TERESA CARREÑO, pupil of Gottschalk and Anton Rubinstein, had given a recital in Minneapolis as early as 1884. She now returned in the Orchestra's fifth and seventh seasons. Around the same time, the Polish pianist and future statesman IGNACY JAN PADEREWSKI made two concerto appearances under Oberhoffer's baton. The legendary JOSEF LHEVINNE played Anton Rubinstein's Concerto No. 5 in January 1909, less than three years after his U.S. debut at Carnegie Hall, and another famous Josef—JOSEF HOFMANN—Rubinstein's renowned Polish pupil, regarded by many as the greatest of all early twentieth-century pianists, played his teacher's Concerto No. 4 in November 1910. The composer-pianist FERRUCCIO BUSONI made his only appearance with the Orchestra, playing Beethoven's *Emperor* Concerto in January 1910.

The fiery, rich-toned violinist MISCHA ELMAN was only eighteen when he first played with the MSO in March 1909. He would return many times up to 1948. The American MAUD POWELL, perhaps the greatest female violinist of the period, made her debut on Valentine's Day 1908. Her compatriot ALBERT SPALDING, another American violinist of that era to achieve international renown, was introduced playing the Saint-Saëns B-minor Concerto. And in November of that year, the 22-year-old Russian sensation EFREM ZIMBALIST arrived in town to introduce the Glazunov Violin Concerto, the work with which he had made his successful U.S. debut a year earlier in Boston. Zimbalist performed with the Orchestra on only one other occasion, in January 1926.

II (from 1914)

During the second half of Oberhoffer's lengthy tenure Minneapolis audiences were treated to a new host of "great voices of the century," which included the delightful Hungarian soprano MARIA IVOGÜN, who sang a Mozart concert aria with the Orchestra in April 1922. What was undoubtedly even more exciting on that evening was her performance of a number in which the composer, Richard Strauss, once described her as being "simply unique and without rival": Zerbinetta's great aria from *Ariadne auf Naxos*. Afterwards, in an interview for the *Minneapolis Tribune*, the delighted artist exclaimed: "It is very seldom the case in the tremendously difficult Strauss opera which I sang Friday night that the director of the orchestra has given me such a sympathetic and masterful accompaniment as Mr. Oberhoffer gave me. I was able to sing exactly as I wanted to, without any worry or concern over the accompaniment."

Most of the vocal immortals made just one local appearance: the magnificent American contralto LOUISE HOMER, aunt of Samuel Barber; the German soprano FRIEDA HEMPEL, one of the Met's greatest artists and regarded as Sembrich's successor; the Czech soprano EMMY DESTINN, Wagner's Senta at Bayreuth in 1901 and the first Minnie in Puccini's *Fanciulla del West* at its Met world première in 1910; the coloratura AMELITA GALLI-CURCI, then Chicago Opera's leading artist; the soprano, later mezzo ELENA GERHARDT; and the superbly endowed Belgian soprano ALICE VERLET,

Marian **Anderson**

Martha **Argerich**

Claudio **Arrau**

Daniel **Barenboim**

Sir Thomas **Beecham**

Joshua **Bell**

whose gown the *Minneapolis Tribune* critic described as "clinging closer to her figure than ivy to a tower . . ." He continued, ". . . as compositions for the coloratura voice ignore the art of real music in order to center aural attention upon vocal acrobatics, the possessors of this kind of voice feel justified in centering ocular attention upon their physical charms." Mention must be made, too, of the beloved Irish tenor JOHN McCORMACK, who sang arias by Beethoven and Puccini with the Orchestra and Irish songs with his own piano accompanist.

Instrumentalists came into their own in Minneapolis during these years as the Orchestra welcomed some of the world's greatest pianists. SERGEI RACHMANINOFF made his debut playing his own Second Concerto in January 1920; ALFRED CORTOT made his only appearance with the Orchestra in March 1921; OSSIP GABRILO-WITSCH came twice (for Chopin's First Concerto and, with Harold Bauer, the Mozart Concerto for Two Pianos); as did LEOPOLD GODOWSKY (for the Tchaikovsky and Liszt No. 1).

IGNAZ FRIEDMAN made his Minneapolis debut in 1922, only a couple of months after his U.S. debut at Carnegie Hall, and there were the first appearances of two further keyboard poets who would continue to grace Twin Cities concerts halls for many decades to come: MYRA HESS, over from London on her first U.S. visit in 1922, and ARTUR RUBINSTEIN in 1921.

Hofmann returned to play the Schumann Concerto, as did Lhevinne (for the last time) to play the Tchaikovsky First. The French-trained, Brazilian poetess of the piano GUIOMAR NOVAES came only once. PERCY GRAINGER, the endearingly eccentric Australian pianist-composer recently settled in the U.S., played the Grieg and a new piece of his own entitled *In a Nutshell*. Featuring a noisy clutch of exotic percussion instruments along with the solo piano and orchestra, Grainger's suite prompted the skeptical *Minneapolis Tribune* reviewer to write, "If you don't care for the shell, go and enjoy the nut."

Two other imposing figures—pianist/composers—came to perform and to hear the Orchestra perform their own music: MRS. H.H.A. (AMY) BEACH, the first successful American woman composer of art music, played her own piano concerto and listened to the Orchestra perform her *Gaelic* Symphony; and ALFREDO CASELLA, an important Italian composer between the wars, played Mozart's D-minor Piano Concerto under Oberhoffer and took the baton himself to direct the MSO in two of his own works.

The roster of guest violinists in that second decade of the Orchestra's history was no less star-studded. FRITZ KREISLER paid four visits, always treating the adoring audiences to several of his famous (later infamous, when the hoax was exposed) encores, those enchanting compositions of his own that he was still passing off as music he'd unearthed from the past. The ingenuous MSO program annotator duly informed the audience that "Kreisler, who is a deep student of the literature of violin music, gave up a great part of his time in years past in hunting up and going over the libraries and musical collections in Italy, France, Austria and Germany, where vast quantities of music by composers long forgotten, and who flourished particularly in Italy during the seventeenth and eighteenth centuries, lay neglected and unknown."

There were three further appearances by Jacques Thibaud, three by Mischa Elman, and two by violinist EUGÈNE YSAŸE, one of the most influential figures in the history of that instrument, shortly before his brief tenure as conductor of the Cincinnati Symphony Orchestra. The Austrian (later naturalized American) violinist ERICA MORINI made her MSO debut as a child prodigy under Oberhoffer in 1922; she would return regularly for the next 30 years. Other violinists included the great JAN KUBELÍK, father of the conductor Rafael Kubelík and acclaimed as "a second Paganini"; VÁŠA PŘÍHODA, admired early in his career by Toscanini but more often remembered today as a Nazi collaborator; and the Pole BRONISLAW HUBERMAN, who played Beethoven, about which the *Journal* effused: ". . . one of the finest renderings of the immortal work ever heard here. He excelled in the ethereal regions where even the most skilled artists are not fully sure of their tone production, and made the lyrical parts of the concerto truly celestial in beauty."

A 1945 photo of the 27-year-old "boy wonder," Leonard Bernstein, with the Orchestra's Principal Cellist and Assistant Conductor Yves Chardon

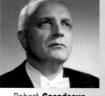

Robert **Casadesus**

Shura **Cherkassky**

Van **Cliburn**

Phyllis **Curtin**

Charles **Dutoit**

Christoph **Eschenbach**

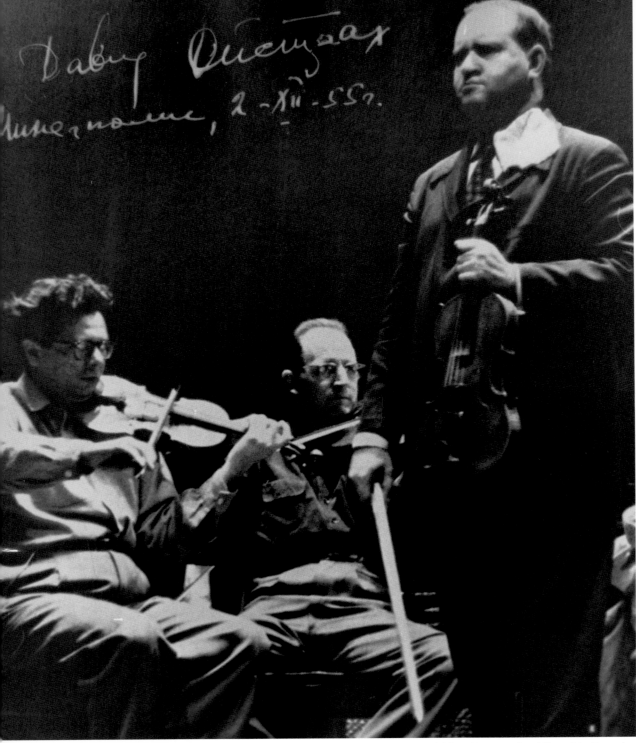

The great Russian violinist David Oistrakh performed with the Orchestra and Music Director Antal Dorati in December 1955. Visible beside Oistrakh are Concertmaster Rafael Druian and Assistant Concertmaster Henry Kramer.

Only a single major cellist made his MSO debut during this period, but he was arguably the greatest of all: PABLO CASALS, who played Lalo's D-minor Concerto and Bruch's *Kol Nidrei* with the Orchestra and Oberhoffer in January 1917.

A new phenomenon—the first guest conductor in the Orchestra's annals—dates from Oberhoffer's sixteenth season. In February 1919, the Austrian ARTUR BODANZKY, who had once been Mahler's assistant at the Vienna Opera and was then one of the leading conductors of the Metropolitan, took the helm of the MSO and reportedly called it the best orchestra he'd ever heard! The significance for the Orchestra, then as now, of this special class of guest artists can hardly be overstated. Just a few years ago, a retired, longtime member of the violin section, Henry Gregorian, put it succinctly in an interview: "I think that all the music directors I've worked with over the years were very good . . . but it was something else to play under the famous visitors."

Interregnum (1922-23)

The Minneapolis Symphony Orchestra's horizons now broadened in this new direction with a whole season of visiting maestros in the aftermath of Oberhoffer's resignation in 1922. One of them, the Belgian violinist-conductor HENRI VERBRUGGHEN, would become the Orchestra's new chief conductor the following season. A pupil of Hubay and Ysaÿe in Brussels, concertmaster then conductor in Glasgow at the beginning of the century, Verbrugghen had been living in Australia. He made his Minneapolis debut on October 20, on an evening that also featured the MSO debut of the Russian-born British pianist BENNO MOISEIWITSCH, another Leschetizky pupil.

Other guest conductors for the season included the pianist Ossip Gabrilowitsch (son-in-law of Mark Twain!), already well-known to local audiences as a soloist, who made his Minneapolis conducting debut in November. Three programs in January 1923 were under the direction of the German-American WALTER DAMROSCH, longtime conductor of the New York Symphony Orchestra (until its merger with—read: absorption by—the Philharmonic under Toscanini in 1928). The English conductor ALBERT COATES (who had recently introduced Holst's *The Planets* with the London Symphony Orchestra) conducted one program in February.

But the most distinguished guest conductor that season was the Berlin-born Mahler protégé BRUNO WALTER, charged with three programs in March 1923. One of the two serious candidates to succeed Oberhoffer was Henri Verbrugghen; the other was Walter, who had just resigned his position as general music director in Munich. Here, in the year of his U.S. debut, was the greatest conductor by far that Minneapolitans had yet heard, conducting *their* Orchestra in *their* auditorium in *his* specialty, the German "classics": Haydn, Mozart, Beethoven, Weber, Schumann, Wagner, and Richard Strauss. Earlier on the day of Walter's rapturously received debut, he conducted the MSO in a radio broadcast heard throughout North America. It was their first time on the air, and his, too. Later during the conductor's nearly month-long stay, Sherman wrote in the *Star*: "Minneapolis concert audiences are receiving first-hand evidence that an orchestra is as good as its conductor. It is doubtful if the Minneapolis Symphony orchestra has ever played with such magnificent spirit as during the last few weeks under Bruno Walter."

But the conductor also had a bone to pick with those audiences, as Victor Nilsson reported in the *Journal* before the concert of March 9: "Mr. Walter has again requested the management of the orchestra to make it known that he would greatly appreciate the courtesy of all patrons being in their seats before the beginning of the concert Friday evening as the Haydn symphony can only shine in its true splendor if he can play the four movements without the interruption caused by the seating of late comers."

Walter would return many times to the Orchestra as guest conductor during the next 30 years and always retained a special affection for it, as we know from his autobiography, *Theme and Variations* (1946): "... a particularly enjoyable period of my first stay in America was spent in Minneapolis.... So cordial a relation between me and the orchestra and so personal a contact with the audience was established during that time that in that icy part of the United States I was made happy by the surprising, the exciting warmth of the musical atmosphere." Walter was also captivated by the place itself: "On my walks along the Mississippi, which separates the twin cities of Minneapolis and St. Paul, and in the vicinity

of the Hiawatha statue inspired by Longfellow's poem, I was struck by the full force of the cold. Yet, I was drawn there again and again by the fascination of the legendary stream." He was particularly struck by Minnehaha Falls, and by the city's beauty, wondering "what must it be in summer?"

Walter's distinguished guest artist on that first occasion, soprano Maria Ivogün, was also smitten with the place. Having asked on a previous visit to be shown the Minnehaha Falls, the diminutive singer decided this time to strike out on her own, but in the course of her walk stepped in a puddle, covering her Parisian pumps with mud, and then proceeded to get lost. Afterwards, the chastened diva confessed to a *Journal* reporter: "But this Minneapolis is so very big! . . . I am going to be very careful. I am not sure I know my way around your town yet."

The Verbrugghen Era (1923-31)

For the next several years, the guest artist roster was highlighted by distinguished "old friends" coming back to play with the Minneapolis Symphony Orchestra at the Auditorium (now known as the Lyceum) under its new conductor. These included pianists Myra Hess, Harold Bauer, Ignaz Friedman, Ossip Gabrilowitsch, and Zeisler. Among the violinists were Spalding, Thibaud, Zimbalist, Elman, and PAWEL KOCHÁNSKI. The period was also marked by a couple of conspicuous absences: Neither Benno Moiseiwitsch nor Fritz Kreisler (firmly settled in Berlin at that point with his American wife) ever played under Verbrugghen.

Major local debuts continued in these years, with vocal artists still figuring prominently. The list includes both up-and-coming singers as well as some of the opera world's hottest divas: Philadelphia-born soprano DUSOLINA GIANNINI; SIGRID ONÉGIN, the greatest contralto of the day; and the Met's leading soprano, ELISABETH RETHBERG, one of the world's outstanding singers between the wars.

A second inaugural concert, this time the Orchestra's gala debut in its new home, the recently completed Northrop Auditorium on the University of Minnesota campus, occurred on October 17, 1930. Like the debut of 1903, this grand occasion demanded a star of grand opera. The Austrian soprano MARIA JERITZA had been

Arthur **Fiedler**

Rudolf **Firkušný**

Maureen **Forrester**

Claude **Frank**

Pamela **Frank**

Miriam **Fried**

the Met's most glamorous artist from the time of her debut in 1924, a stunning beauty as well as one of the most magnetic vocal artists of the century. Strauss created the roles of Ariadne and the Empress in *Die Frau ohne Schatten* for her, and she was also one of the era's outstanding Puccini singers. At Northrop on that evening, Jeritza "swept from the wings in a canary yellow Grecian-style gown with belts of brilliants and necklace of pearls" to sing "Dich, teure Halle," the rapturous greeting to the Hall of Song of the heroine Elisabeth in *Tannhäuser* and thus an obvious choice for this occasion.

Another legendary singing-actress—and famous beauty—MARY GARDEN, Debussy's first Mélisande, opened the following season in October. Sherman relates that Garden "performed with a battery of specially installed lights to illuminate a new coiffure of reddish hair, a sylphlike figure and a breathtaking gown." The players, and presumably the audience, were distracted from the music, and perhaps just as well, for Garden was reportedly not in best voice that evening.

The visiting male singers were less colorful, a possible exception being the famous American baritone LAWRENCE TIBBETT, for decades not only a star of the Met, but also of Broadway, radio, and Hollywood movies. RICHARD CROOKS, described in 1974 by the esteemed critic J. B. Steane as "probably the best lyric tenor America has produced," made three appearances with the MSO between 1927 and 1932. The American-born and -trained baritone JOHN CHARLES THOMAS was still better known in the opera houses of Europe than of the U.S. when he made his MSO debut in 1929, but he was one of the Met's leading artists by the time of his fourth and last visit eleven years later. Another celebrated baritone visitor to the MSO was HEINRICH SCHLUSNUS from the Berlin State Opera.

Some of the world's finest instrumentalists made their debut appearances with the Orchestra during Verbrugghen's tenure, including the Scottish pianist FREDERIC LAMOND, who had attended Liszt's master classes; the nineteen-year-old Minneapolis native EUNICE NORTON, who had already made her reputation in Europe; and the legendary Polish virtuoso MORIZ

ROSENTHAL, who had been a private pupil of Liszt for nine years.

On January 12, 1928, the sensational Russian pianist VLADIMIR HOROWITZ made his U.S. debut playing the Tchaikovsky Concerto with the New York Philharmonic under Beecham (and, shortly thereafter, his Twin Cities debut in St. Paul at a Schubert Club recital). Two years later, Horowitz brought his astonishing Tchaikovsky fireworks display to Northrop with the MSO, igniting it again three years later at a Sunday afternoon "Popular Concert."

Horowitz's famous compatriot the virtuoso violinist JASCHA HEIFETZ also made his MSO debut that season, in the first U.S. performance of the Violin Concerto No. 1 by Castelnuovo-Tedesco. Heifetz no doubt disappointed some Minneapolitans by coming without his new wife, Hollywood actress Florence Vidor—probably a wise decision, given the 20-below-zero February weather.

One of the most memorable of all the debuts in these years came in March 1930 when the twelve-year-old violin prodigy YEHUDI MENUHIN played the Brahms Concerto at Northrop Auditorium, with first-movement cadenza by his teacher Georges Enesco. Following the public final rehearsal, the *Tribune* reviewer reported: "Sixty blasé musicians forgot their dignity and took part in a mad demonstration. Tears tickled down grizzled chins and splashed into the bass horns. Music stands were upset as musicians leaped to their feet and shook the rafters with a chorus of 'Bravos' . . . Yehudi grinned happily and boyishly and offered to try it again if they liked."

The concert itself, alas, did not go quite as brilliantly. In the second movement, a few bars into his solo, his biographer Humphrey Burton writes, Menuhin "stopped playing. For the first time in his performing career he had lost the thread. . . . He turned to the conductor Henri Verbrugghen, a violinist himself, and whispered, 'We must not bluff Brahms!' Verbrugghen stopped the Orchestra and told the audience 'in the kindliest manner,' according to the Minneapolis *Journal*, 'that the little lapsus was caused by the fact that he had never played it in public before.'" The *Tribune* critic charmingly asserted that "greatly to the youngster's credit was his calm ability

Pianist André Watts in his January 1964 debut, playing the Liszt Piano Concerto No. 1 with the Orchestra and guest conductor Vladimir Golschmann

James **Galway**

Dusolina **Giannini**

Richard **Goode**

Susan **Graham**

Reri **Grist**

Franco **Gulli**

to think his way through the crisis and bring the movement to a splendid conclusion."

After the concert, Menuhin was invited home by Verbrugghen to play chamber music. ("Fortunately I could sight-read well and did not disgrace myself," the violinist relates in his autobiography.) Four years later, Menuhin, at sixteen a seasoned veteran of the concert hall, returned to Northrop to play, without mishap, the Beethoven Concerto. And he would come back regularly after that, for nearly the next half century, becoming one of the most faithful and frequent visiting soloists in the Orchestra's history.

Perhaps the biggest ballyhoo to erupt at the MSO during Verbrugghen's tenure surrounded a Northrop visit by legendary pianist Ignacy Jan Paderewski in December 1930. With the house sold out well in advance, the great man received a standing ovation as he entered, before playing a single note. Sherman in the *Star* wrote that "no one who went to the campus auditorium last night, we dare say, was aloof enough not to . . . realize that the event, somehow, was among the major experiences of life. . . . Paderewski, in his seventieth year, is still the genius who works miracles on the sensibilities and emotions of his listeners. His presence now has become almost that of the seer, the philosopher, and the notes from his Steinway are awaited as words from an oracle." Paderewski, who had first played with the Orchestra more than two decades earlier, was reportedly charmed on this, his final visit, by the Christmas lights on Nicollet Avenue. "It's the most beautiful civic display I have ever seen," he declared.

The Ormandy Era (1931-36)

Eugene Ormandy's five years with the Minneapolis Symphony Orchestra, though the shortest tenure of any of its chief conductors, was a decisive period in the Orchestra's development and the spread of its reputation. For his debut concert Ormandy brought ELISABETH SCHUMANN, one of history's most delightful and adored sopranos. (She and Ormandy would team up once again in January 1935, Schumann's only other appearance with

the Orchestra, for arias from *Don Giovanni* and *Figaro* and lieder by Mahler and Hugo Wolf.)

In just *one* season during Ormandy's tenure, the MSO's 31st (1933-34), its roster of guest artists included the local debuts of the Austrian pianist ARTUR SCHNABEL and the immensely popular Hungarian bass-baritone FRIEDRICH SCHORR, one of history's greatest Wagner singers. Another matchless Wagner singer, one of Richard Strauss's favorite artists—perhaps the finest Marschallin ever in his *Rosenkavalier*—was the German soprano LOTTE LEHMANN. Engaged by the Met for the 1933-34 season, Lehmann was soon heard by MSO audiences, too ("gorgeous of voice and magnificent in appearance"—Davies).

Among the returning soloists that season were two legendary violinists: Heifetz, this time with his glamorous wife in tow, and sporting a new mustache; and Kreisler, who arrived late—his flight from Louisville delayed by fog—and played the Beethoven Concerto without a rehearsal. The pianists included Myra Hess and WALTER GIESEKING. Rachmaninoff was back to play his Second Concerto again, with Ormandy conducting a performance of his Second Symphony after intermission. Another great pianist, Moiseiwitsch, performed with the Orchestra for the last time, while yet another, the inimitable SHURA CHERKASSKY, came for the first and only time, still early in his unusually long career.

ADOLF BUSCH, arguably the supreme chamber-music player of the last century and one of its greatest interpreters of Beethoven's Violin Concerto, presented that work in his sole appearance with the MSO. Debuting in March 1935, another outstanding soloist, NATHAN MILSTEIN, made the first of many visits, this time with the Tchaikovsky Violin Concerto. His last appearance here would, amazingly, come nearly half a century later, when he played the Tchaikovsky again.

In addition to Schumann and Lehmann, Ormandy and the Orchestra attracted other outstanding singers: TITO SCHIPA, the greatest Italian lyric tenor of his generation; the French coloratura LILY PONS, not long after she conquered the Met with her Lucia; the outstanding American tenor ROLAND HAYES, performing works that,

At a special concert in November 1963, comedian and violinist Jack Benny performed music of Sarasate and Wieniawski with the Orchestra and Music Director Stanislaw Skrowaczewski.

Ida **Haendel**

Lynn **Harrell**

Roland **Hayes**

Vladimir **Horowitz**

Young-Uck **Kim**

Igor **Kipnis**

tragically, he would not have been allowed to sing in an American opera house in those days because of his race; and KIRSTEN FLAGSTAD, fresh from her triumphant debut at the Met and just beginning her reign as the outstanding Wagnerian soprano of the day.

In a performance that must have had Minneapolitans buzzing for weeks, FEODOR CHALIAPIN, regarded as the greatest singing actor of his time, but nearing the end of his career, offered arias by Rossini, Borodin, and Mozart. In a concert described by Sherman, rather priggishly, as "the most shocking and ludicrous evening of the Ormandy reign, and one of the most curious in the orchestra's history . . . the aging Russian basso [who had been heard several times before in Minneapolis] . . . threw a dignified Friday evening program out of gear, much to the suppressed fury of Conductor Ormandy . . . served as his own announcer . . . rearranged the order of his songs and interpolated new ones." After intermission Chaliapin "sang encores in which he simulated drunkenness and mimicked an explosive kiss to the last row of the balcony." More egregious was his repeatedly turning his back to the audience, waving his hands at the Orchestra to shush them in loud passages, and generally interfering with the outraged Ormandy.

In March 1936 the American matinee idol NELSON EDDY, opera singer turned Hollywood star (his first movie with Jeanette MacDonald, *Naughty Marietta*, had recently been released), sang Mahler's *Wayfarer* Songs, "Non più andrai" from *Le nozze di Figaro* and an aria from Meyerbeer's *L'Africaine* and nearly caused a riot. According to Sherman, his appearance created "the largest female stampede in local musical memory . . . his only major competition . . . another male blond, Eugene Ormandy, whose luster paled somewhat beside that of the glamorous Eddy."

In Ormandy's final season before leaving the MSO for The Philadelphia Orchestra, he conducted only the first three programs, with the remaining concerts entrusted to guests. They began at the end of November 1936 with a return visit by conductor Artur Bodanzky with the American tenor CHARLES KULLMAN singing selections from *Meistersinger*. Bodanzky was praised by a local critic

for "lucidity and certainty, free of temperamental distortions . . . a tonic . . . especially in his Wagner," but he was eclipsed completely two months later by what was probably the most memorable appearance by any guest conductor in the Orchestra's history.

On January 29, 1937, DIMITRI MITROPOULOS, in his MSO debut concert, "turned the normally phlegmatic Minneapolis audience into an excited mob," as his biographer William R. Trotter has written. Eyewitness John K. Sherman reported: "Mitropoulos . . . conducted the orchestra like a man possessed. . . . It was especially memorable because the sound that went with it was intensely compelling, music so full of blood, muscle, and nerves as to seem alive and sentient, and bearing unmistakable overtone of great thought and aspiring spirit." The announcement at a concert ten days later of Mitropoulos's appointment as the Orchestra's next permanent conductor set the audience to cheering.

The Mitropoulos Era (1937-49)

Dimitri Mitropoulos brought the Minneapolis Symphony Orchestra to the pinnacle of its fame and he stamped his twelve seasons at the helm with the force of his own magnetic personality and electrifying musicianship. Meanwhile, the influx of famous visiting artists continued unabated, especially during the war years. Great talents yearned to perform with him. As retired double bassist Clifford Johnson, a member of the Orchestra for nearly half a century, recently recalled, Mitropoulos "had a 'sixth sense' when accompanying and seemed to know even before rehearsing with a soloist what they were going to do."

Wagnerian singers came out in full force, including Flagstad, who appeared on two further occasions with the Orchestra—in 1939, with Crown Prince Frederick and Princess Ingrid of the Danish royal family present in the audience, and at the beginning of 1941, before the singer's controversial return home to Nazi-occupied Norway. In April 1938 the season's climax had Mitropoulos and the Orchestra performing with HELEN TRAUBEL, LAURITZ MELCHIOR, and EMANUEL LIST in the complete first

Kirill **Kondrashin**

Alicia **de Larrocha**

Erich **Leinsdorf**

Yo-Yo **Ma**

Dorothy **Maynor**

Yehudi **Menuhin**

Polish composer Krzysztof Penderecki, Music Director Stanislaw Skrowaczewski, violinist Isaac Stern, and the Orchestra accept applause in Orchestra Hall after the premiere of Penderecki's Violin Concerto in January 1978.

act of *Die Walküre*. After the war, the great Swedish-American Wagner soprano ASTRID VARNAY sang her local debut with the Orchestra.

Other famous voices heard during those years included Met favorite ELEANOR STEBER, DOROTHY MAYNOR (barred from that stage because of her race), and the inimitably elegant Viennese tenor RICHARD TAUBER. His "buttery tone and rubber phrase" was not to John Sherman's taste, however, and another local skeptic found "his manner that of a man whom audiences have given too much adulation." PAUL ROBESON came in 1943, the year of his triumph as Shakespeare's *Othello* on the New York stage. EZIO PINZA sang the "Death of Boris" and other excerpts from Mussorgsky's opera and returned for Mozart and Verdi; the Ukrainian-born bass ALEXANDER KIPNIS presented two substantial Verdi arias and an orchestrated version of Brahms's *Four Serious Songs*; and the revered American contralto MARIAN ANDERSON made her debut in the same era.

Debuting pianists included RUDOLF SERKIN, who quickly became a regular, with six concerto appearances during the Mitropoulos period alone. Years later, after a concert at Carnegie Hall with Mitropoulos and the New York Philharmonic, Serkin mused about his long association with the conductor: "Yes . . . it was extraordinary, but it was even more so in Minneapolis than in New York. There was less pressure—the orchestra was not so tired. Somehow, we enjoyed it more in Minneapolis."

CLAUDIO ARRAU performed with the Orchestra three times in this period, and ROBERT CASADESUS, who came four times, joined the Orchestra in 1945 on a tour of the South. In 1949, the remarkable Italian pianist ARTURO BENEDETTI MICHELANGELI, on his first American tour, performed Franck's Symphonic Variations and the First Liszt Concerto with the MSO under Mitropoulos. Among the keyboard legends returning to perform with Mitropoulos were Rachmaninoff, Josef Hofmann, Horowitz, and Myra Hess.

The brilliant young American pianist WILLIAM KAPELL, whose career was cut tragically short by a fatal plane crash in 1953, made his debut in the first local performance of the Concerto No. 1 of Khachaturian in January 1944, a "high-speed romp," reported Sherman, who also tells us that Kapell "split a fingertip while playing this highly percussive concerto but continued despite pain and slippery bloody keys." Kapell came again a year later to play the Brahms First.

Pianist Artur Schnabel came twice: for Brahms 1 on an all-Brahms program and for Beethoven 1, followed after intermission by the world premiere of the pianist's own composition, the thorny First Symphony. About Schnabel's Symphony, the *Tribune* critic reported: "It was too strenuous an adventure on uncharted seas for some of the audience, who struck out for familiar shores. I mean they got up and walked out."

During the performance, at least a hundred listeners headed for the exits, according to Mitropoulos's biographer, and the musicians weren't much happier. After the Symphony ended and Mitropoulos had left the stage, a member of the violin section remarked: "Gee, is it over? I still had half a page of notes to play." "I don't know what they're complaining about," the conductor is quoted as saying, "*I* had to memorize the bloody thing." The composer, who had never before heard a performance of one of his orchestral works, on the other hand, was delighted, calling Mitropoulos's conducting "astonishing" and the Orchestra's playing "magnificent."

The most frequent return visitor among the great pianists during this period was the MSO's idolized Artur Rubinstein, who appeared in no less than six seasons and recorded the Tchaikovsky First Concerto with the Orchestra for RCA Victor. Rubinstein and Mitropoulos liked to go to the moving pictures together in downtown Minneapolis and, according to Trotter, ". . . the two musicians were once overheard in a spirited argument about the proper symbolism of a small dog which was featured in a Fred MacMurray-Claudette Colbert movie."

Under Mitropoulos, returning fiddlers included Milstein (five times), Menuhin (four times, including, in 1943, a performance in which he introduced Bartók's Violin Concerto to Minneapolis audiences), Josef Szigeti (also four), Kreisler (three times), and Heifetz (also three

Nathan **Milstein**

Shlomo **Mintz**

Anne-Sophie **Mutter**

Igor **Oistrakh**

Itzhak **Perlman**

Roberta **Peters**

Music Director Neville Marriner conducted the musical forces assembled for a gala concert, Tonight Scandinavia, televised in Orchestra Hall in September 1982. Performers included soloists (from left) Martti Talvela, Håkan Hagegård, Judith Blegen, and Birgit Nilsson, and three choirs: Icelandic Male Chorus, St. Olaf Choir, and The Tapiola Choir of Finland.

Composer and conductor Aaron Copland in rehearsal with the Orchestra in Orchestra Hall

times), who came into his own in later seasons introducing Minneapolis audiences to the concertos by Elgar and Walton. The distinguished cellist GREGOR PIATIGORSKY, who had made his MSO debut with the Dvořák Concerto in 1936, repeated that work twice under Mitropoulos. There were some new faces, too, including three outstanding violinists: ZINO FRANCESCATTI, ISAAC STERN, and the superb young French player GINETTE NEVEU, who came only once, in 1948, before a plane crash claimed her life the following year.

Mention must be made of the MSO's extraordinary concertmaster LOUIS KRASNER, who introduced Minneapolis in 1945 (before New York had heard them) to the concertos by Berg and Schoenberg, both of which he had given their world premiere performances several years earlier (indeed Krasner had commissioned the Berg). After the Schoenberg Concerto the *Tribune* reviewer wrote: "Underneath the complex surface of this difficult piece . . . was not nonsense, but order, and as much emotion as can be discovered in any romantic composition, which this concerto essentially is. . . . I sincerely hope we are aware of the enormous debt we owe to Dimitri Mitropoulos and Louis Krasner. It is Mr. Mitropoulos's forward looking that makes Minneapolis an important music center."

Two years later, Krasner, Mitropoulos, and the Orchestra gave the first Minneapolis performance of the difficult but deeply rewarding Violin Concerto by the great American composer Roger Sessions. "The stone-faced reactionaries," writes William Trotter, "were, on this occasion, vastly outnumbered by an audience that listened with respect and sincere concentration." Sherman noted that the work "won a decent measure of applause and even a bravo or two for the composer, who was present for the performance."

Such an important musical center was also attracting some exceptional guest conductors. In December 1940, a year after settling in the U.S., IGOR STRAVINSKY came for a concert of his own works: the Divertimento from *The Fairy's Kiss*, *Jeu de cartes* and the *Petrushka* and *Firebird* suites. Sherman in his book called this "one of the historic evenings in Symphony annals." The "short, prim, bespectacled gentleman with a calm, measured beat and a self-possessed, entirely unferocious manner . . . exhibited a precise baton style and an almost pedagogical method that gave shining clarity to works which, as he remarked at the time in an interview, were too often 'sensationalized' by prima donna conductors."

Beginning in January 1941, Bruno Walter made return appearances in three consecutive seasons to "the city that welcomed him so eagerly in 1923" (Sherman), and SIR THOMAS BEECHAM came to Minneapolis in December 1942. Beecham liked the Orchestra, calling it "plastic, experienced, and well disciplined." For the first time at an MSO concert, the audience applauded the national anthem, which Beecham in rehearsal likened to 'a battle cry . . . not a widow's dirge as played by the Metropolitan Opera orchestra.'"

In January 1943, conductor WILLIAM STEINBERG, then Arturo Toscanini's associate with the NBC Symphony Orchestra, made "a good impression" (Sherman) conducting Mozart and Strauss. In December 1944 the young Hungarian conductor ANTAL DORATI, who had already stood before the Minneapolis Symphony several times accompanying the annual visits to Northrop of the Ballet Russe de Monte Carlo, conducted Beethoven, Mozart, Ravel, and Strauss; and ARTHUR FIEDLER conducted a Christmas Pops Concert. December 1945 saw two new faces on the Northrop podium. A young protégé of Mitropoulos named LEONARD BERNSTEIN, composer of the brand-new hit Broadway musical *On the Town*, led the Orchestra in Beethoven, Strauss, Copland, and Brahms. "The 27-year-old . . . 'boy wonder' in the conducting-composing field . . . punched out the music with right hooks and left jabs and gave it kindling warmth and eloquence." (Sherman) A week later ERICH LEINSDORF conducted an all-Wagner program with soprano Helen Traubel.

The Alsatian conductor CHARLES MUNCH made his MSO debut in December 1947 in an all-French program. FRITZ REINER, having just left the Pittsburgh Symphony after ten years, conducted a series of MSO concerts in October and November 1948. Reiner's Minneapolis repertoire ranged from Wagner excerpts (with Astrid Varnay), through Tchaikovsky's Fourth Symphony and Ravel's second *Daphnis et Chloë* suite and, would you believe, the *Carousel* Waltz by Richard Rodgers. And, finally, in December 1948, Eugene Ormandy, starting a welcome, sentimental tradition, came back to his old haunt for the first time in years to conduct Bach-

Ormandy, Brahms, the Strausses (Johann and Richard), and Debussy.

The Dorati Era (1949-60)

With Mitropoulos's successor, Antal Dorati, the MSO continued to attract the cream of the international musical scene. To play the big concertos the ensemble collaborated with pianists of the caliber of Horowitz's pupil BYRON JANIS; RUDOLF FIRKUŠNÝ, who had toured with the Orchestra under Mitropoulos; FRIEDRICH GULDA; GÉZA ANDA; two great Schnabel pupils, CLIFFORD CURZON and LEON FLEISHER; PHILIPPE ENTREMONT; the 21-year-old VLADIMIR ASHKENAZY, on his first U.S. tour; JORGE BOLET; VAN CLIBURN (playing Tchaikovsky, ten months after his triumph at the Tchaikovsky Competition in Moscow, and frequently returning in the 1960s and 70s); EUGENE ISTOMIN; and the iconoclastic GLENN GOULD, at the mid-point of his single decade of international public appearances. Other familiar faces included Casadesus (five visits), Rubinstein and Arrau (four each), Serkin (three), Kapell (two), and Myra Hess (for the last time in 1954).

The great Hungarian pianist-composer ERNÖ DOHNÁNYI gave Mozart's C-major Concerto K.503 an astonishingly belated first MSO performance. Michelangeli returned in February 1950, eliciting from local reviewers the sort of split decision that followed the controversial artist throughout his career: John Harvey in the *Pioneer Press* found everything about his playing "clean, shipshape, balanced, vital and thoroughly beautiful," while John Sherman in the *Star*, although struck by the "marvel of precision, of crisp fingerwork, of explicit and always positive exposition," thought that "the performance as a whole had fine balance and shape, but no stature."

The roster of violinists also showed no signs of slacking off. Within a single season, the Orchestra's 53rd (1955-56), it offered MSO audiences DAVID OISTRAKH and Jascha Heifetz, as well as Menuhin and Stern. First-timers under Dorati were violinists ARTHUR GRUMIAUX and SZYMON GOLDBERG, cellist LEONARD ROSE, and guitarist ANDRÉS SEGOVIA. In December 1949 the outstanding violist of the era, WILLIAM PRIMROSE, gave the world premiere of the Bartók Viola Concerto (com-

Gregor **Piatigorsky**

Sergei **Rachmaninoff**

Helmuth **Rilling**

Paul **Robeson**

Mstislav **Rostropovich**

Artur **Rubinstein**

Eminent guest conductor Robert Shaw led the Orchestra, choruses (Minnesota Chorale, Warland Symphonic Chorus, and Metropolitan Boys Choir), and soloists (Richard Clement, left, Carol Vaness, center, and Bo Skovhus, right) in March 1998 performances of the Benjamin Britten War Requiem.

pleted posthumously by the composer's friend Tibor Serly) and a few years later returned for the Walton Concerto.

The great fiddlers of the day came back again and again. Heifetz played in two other seasons during the Dorati tenure, Milstein in three, Francescatti in four, and Stern in six. In February 1957, Menuhin joined Dorati and the Orchestra for the Bartók Concerto at Carnegie Hall, with the famous Mercury recording taking place between midnight and 5 a.m. directly following the concert, although the MSO had an engagement out on Long Island later that day!

Dorati created some notable Wagner events. He brought Traubel and Melchior back to perform a con-

cert abridgment of *Tristan und Isolde*; and Flagstad came back after a long absence to sing excerpts from Acts I and III of *Tristan* and Brünnhilde's "Immolation." Marian Anderson returned twice, and there were visits by BLANCHE THEBOM, GEORGE LONDON, ROBERTA PETERS, LISA DELLA CASA, PHYLLIS CURTIN, and GIULIETTA SIMIONATO.

The Dorati years featured an impressive line-up of guest conductors. FRITZ BUSCH, already familiar to Twin Cities audiences from visits by the touring Metropolitan Opera and Leopold Stokowski, who praised the MSO in an interview in the *Star*: "In my opinion the orchestra is truly great. Antal Dorati . . . and Dimitri Mitropoulos, before him, have done wonderful things in developing it to a high state. It is full of very fine musicians and moves from one style to another with the greatest ease."

PIERRE MONTEUX appeared with the Orchestra three times. Sherman in the *Star* eulogized the great French maestro's Minneapolis performances: "The thing you notice most in his utterly unostentatious direction is his expansive touch, which draws out the phrase in full grace and beauty—not only the phrase but the long line and whole design, all made to flower and mature fully. . . ."

Other conducting highlights of the Dorati era included The Cleveland Orchestra's GEORGE SZELL, composer PAUL HINDEMITH, KARL BÖHM (on his first American tour), and debuts by THOMAS SCHIPPERS, PAUL KLETZKI, and EUGEN JOCHUM, as well as a return visit by Bruno Walter.

The significance of these events can be gauged by the recollections of Orchestra members themselves. Marvin Dahlgren, principal percussionist at the time, replying to a query of the Orchestra's longtime program annotator Mary Ann Feldman, recently named the three Monteux concerts as the ones he would choose to play again: "After all, he was the original conductor of *Rite of Spring*, the piece that got me into classical music in the first place. When he broke his baton during rehearsal, he left the part that did not fly off on the podium. After rehearsal I retrieved it, and I've kept it ever since."

Retired violinist Henry Gregorian, without faltering, declared his two choices: "The Beethoven Seventh under the great Eugen Jochum, who first came here in my fifth season . . . and the Bruckner Fourth we did under him when he came back one more time, just two years later. He had such poise on the podium, and such a sense of style." Other musicians have also singled out Jochum's Bruckner as the high point of their years in the Orchestra.

The Skrowaczewski Era (1960-79)

Under Music Director (the formal title was introduced at this time) Stanislaw Skrowaczewski, many well-loved older figures continued to grace the Orchestra's programs, and no visitor was more faithful than Artur Rubinstein. In December 1960, he and his compatriot Skrowaczewski

presented an all-Polish evening, which included Chopin's Second Piano Concerto and the fascinating Sinfonia Concertante, composed for Rubinstein by Szymanowski. The great pianist played both of the Brahms concertos with the MSO a few years later and returned again in January 1972, a few days shy of his 85th birthday, nearly 51 years after his debut with the Orchestra, to play the Mozart D-minor and Schumann concertos.

Other favorite pianists—Ashkenazy, Curzon, Fleisher—came back again during these two decades, and many returned a number of times: Serkin, Janis, Firkušný, Istomin, Casadesus, and Arrau. Glenn Gould had been scheduled to play the Mozart C-minor Concerto in April 1964, but that date was one of many he cancelled after abruptly ending his public career. Among the seasoned violinists, Isaac Stern was the most frequent visitor, playing no fewer than eight engagements in this period alone, and Menuhin, Ruggiero Ricci, Francescatti, and Milstein, too, were often to be heard. David Oistrakh came only once again, in December 1965, to play the Beethoven Concerto under Skrowaczewski.

Two distinguished violinists debuted during these years: legendary Soviet violinist LEONID KOGAN, who appeared with the Orchestra only once, and the great Polish virtuoso HENRYK SZERYNG, who in nine appearances treated lucky Twin Cities audiences to performances of concertos by Bach, Mozart, Beethoven, Schumann, Paganini, Brahms, Tchaikovsky, Sibelius, Bartók, and Szymanowski. Other important newcomers included CHRISTIAN FERRAS, IDA HAENDEL, KYUNG-WHA CHUNG, ITZHAK PERLMAN, PINCHAS ZUKERMAN, and GIDON KREMER. There was even a concert in November 1963 devoted to the unusual fiddling talents of JACK BENNY, who ventured to display his virtuosity in Sarasate's *Zigeunerweisen* and a condensed version of Wieniawski's warhorse Second Violin Concerto.

This period's distinguished list of first-time pianists with the Orchestra included, chronologically by debut, GINA BACHAUER, GARY GRAFFMAN, NIKITA MAGALOFF, JOHN BROWNING (introducing the Barber Piano Concerto), ANDRÉ WATTS, JULIUS KATCHEN, CLAUDE FRANK, EMIL GILELS, DANIEL BARENBOIM, WILHELM KEMPFF, PETER SERKIN, JOHN OGDON, CHRISTOPH ESCHENBACH, ALICIA DE LARROCHA, GARRICK OHLSSON, MARTHA ARGERICH, MURRAY PERAHIA, ALFRED

Esa-Pekka **Salonen**

Alexander **Schneider**

Rudolf **Serkin**

Robert **Shaw**

Janos **Starker**

Isaac **Stern**

BRENDEL, KRYSTIAN ZIMERMAN, YEFIM BRONFMAN, and WALTER KLIEN (Mozart Concertos No. 17 and No. 27—alert, stylish readings that he subsequently recorded with Skrowaczewski and the Orchestra).

A new crop of outstanding cellists also made their first appearances in Minnesota with the Orchestra: MSTISLAV ROSTROPOVICH (five seasons), JACQUELINE DU PRÉ and LYNN HARRELL (each twice), PIERRE FOURNIER, JÁNOS STARKER, ZARA NELSOVA, and YO-YO MA, with Rostropovich playing both the Shostakovich First Cello Concerto (local premiere) and the Dvořák Concerto on one program in November 1965, and Du Pré offering her incomparable reading of the Elgar Concerto in December 1968 (another local premiere).

In October 1974 the Orchestra performed the third major gala opening of its life: the first concert in its own home, the newly constructed Orchestra Hall. This time the featured guest artist honor went to cellist Lynn Harrell, who performed Haydn's D-major Concerto as the first soloist in the brand-new concert hall.

In the Hall's second season, another brilliant virtuoso, the Australian-born, British horn player BARRY TUCKWELL made his Orchestra debut playing a Mozart concerto. He returned twice during the next several seasons with another Mozart, as well as concertos by Hindemith and Thea Musgrave.

Skrowaczewski's era was another good period for singers. RICHARD TUCKER sang arias by Beethoven, Handel, Verdi, Wagner, and Mascagni; BIRGIT NILSSON sang Wagner; JUDITH RASKIN sang Bach, Mozart, Mahler, and Ravel; MARILYN HORNE, CESARE VALLETTI, and GÉRARD SOUZAY were the soloists in Berlioz's *Damnation of Faust*, JANET BAKER was heard in Mahler's *Das Lied von der Erde*; EVELYN LEAR and THOMAS STEWART sang Bartók's *Bluebeard's Castle*; and ROBERTA PETERS sang just about everything, including *Lucia*'s Mad Scene. This era's treasury of singers also included soprano ANNA MOFFO, JESS THOMAS with EILEEN FARRELL, LEONTYNE PRICE, SHIRLEY VERRETT, JANE BERBIÉ with STUART BURROWS, and BEVERLY SILLS.

Skrowaczewski invited a remarkable coterie of guest conductors to share the podium duties: PETER MAAG,

ISTVÁN KERTÉSZ, RAFAEL KUBELIK, BERNARD HAITINK, Paul Kletzki, HERMANN SCHERCHEN, VLADIMIR GOLSCHMANN, JASCHA HORENSTEIN, JOSEF KRIPS, KARL RICHTER, HANS SCHMIDT-ISSERSTEDT, and COLIN DAVIS, who made his U.S. debut at Northrop in December 1960. Eugen Jochum returned to conduct Bach, Mozart, and the performance, already mentioned, of Bruckner's Fourth.

Other distinguished guests in this huge array of international conducting talent included AARON COPLAND, the doyen of American composers, conducting surprisingly broad programs (works by Brahms, Busoni, Chavez, Bernstein, Ives, and Schuman, as well as his own compositions). His July 4, 1976, concert in Orchestra Hall stands as a landmark performance in Orchestra history.

Orchestra Hall audiences also heard SEIJI OZAWA, ANDRÉ PREVIN (twice), ROBERT SHAW (six times to conduct major choral works, including memorable *Messiah* performances), GARY BERTINI, Charles Munch, THOMAS SCHIPPERS, Eugene Ormandy (back again three times), RAFAEL FRÜHBECK DE BURGOS (three times), JAMES LEVINE (twice), Yehudi Menuhin playing and conducting (twice), MICHAEL GIELEN (twice), ANDREW DAVIS, ZDENĚK MÁCAL, KIRILL KONDRASHIN, ALEXANDER SCHNEIDER playing the violin and conducting (twice), SARAH CALDWELL, JERZY SEMKOW, Erich Leinsdorf, DENNIS RUSSELL DAVIES, RAYMOND LEPPARD (three times), YURI TEMIRKANOV, and DAVID ZINMAN (who would become an artistic director of the Orchestra's summer season).

Skrowaczewski also invited Igor Stravinsky to return. He shared the podium with his amanuensis ROBERT CRAFT (*Fireworks, Rite of Spring*, Divertimento from *The Fairy's Kiss*). Further distinguished conductors included former music director Antal Dorati, future music directors NEVILLE MARRINER and EDO DE WAART, and . . . Danny Kaye? Yes, Danny Kaye!

A separate mention must be reserved for LEONARD SLATKIN, who became the Orchestra's first principal guest conductor in 1974 and occupied that position for five seasons. Slatkin, who initiated the popular Rug Concerts series, also founded the Orchestra's Viennese Sommerfest

Igor **Stravinsky**

Gladys **Swarthout**

Jeffrey **Tate**

Michael Tilson **Thomas**

Alexander **Toradze**

Giorgio **Tozzi**

Concertmaster Jorja Fleezanis and guest violinist (Nigel) Kennedy onstage at Orchestra Hall in 1992 for the premiere of Dave Heath's Alone at the Frontier, *a Concerto for Improvised Instrument and Orchestra*

*Minnesota Orchestra Music Director Neville
Marriner (wiping tears of laughter from
his eyes, left) and The Saint Paul Chamber
Orchestra Music Director Pinchas Zukerman sat
for a promotional photo in advance of a joint
concert of the two orchestras in March 1984.*

and then was engaged to succeed Slatkin as principal guest conductor. In that period, 1979-1982, he conducted indelible performances of Beethoven's *Eroica*, Fourth, Eighth, and Ninth; the Mahler Third and Seventh; the Bruckner Fourth; Dvořák's *New World* and Stravinsky's *Firebird*, as well as Haydn, Weber, Johann Strauss, Falla, Ravel, and much else. He returned in January 1984 with his own orchestra, the London Philharmonic.

As anyone who heard his concerts will surely testify, Tennstedt was a galvanizing force and an object of great affection in Minneapolis. The *Eroica* he conducted in Orchestra Hall, for example, was one of amazing intensity and power, magnificently played by the Minnesota Orchestra, tempting one to reach for interpretations like Furtwängler's or Klemperer's for comparison. That the Orchestra musicians in Minneapolis revered him is confirmed by the testimonials that followed his death in 1998, including this one from Co-Principal Clarinet Joseph Longo: "He made us all play way over our heads. He'd say, 'This pianissimo must be *unbelievable. Everything* must be unbelievable.' And it was—we were on the edge of our seats when we played for him. I've never seen that kind of excitement, in the players and in the audiences. And he was a nice fellow, a real *mensch*."

Tennstedt's successor as the Orchestra's principal guest conductor was the distinguished Swiss conductor CHARLES DUTOIT, then music director of another of North America's finest orchestras, the Montreal Symphony (which he brought to Orchestra Hall in January 1989). Minnesotans were lucky enough to hear Dutoit regularly with their own Orchestra from 1983 to 1986, conducting such works as Tchaikovsky's Fourth and Fifth Symphonies, Saint-Saëns's *Organ* Symphony, Mahler's Third, Prokofiev's Fifth, Ravel's *Mother Goose* Suite, Stravinsky's *Petrushka*, Strauss's *Don Quixote*, and the Bach Mass in B minor.

Other notable guest conductors of the last two decades (in alphabetical order, with visitors appearing on multiple occasions indicated in boldface) include **Roberto Abbado, Jiří Bělohlávek, Paavo Berglund, Harry Bicket, Herbert Blomstedt,** Frans Brueggen, Semyon Bychkov, Sian Edwards, Mark Elder, Adam Fischer, Iván Fischer, **Claus Peter Flor,** Jean Fournet, **Valery Gergiev, Günther Herbig, Eliahu Inbal, Neeme Järvi, Bernhard Klee, Yakov Kreizberg, Bernard**

and was its inspiring artistic director and principal conductor for a decade starting in 1980. He has stood on the Orchestra's podium more often than any other guest conductor in its history.

Recent Past: the Eras of Marriner, de Waart, and Oue (1979–2002)

As this chronicle approaches its end, the names become largely those of performers who still figure prominently, as of the 2002-03 season, in the musical scene. Many of them continue to grace Orchestra Hall with their artistry.

One especially important figure from this era, sadly, is no longer among us. KLAUS TENNSTEDT appeared with the Orchestra during two seasons in the late 1970s

Labadie, **Zdeněk Mácal, Eduardo Mata,** Paul McCreesh, **Ingo Metzmacher, Kent Nagano, Roger Norrington, Sakari Oramo, Arnold Östman,** Andrew Parrott, **Libor Pešek, Helmuth Rilling,** Donald Runnicles, Esa-Pekka Salonen, Kurt Sanderling, **Jukka-Pekka Saraste,** Calvin Simmons, **Leonard Slatkin, Robert Spano,** Emil Tchakarov, **Christian Thielemann,** Michael Tilson Thomas, **Yan Pascal Tortelier, Hans Vonk, and Mark Wigglesworth.**

David Zinman and **Jeffrey Tate** were frequent visitors as directors of Viennese Sommerfest and conductors of enterprising programs such as semi-staged, full-length opera performances. Zinman, for example, presided over Leonard Bernstein's *Candide*, and Tate over Strauss's *Ariadne auf Naxos* and Verdi's *Falstaff*.

Singers during these seasons included **John Aler,** Roberta Alexander, June Anderson (replicating Sembrich's entire 1903 inaugural program, with Skrowaczewski conducting and Margo Garrett at the piano, in celebration of the Orchestra's 90th birthday), Vladimir Atlantov, **Arleen Augér,** Juliane Banse, Jules Bastin, **Kathleen Battle,** Judith Blegen, **John Cheek,** Pamela Coburn, Barbara Daniels, **Michelle DeYoung, Susan Dunn, Jane Eaglen, Renée Fleming,** Maureen Forrester, **Matthias Goerne, Susan Graham,** Barbara Hendricks, **Heidi Grant Murphy, Håkan Hagegård, Ben Heppner,** Gwynne Howell, Robert Lloyd, Frank Lopardo, Benjamin Luxon, **Sylvia McNair,** Alessandra Marc, Charlotte Margiono, Margaret Marshall, **Jessye Norman,** Adrianne Pieczonka, Leontyne Price, Thomas Quasthoff, **Florence Quivar, Kenneth Riegel,** Michael Schade, Peter Schreier, Nadine Secunde, Lucy Shelton, Joanna Simon, Bo Skovhus, Thomas Stewart, **Kurt Streit, Martti Talvela,** Ruth Ann Swenson, Robert Tear, **Tatiana Troyanos, Dawn Upshaw, Benita Valente, Carol Vaness, Jon Villars,** Jard van Nes, **Deborah Voight, Frederica Von Stade,** and Carolyn Watkinson.

Scores of distinguished instrumentalists have performed with the Orchestra; among those who have returned repeatedly are (in alphabetical order): Emanuel Ax, Joshua Bell, Alfred Brendel, Yefim Bronfman, Rudolf Buchbinder, Sarah Chang, Bella Davidovich, Malcolm Frager, Pamela Frank, Miriam Fried, James Galway, Richard Goode, Hélène Grimaud, Andreas Haefliger, Lynn Harrell, Stephen Hough, Sharon Isbin, Steven

Isserlis, Joseph Kalichstein, (Nigel) Kennedy, Zoltan Kocsis, Alicia de Larrocha, Cho-Liang Lin, Radu Lupu, Yo-Yo Ma, Midori, Shlomo Mintz, Truls Mørk, Viktoria Mullova, Anne-Sophie Mutter, Garrick Ohlsson, Jon Kimura Parker, Murray Perahia, Itzhak Perlman, Jean-Pierre Rampal, Vadim Repin, Nadja Salerno-Sonnenberg, András Schiff, Peter Serkin, Gil Shaham, Christian Tetzlaff, Jean-Yves Thibaudet, Alexander Toradze, Maxim Vengerov, Lars Vogt, Jian Wang, André Watts, Thomas Zehetmair, and Pinchas Zukerman.

As the Orchestra enters its 100th season, 2002-2003, the guest artist roster will swell with names from the Orchestra's past, present, and future. The centennial season offers a unique opportunity to celebrate artistic liaisons from the past, while planning for a second century of outstanding concert programs.

Taking their places on the centennial podium will be several of the Orchestra's titled conductors: former music directors Stanislaw Skrowaczewski, Sir Neville Marriner, Edo de Waart, and Eiji Oue; former principal guest conductors Leonard Slatkin and Charles Dutoit; Henry Charles Smith, former associate and resident conductor; and current Associate Conductor Giancarlo Guerrero, Principal Pops Conductor Doc Severinsen, and Assistant Conductor Scott Terrell.

In addition, and continuing a century-long tradition of offering its audiences the very finest guest artists, the Orchestra will welcome such outstanding visitors as Renée Fleming, Yo-Yo Ma, Midori, Thomas Quasthoff, André Watts, Viktoria Mullova, Jean-Yves Thibaudet, Yakov Kreizberg, Roberto Abbado, James Conlon, and many more.

As for the future, Music Director Designate Osmo Vänskä—who himself began his association with the Orchestra as a distinguished guest artist—will conduct the Orchestra four weeks during the centennial season. Measured by the visiting artists it has attracted, the Minnesota Orchestra has been a major player on the classical music scene from its very inception. Under Vänskä's leadership, which begins with the 2003-2004 season, the Orchestra shows every sign of maintaining that stature in its second century.

Barry **Tuckwell**

Benita **Valente**

Deborah **Voight**

Frederica **Von Stade**

André **Watts**

Pinchas **Zukerman**

The Musicians of the Minnesota Orchestra
1903 through 2003

NEARLY ONE THOUSAND MUSICIANS have performed as permanent Minnesota Orchestra members in the ensemble's 100-year history. They came from vastly disparate backgrounds and played under widely different circumstances, but each was part of the same lineage and each served the same mission: sharing great music with their community. The musicians are the heart and soul of the Minnesota Orchestral Association. We salute each of them, past and present, on these pages.

Adam, Claus	Atkins, Leslie	Barton, Leland S.	Betts, Kendall	Braun, Harry
Adams, Merle S.	Atkins, Stanley	Bartz, Ernest B.	Beyer-Hane, Hermann	Breeskin, Elias
Adams, Michael	Ayer, Julie	Bartz, William L.	Biggs, Clifford	Bregman, Mischa
Adams, Richard	Ayres, Harold	Basinger, Emily	Bily, John F.	Bregmann, Joseph
Adelstein, Bernard	————	Bass, Jack	Binstock, Paul	Bright, Earl M.
Akos, Francis		Basso, Alexander B.	Bladet, Robert	Brissey, Paul
Albrecht, John Fred	Babst, August	Bates, Margaret	Blakkestad, Julius	Britt, Cynthia Eddy
Alexander, Joseph P.	Badollet, F. V.	Bauer, Jaraslov K.	Blinoff, Nicholas	Britt, Roger
Allard, Susan	Bagwell, William	Baum, George C.	Blitz, Edouard	Brooke, William E.
Allen, Blain	Baker, Rose-Marie	Beck, Barbara	Bloch, Robert	Brown, John
Alpert, Dorothy	Balazs, Ronald	Beckerman, Bernice	Blume, R.	Bruckner, Albert
Alpert, Victor	Baldwin, J. W.	Beckerman, Martin	Blunck, Victor H.	Brunelle, Philip
Andersen, Robert	Balian, Haig	Behr, J.	Bockman, Sigurd	Brunzell, Clifford
Andersen, Vigo	Baltrusch, Franz	Bellino, Frank	Boehle, Gustav	Bruzek, Frank J.
Anderson, Betty	Barach, Daniel	Benfield, Warren	Boessenroth, Herman	Buchbinder, Kay
Anderson, Robert	Barbier, Henri Le	Benoit, Isidore	Boettcher, William	Bures, Adolph
Angelucci, Rhadames	Barnard, Floyd P.	Benthin, Betty	Bohnen, John	Burkey, Charles E.
Antoun, Alison	Baron, James	Berdahl, James	Bonecutter, Max	Burkhart, Gloria
Arado, Stephanie	Baron, Samuel	Bergh, Arthur	Bonelli, Nicolo	Buschardt, Karl
Arkis, Jason	Barrows, John	Berglund, Carl E.	Booth, Clarence E.	Buskirk, John Van
Arnstein, Pamela	Barrus, Clyn Dee	Bergman, Samuel	Booth, Lester E.	Busse, Henry H.
Askegaard, Arthur C.	Barton, A. Russell	Best, Crawford	Brader, Harry	————

2001-2002 Season: Musicians, stage managers, and music librarians toss confetti in anticipation of the Orchestra's centennial season.

Calkins, Charles E.
Campbell, Chester
Capps, Ferald
Carlini, Louis
Carlsen, Douglas C.
Carmen, Elias
Carol, Norman
Caruthers, Annette
Cassetta, Louis
Celentano, Rosario
Chabr, Joseph
Chadwick, Arthur B.
Chalfant, Paul
Chappuis, Alphonse
Chardon, Yves
Chausow, Leonard
Chen, Taichi
Chenette, Stephen
Cheng, Sifei
Chickering, Robert
Christian, Andrea J.
Clavadetscher, John B.
Clute, James
Coleman, Avron
Coletti, Charles
Colf, Howard
Conradi, Otto
Consoli, Leonardo
Constant, Henriette de
Cooke, Glenn R.
Cooper, J. Andrew
Costa, Benedetto
Cote, E. E.
Crassas, Stelly
Cullen, Jenny
Culp, Paula
Cunnington, Henry
Cunnington, Syd
Currier, Frank S.
Czerwonky, Richard

D'Este, Charles
D'Isere, Guy
Dahl, Anton
Dahlgren, Marvin
Dalman, Conrad
Damm, Alfred, Jr.
Damm, Alfred, Sr.
Danz, Frank, Jr.
Davenport, Kenneth
Davis, Lester
Dawson, David P.
Dellone, Loretta
Demkier, Albert F.
Denecke, Henry, Jr.
Denecke, Julia
Denesuk, Michael
Díaz, Roberto
Dicks, Franz
Dircks, William E.
Docter, Kari Jane
Dorer, Robert
Dosch, William M.
Dost, Oscar
Dotzel, John
Doucet, Alfred
Doucet, Louis L.
Douglas, Meyer
Downs, Donald
Druian, Rafael
Dubois, Gaston
Dumont, Adolphe
Dupuis, Andre
Duvoir, Alexandre

Eager, James
Edmunds, F. T.
Eleftherakis, Eleftherios
Elliott, Anthony
Elst, Richard O.
Elworthy, Robert
Erck, Christian

Erck, Edward J. "Bill"
Esser, Walter
Eurist, Harry
Evenson, P. E.
Evenson, S.
Evers, Hermann
Ewart, Hugh

Faetkenheuer, William L.
Fafard, Joseph
Fallick, Louis
Fantozzi, William
Farmer, Virginia
Feiler, Maurice
Feit, Robert
Ferris, Kirkland D.
Fields, Dall
Filerman, H.
Filerman, Peter
Fine, Elliot
Finney, Theodore M.
Fisch, Burton
Fischer, Carlo
Fisher, Mina
Fishman, Bernard
Fitch, Ray W.
Fitzgerald, James
Fleezanis, Jorja
Fleminger, Gerald
Flor, Samuel
Foli, Lea
Fox, Fred
Frank, Joseph E.
Frankson, Roy E.
Freed, Kenneth
Freeman, Charles
Freiwald, Arthur
Frengut, Leon
Frisch, Roger
Frischman, Matthew
Frohn, Otto M.

Frommelt, Alfred
Fulginiti, Anthony C.
Fuller, Angela
Funnekotter, Adrian
Fust, Carl J.

Gallicchio, Joseph
Gangelhoff, John
Garfinkle, Paul
Gast, Michael
Gatscha, John
Gauthier, Roger
Geankoplis, Deno
Gebhart, Otto
Gebhart, Victor
Gentile, Flavio
Gerstel, Alan
Gibson, Daryl J.
Gietzen, Alfred
Gilbert, Folke
Gilombardo, Anthony
Glemming, Ivar A.
Gluck, Alexander
Gluschkin, Mischa
Glynn, Franklin
Goffin, M. D.
Gold, Arthur
Goldbaum, Martin
Goldberg, Abe
Golden, Joseph
González, Rubén
Gottesman, Andrew
Graef, Richard
Graffman, Vladimir
Granat, Wolfgang
Grapentin, Egon
Graudan, Nikolai
Graves, Clarence C.
Greco, James B.
Green, Laurel
Greenberg, Herbert

Gregorian, Henry
Grisez, Georges
Grosbayne, Edward
Grubner, James
Gruppe, Paulo M.
Guetter, Max
Gunther, Paul
Gunvalson, Otto

Habberstad, George
Hagen, Edward A.
Haigh, Bertram N.
Halpern, Sidney
Hals, Olaf
Halten, Olaf
Han-Gorski, Adam
Hancock, Walter S.
Handlon, Earl A.
Hanford, Robert
Hanks, Thompson W., Jr.
Hara, Burt
Harrison, H. K.
Hartl, John
Hasselmann, Ronald
Hays, Vivian
Hedberg, Earl
Hedges, William
Hedling, Fredrik
Heidemann, Donald
Heiderich, Jacob
Heiseke, John Frederik
Hendricks, Herbert
Henrotte, Pierre
Herring, David
Hersh, Stefan
Heynen, Achille
Hines, Frank
Hipps, Merrimon, Jr.
Hoevel, Heinrich
Holguin, David
Holskin, Jacob

Holub, Carl
Holzinger, Raymond
Horak, Edward
Horvath, Janet
Hoskins, Adelmour M.
Hosmer, Eugene A.
Hougham, Marni J.
Howell, John
Hranek, Carl
Hubert, Marcel
Huff, Henry
Huff, J. A.
Hughart, Frederick S.
Humphrey, George N.
Hunt, Hamlin
Hurt, Martin
Hurt, Robert
Hustana, Allan
Hyna, Otto

Iglitzin, Alan
Ikeda, Eiji
Illions, Seymour
Ingraham, Paul
Isaeff, Eugene
Isomura, Sachiya
Isuf, Sami

Jackson, Clifton
Jacobs, Harry M.
Jacobsen, Edmund
James, Dennis
Jamieson, Robert
Janossy, Gus S.
Janossy, William J.
Janse, Aaron
Janss, Albert
Jeffery, George J.
Jensen, Richard
Jerabek, Frank

Johnson, Alvin
Johnson, Clifford
Johnson, Joseph
Johnson, Rose-Marie
Johnstone, Donald
Jordan, Clarence S.

Kaltschmidt, Eugen
Kamins, Benjamin
Kamminga, David
Kasanoff, Michael
Kast, George
Katzsch, Theodore
Keller, Carole Marie
Keller, William C.
Kelley, Mark
Kemper, Kristin
Kennedy, James
Kenny, Ralph E.
Kershaw, Clarence B.
Kesnar, Maurits
Kienzle, Kathy
Kirksmith, Karl
Kishkis, Alfred
Klanfer, Morton
Klass, George
Klatzkin, Benjamin
Klimitz, Richard
Knapp, Roy C.
Knardahl, Eva
Knutsen, Kristian
Knutson, Erling
Koch, Jean
Koch, Oscar
Kocsis, Leslie
Koehler, Albert
Koehler, George
Koehler, Lawrence
Kogan, Peter
Kogen, Ronald
Kolker, Phillip

Koltun, Alexander
Komarovsky, Constanin
Konrad, Robert
Kopp, Edouard C.
Korb, Fram Anton
Kostelecky, Gustave
Kovarick, Frank J.
Kovarik, John P.
Kramer, Henry
Krasner, Elsa
Krasner, Louis
Krausse, Otto H.
Kreston, Aimee
Kruczek, Leo
Krueger, Arnold
Kruse, Paul
Kuchynka, Frank
Kuehle, Alfred
Kuehne, Carl
Kuenzel, Adam
Kurtz, Arthur
Kurz, George A.
Kuypers, John
Kwak, Sarah

Labate, Bruno
Lah, Radivoj
Lambert, John C.
Lamping, Willy
Langstadt, Moritz
Lantz, William H.
Larsen, T. Nils
Larusson, Harry
Latisch, Emil
Latisch, Isa
Lau, Paul
Laureano, Manuel
Lawrence, P. J.
Lazarus, Charles
Leathead, Celine
Lee, Frank

Leibundguth, Barbara
Lekhter, Rudolf
Lemay, Paul
Letvak, Phillip
Leuba, Christopher
Levakoff, Lawrence
Levine, Harold
Levinson, Eugene
Levitski, Vladimir
Levy, Amnon
Levy, Harry
Lewis, Scott
Lhoest, Fernand
Liddle, Brian
Lieberman, Harold
Liegl, Ernest
Liegl, Leopold
Lind, Carl M.
Lindaman, John R.
Linden, Anthony
Lindenhahn, Richard
Linder, Waldemar C.
Lindholm, Fridolph
Linfield, Katja
Linke, Charles
Lisowsky, Peter
Llewellyn, E. B.
Lloyd, Peter
Loeserman, Arthur
Lombardi, Astorre
London, James
Long, R. J.
Longo, Joseph
Lorenzo, Leonardo de
Lorraine, Adele
Loughran, Hugh
Luboviski, Calmon

MacKay, James S.
MacKay, John "Jack" G.
MacPhail, William S.

Madden, Claude
Maddy, Harry D.
Maddy, Joseph E.
Madson, Lawrence
Magendanz, Felice
Mainzer, Joan
Majeske, Stephen
Mala, Stephen
Margolis, Sanford
Marlow, William C.
Marshall, J. Christopher
Marshall, Richard
Marshall, W. S.
Marshall, William
Martin, Theodore
Martinez, Genaro
Mathieu, Harvey F.
Mathieu, Max
Matson, Ralph
Maurer, C. C.
Mauricci, Vincent
May, Louis L. J.
Mayr, Edward
McDonald, Charles
McIver, Felix
McReynolds, George W.
Megerlin, Alfred
Melby, Chester D.
Meltzer, Jess
Mermelstein, Sally
Messeas, James
Meyer, Otto
Midtmoen, Forrest
Migli, Umberti
Miller, Charles
Miller, Dean
Miller, Frank
Miller, John, Jr.
Miller, Joseph L.
Miller, Wilhelm
Milosovich, Chester
Min, Chouhei

Minsel, Robert K.
Molieri, Gaetano
Mollers, Mathias
Molzahn, Fred
Moore, Jack
Morgan, Byron
Moroni, Alfred
Moses, Hilbert D.
Mount, Brian
Mount, Jill
Muelbe, William
Mueller, E.
Muetze, Felix
Muetze, Moritz
Munroe, Lorne
Murphy, Paul
Murray, Edward
Myers, Philip

Nash, Maurice W.
Nashan, Carl
Nelson, H. J.
Nelson, Josef
Nelson, Lisa
Nelson, William Warvelle
Nichols, David E.
Nielubowski, Norbert
Niosi, Emil J.
Nirella, Salvatore
Nisbet, Ann
Noack, Harvey
Nolton, George H.
Noonan, Charles
Nordstrom, Harry
Nowinski, William
Nyberg, Gosta Carl

Obermann, Frank
Obermann, Rudolph
Okel, J. D.
Ollerhead, Hubert

Olsen, Clarence E.
Olson, Harry W.
Olson, Robert
Opava, Emil B.
Opgenorth, Joanne
Opland, Bradley
Orzechowski, Henry
Osborn, George
Ostrowsky, Robert
Oulie, Erik

Paananen, Ernest
Palma, Emilio de
Patek, Jaroslav
Paulsen, C.
Pauly, Francis
Peck, Marcia
Perez, Heinz
Perkins, Harry
Perrier, Pierre
Perry, Lyle H.
Persinger, Rolf
Person, Virgil H.
Petersen, Hans J.
Petersen, Lennard N.
Peterson, Edwin
Peterson, J. R.
Peterson, Jack
Pezzi, Vincenzo
Pfeil, Walter
Phelps, Cynthia
Phillips, Vali
Pikler, Charles
Pinto, Charles
Plagge, Egon
Plagge, Frank
Pleier, Ludwig
Policoff, Ivan
Pomero, Giovanni
Portnoi, Nathan
Prior, Ferdinand

Promuto, Albert
Ptashne, Theodore

Rabis, Martin
Rahn, William
Rakov, A.
Ransom, George
Rapier, Beth
Rapp, James
Rardin, Bruce
Rateau, René
Reckow, Clifford Karl
Reeve, Basil
Reiche, Milana
Reichenbach, Paul
Reiner, Sam
Reines, Nat
Remfrey, James
Remsen, Dorothy
Renzi, Renzo
Riccardo, James
Rice, George
Rich, Leon
Ricketts, Ronald
Riedelsberger, Carl
Riggs, M. Geraldine
Rimanoczy, Jean de
Rishovd, S. G.
Rissland, Karl
Rittmeister, Heinrich
Ritzler, Alexander
Rivera, Manuel
Roberts, Richard
Robinson, J. W.
Roche, Joseph
Rockler, Sheldon
Rodenkirchen, B.
Rodenkirchen, John
Rodrigues, Carla-Maria
Roeder, Robert
Roentgen, Engelbert
Rosander, A. R.
Rosansky, Leo

Rose, B. A.
Rosen, Abraham
Rosen, Kensley
Rosen, Myor
Rosen, Nancy
Ross, Anthony
Rubin, Benjamin
Rudd, Albert
Rudd, Charles
Rudolf, Carl P.
Ruhoff, Frederick
Ruhoff, Herman A.
Ryan, Kerri

Salathiel, Donald
Salgado, Frank
Sambuco, John
Samuel, Gerard
Santucci, William
Sarli, Louis E.
Saslav, Isidor
Sauser, Martin
Schaeffer, Ralph
Scheld, Fred
Schellner, Max
Scheurer, Frederik
Scheurer, Karl
Schinner, Carl A.
Schlossberg, Benjamin
Schlueter, Charles E.
Schmidt, Robert E.
Schmidt, Roy O.
Schoen, Curt
Schoenlein, Julius L.
Schotta, Joseph
Schrickel, William
Schroetter, Josef
Schubert, Gustave A.
Schubilske, Catherine
Schubring, Clarence
Schugens, Edward M.
Schulz, Emil
Schutte, Herman C.

Schwarzmann, Jascha
Seddon, Tom
Segal, Samuel W.
Seidenberg, Stella
Seidl, Rudolph
Selinger, Henry
Senescu, Bernard M.
Serafini, Deborah
Serulnic, George J.
Sery, Miles B.
Shadwick, E. Joseph
Shaffer, Pamela
Shin, Pitnarry
Shlutz, Harry
Shoemaker, William
Shryock, Raymond F.
Sidwell, William W.
Siegert, B. W.
Silver, Eli
Sindelar, Charles
Sjolander, Erick Edward
Sjostrom, Eric
Skerlong, Richard
Smith, Barrett
Smith, Ellen Dinwiddie
Smith, Stephanie
Snow, John
Soergel, Albert
Sokol, Paula
Speil, Alfred J.
Speil, Ernest
Sperzel, John
Sperzel, Peter
Speyer, Andre
Spiga, Carlo
Spoor, Simon
Stack, Edward
Stacy, Thomas
Stagliano, Vincent
Stahl, George
Stamp, James
Stanisha, Ladi
Starr, Elizabeth
Steffensen, Carl

Stein, William
Steinberg, Sherry
Stephan, A.
Steuck, Louise
Stewart, Cheryl Minor
Stolurow, Emanuel M.
Straka, Emil, Jr.
Straka, Herman
Sullivan, John
Sundström, Kari
Sustad, Fred T.
Sutton, Michael
Sutyak, Geraldine
Swalin, Benjamin
Swanson, George
Swanson, Robert E.

Tafoya, John
Targ, Walter
Tartaglia, John
Teply, John
Tetzlaff, Daniel
Tetzlaff, Jane
Tetzner, Henry
Thalin, Walter R.
Thevenin, Francis
Thieck, William A.
Thies, Fred
Thomas, Paul
Thompson, Jane
Thordarson, Lorado
Tinlot, Gustave
Tlucek, Hyacinthe
Tolbert, Ross
Tongeren, Helen Van
Tonkin, Milton
Tower, W. L.
Trebacz, Leon
Triebel, August
Trnka, Alois
Trobaugh, Joan
Tsaggaris, Thomas
Tucker, Irwin

Tung, Ling
Turner, Thomas
Tweedy, Robert
Tweedy, Rose-Marie

Ulfeng, David
Uterhart, Carl

Vere, Jean Marker De
Vianello, Hugo
Vitale, Valerie
Vliet, Cornelius van
Voigt, A.
Vollmer, Harry
Voloninis, Frederick
Volpe, Clement

Wade, Eugene
Wagner, Frank
Wagner, Harold B.
Wagner, Richard
Wahlin, Eric
Walker, Ernest
Walker, Kirke
Walston, Cragg
Walton, Paul
Wanka, Karl
Wardle, George P.
Warmelin, C.
Waterhouse, John
Watkins, Kevin
Waxman, Henri
Weckl, Christian
Weflen, Emil
Weinman, Lawrence
Weinstine, Heimann
Weisel, Clay
West, Walter W.
Wheeler, Lawrence
Whitaker, Ronald
Widoff, Gerald

Wiedrich, Fernand
Wiegand, F. G.
Wigler, Jerome
Wilber, Weldon G.
Wilczek, Janusz
Will, Fred
Williams, Cloyde
Williams, Henry J.
Williams, Wendy
Williamson, David
Willoughby, Clarence
Winkler, Anton
Winslow, Irving L.
Winsor, Frank
Wirth, Robert
Wistrum, Emanuel
Wittmar, Friedrich von
Witz, Victor
Woempner, Carl, Jr.
Woempner, Carl, Sr.
Woempner, Henry C.
Wohl, Harry
Wolfe, Joseph
Wolff, Louis
Woodard, Guy H.
Wright, David
Wright, R. Douglas
Wrigley, William
Wuerz, Herman

Xiao, Hong-Mei

Zaplatynsky, Andrew
Zawisza, Leon
Zedeler, Franz
Zeitlin, Sidney "Sid"
Zellmer, Steven
Ziebel, Sigmund
Zinn, William
Zupnik, Marilyn
Zwolanek, Joseph

2002-2003 Minnesota Orchestra Musician Roster

Osmo Vänskä, *Music Director Designate*
Stanisław Skrowaczewski, *Conductor Laureate*
Doc Severinsen, *Principal Pops Conductor*
Dominick Argento, *Composer Laureate*
Aaron Jay Kernis, *New Music Advisor*
Giancarlo Guerrero, *Associate Conductor*
Scott Terrell, *Assistant Conductor*

FIRST VIOLINS
Jorja Fleezanis
  Concertmaster
  Elbert L. Carpenter Chair
Sarah Kwak
  First Associate
  Concertmaster
  Lillian Nippert and Edgar F. Zelle Chair
Roger Frisch
  Associate Concertmaster
  Frederick B. Wells Chair
Stephanie Arado
  Assistant Concertmaster
  Loring M. Staples, Sr. Chair
Celine Leathead
Pamela Arnstein
Deborah Serafini
Milana Reiche
Angela Fuller
Hyacinthe Tlucek
Joanne Opgenorth
Chouhei Min
Rudolf Lekhter
Frank Lee
Pamela Shaffer
Emily Basinger

SECOND VIOLINS
Vali Phillips
  Principal
  Sumner T. McKnight Chair
Robert Hanford
  Associate Principal
Julie Ayer
  Assistant Principal
Laurel Green
Catherine Schubilske
Kristin Kemper
Aaron Janse
Edward Stack
Jean Marker De Vere
Arnold Krueger
David Wright

Taichi Chen
Michael Sutton

VIOLAS
Thomas Turner
  Principal
  Reine H. Myers Chair
Richard Marshall
  Co-Principal
  Douglas and Louise Leatherdale Chair
Kerri Ryan
  Assistant Principal
Michael Adams
David Ulfeng
Kenneth Freed
Sifei Cheng
Samuel Bergman
Eiji Ikeda
Myrna Rian

CELLOS
Anthony Ross
  Principal
  John and Elizabeth Bates Cowles Chair
Janet Horvath
  Associate Principal
  John and Barbara Sibley Boatwright Chair
Beth Rapier
  Assistant Principal
  Marion E. Cross Chair
Marcia Peck
Mina Fisher
Katja Linfield
Joseph Johnson
Sachiya Isomura
Kari Jane Docter *
Pitnarry Shin
  Roger and Cynthia Britt Chair

BASSES
Peter Lloyd
  Principal
  Jay Phillips Chair

Clifford Biggs
  Associate Principal
  Mr. and Mrs. Edward E. Stepanek Chair
William Schrickel
  Assistant Principal
David Williamson
Brian Liddle
Matthew Frischman
Robert Anderson
James Clute

FLUTES
Adam Kuenzel
  Principal
  Eileen Bigelow Chair
Barbara Leibundguth
  Co-Principal
  Chair Funded by an Anonymous Donor
Wendy Williams

PICCOLO
Unoccupied
  Alene M. Grossman Chair

OBOES
Basil Reeve
Marilyn Zupnik
  Co-Principals
  Grace B. Dayton Chair
John Snow
Marni J. Hougham

ENGLISH HORN
Marni J. Hougham
  John Gilman Ordway Chair

CLARINETS
Burt Hara
  Principal
  I.A. O'Shaughnessy Chair
Joseph Longo
  Co-Principal
  Ray and Doris Mithun Chair
Chester Milosovich
Fredrik Hedling

E-FLAT CLARINET
Joseph Longo

BASS CLARINET
Fredrik Hedling

BASSOONS
John Miller, Jr.
  Principal
  Norman B. Mears Chair
Mark Kelley
  Co-Principal
  Marjorie F. and George H. Dixon Chair
J. Christopher Marshall
Norbert Nielubowski

CONTRABASSOON
Norbert Nielubowski

HORNS
Kendall Betts
  Principal
  John Sargent Pillsbury Chair
Michael Gast
  Associate Principal
  Gordon C. and Harriet D. Paske Chair
Brian Jensen
Ellen Dinwiddie Smith
David Kamminga

TRUMPETS
Manuel Laureano
  Principal
  Mr. and Mrs. Archibald G. Bush Chair
Douglas C. Carlsen
  Associate Principal
  Rudolph W. and Gladys Davis Miller Chair
Robert Dorer
Charles Lazarus

TROMBONES
R. Douglas Wright
  Principal
  Star Tribune Chair
Kari Sundström

BASS TROMBONE
David Herring *

TUBA
Ross Tolbert
  Principal
  Robert Machray Ward Chair

TIMPANI
Peter Kogan
  Principal
  Dimitri Mitropoulos Chair
Jason Arkis
  Associate Principal

PERCUSSION
Brian Mount
  Principal
  WAMSO Chair
Jason Arkis
  Associate Principal
  Opus Chair
Kevin Watkins

HARPS
Kathy Kienzle
  Principal
  Bertha Boynton Bean Chair

PIANO, HARPSICHORD AND CELESTA
Vladimir Levitski
  Principal
  Markell C. Brooks Chair

LIBRARIANS
Paul Gunther
  Principal
Eric Sjostrom
  Associate Principal
Jill Mount
  Assistant Principal

PERSONNEL MANAGER
Julie Haight-Curran

ASSOCIATE PERSONNEL MANAGER
Matthew Ritter

STAGE MANAGER
Timothy Eickholt

ASSISTANT STAGE MANAGERS
Gail Reich
Dave McKoskey

AUDIO ENGINEER
Terry Tilley

* On leave 2002-2003

Orchestra on Wheels and Wings

Principal Tuba Ross Tolbert warms up backstage somewhere in the world.

As historian Mary Ann Feldman points out in her essay on touring, the Minnesota Orchestra has an extraordinary record on the road. During its first 99 years, the ensemble has performed in more cities, towns, and villages in the United States and abroad than has any other U.S. orchestra. Because of tours to distant foreign lands, The Philadelphia Orchestra and New York Philharmonic have traveled a greater total number of miles, but the Minnesota Orchestra has an unmatched record for the number of places to which it has traveled: 658 towns in 22 countries. This number has value, not because it belongs in a book of world records, but rather because it represents hundreds of thousands of music lovers whose lives have been enriched because they heard the Minnesota Orchestra in their community. As Feldman has written in her essay, audiences have responded by applauding, cheering, and honking their horns in pleasure.

The following cities have provided venues as disparate as circus tents and concert halls: the Herodicus Atticus amphitheater in Athens, the basketball court at the University of Oregon in Eugene, the venerable Tanglewood shed in Massachusetts, the hallowed stage at Carnegie Hall, and many, many more. As the Orchestra enters its 100th season it looks forward to a tour of the State of Minnesota that will add Perham as town #659, while returning to Bemidji, Grand Rapids, Monticello, Moorhead, and Pipestone.

The figure in parentheses indicates the number of performances in that community.

A & M College, Mississippi (3)	Albert Lea, Minnesota (18)	Anderson, Indiana (1)
Aberdeen, South Dakota (26)	Albuquerque, New Mexico (1)	Ankara, Turkey (2)
Aberdeen, Washington (2)	Alexandria, Louisiana (3)	Ann Arbor, Michigan (9)
Abilene, Kansas (1)	Alexandria, Minnesota (4)	Appleton, Wisconsin (29)
Abilene, Texas (2)	Algona, Iowa (1)	Arlington, California (1)
Adrian, Michigan (1)	Allentown, Pennsylvania (1)	Asheville, North Carolina (6)
Afton, Minnesota (2)	Alton, Illinois (4)	Ashland, Wisconsin (1)
Akita, Japan (1)	Altoona, Pennsylvania (2)	Aspen, Colorado (10)
Akron, Ohio (7)	Amery, Wisconsin (1)	Atchison, Kansas (3)
Albany, Georgia (1)	Ames, Iowa (45)	Athens, Georgia (2)
Albany, New York (2)	Amherst, Massachusetts (6)	Athens, Greece (2)

Athens, Ohio (2)
Atlanta, Georgia (19)
Atlantic City, New Jersey (1)
Auburn, Alabama (5)
Augusta, Georgia (3)
Aurora, Illinois (7)
Aurora, New York (2)
Austin, Minnesota (14)
Austin, Texas (4)
Baghdad, Iraq (1)
Bakersfield, California (2)
Barcelona, Spain (1)
Bartlesville, Oklahoma (1)
Baton Rouge, Louisiana (4)
Battle Creek, Michigan (4)
Bay City, Michigan (6)
Beatrice, Nebraska (1)
Beaumont, Texas (2)
Beaver Falls, Pennsylvania (1)
Beirut, Lebanon (2)
Belgrade, Yugoslavia (1)
Bellingham, Washington (2)
Beloit, Wisconsin (5)
Belvidere, Illinois (1)
Bemidji, Minnesota (18)
Benton Harbor, Michigan (7)
Berkeley, California (1)
Berlin, Germany (1)
Bethlehem, Pennsylvania (3)
Beverly Hills, California (1)
Beverly Hills, Illinois (2)
Billings, Montana (7)
Binghamton, New York (2)
Birmingham, Alabama (26)
Birmingham, England (2)
Bismarck, North Dakota (10)
Bloomington, Illinois (8)
Bloomington, Indiana (10)
Bloomington-Normal, Illinois (3)
Blue Earth, Minnesota (3)
Bluffton, Ohio (1)
Boise, Idaho (4)

Bombay, India (2)
Boone, North Carolina (1)
Boston, Massachusetts (7)
Boulder, Colorado (9)
Bowling Green, Kentucky (1)
Bowling Green, Ohio (6)
Bozeman, Montana (4)
Bradenton, Florida (1)
Brainerd, Minnesota (6)
Brandon, Canada (3)
Brisbane, Australia (1)
Brookfield, Missouri (1)
Brookings, South Dakota (6)
Brooklyn, New York (8)
Brownsville, Texas (2)
Brunswick, Georgia (2)
Buffalo, Minnesota (1)
Buffalo, New York (11)
Burlington, Iowa (20)
Burlington, Vermont (2)
Butte, Montana (5)
Calgary, Canada (10)
Canberra, Australia (2)
Canton, Illinois (1)
Cape Girardeau, Missouri (2)
Carbondale, Illinois (4)
Carlisle, Pennsylvania (1)
Cedar Falls, Iowa (15)
Cedar Rapids, Iowa (55)
Centerville, Iowa (1)
Centralia, Illinois (3)
Centralia, Washington (1)
Chanute, Kansas (4)
Chapel Hill, North Carolina (3)
Charles City, Iowa (1)
Charleston, Illinois (6)
Charleston, South Carolina (4)
Charleston, West Virginia (3)
Charlotte, North Carolina (3)
Charlottesville, Virginia (3)
Chattanooga, Tennessee (4)
Cheyenne, Wyoming (3)

Chicago, Illinois (39)
Chico, California (1)
Cicero, Illinois (1)
Cincinnati, Ohio (2)
Claremont, California (1)
Clarinda, Iowa (2)
Clearwater, Florida (1)
Clemson, South Carolina (3)
Cleveland, Ohio (8)
Clinton, Iowa (3)
Collegeville, Minnesota (1)
Cologne, Germany (2)
Colorado Springs, Colorado (5)
Columbia, Missouri (24)
Columbia, South Carolina (2)
Columbus, Georgia (5)
Columbus, Mississippi (6)
Columbus, Ohio (38)
Concord, New Hampshire (1)
Concordia, Kansas (2)
Corning, New York (2)
Corpus Christi, Texas (2)
Corsicana, Texas (2)
Cortland, New York (1)
Corvallis, Oregon (2)
Costa Mesa, California (3)
Crookston, Minnesota (7)
Croydon, England (1)
Cumberland, Maryland (1)
Dallas, Texas (6)
Danbury, Connecticut (1)
Danville, Illinois (3)
Danville, Virginia (1)
Darmstadt, Germany (1)
Davenport, Iowa (4)
Dayton, Ohio (14)
Daytona Beach, Florida (11)
De Kalb, Illinois (1)
De Pere, Wisconsin (1)
Dearborn, Michigan (1)
Decatur, Illinois (18)
Decorah, Iowa (3)

Deer Lodge, Montana (1)
Delaware, Ohio (7)
Denton, Texas (4)
Denver, Colorado (13)
Des Moines, Iowa (46)
Detroit, Michigan (11)
Detroit Lakes, Minnesota (1)
Devil's Lake, North Dakota (5)
Dubuque, Iowa (15)
Duluth, Minnesota (17)
Durant, Oklahoma (1)
Durham, North Caroloina (4)
Düsseldorf, Germany (2)
East Lansing, Michigan (3)
Eau Claire, Wisconsin (30)
Eden Prairie, Minnesota (1)
Edmond, Oklahoma (2)
Edmonton, Canada (13)
Edwardsville, Illinois (1)
El Dorado, Arkansas (4)
El Paso, Texas (4)
Elgin, Illinois (3)
Elkhart, Indiana (2)
Elmhurst, Illinois (2)
Elmira, New York (3)
Elyria, Ohio (1)
Emmetsburg, Iowa (1)
Emporia, Kansas (13)
Englewood, New Jersey (2)
Erie, Pennsylvania (3)
Escanaba, Michigan (1)
Eugene, Oregon (6)
Evanston, Illinois (23)
Evansville, Indiana (15)
Everett, Washington (2)
Fairfield, Iowa (1)
Fairmont, Minnesota (5)
Falls City, Nebraska (2)
Fargo, North Dakota (15)
Faribault, Minnesota (15)
Fayetteville, Arkansas (1)
Fergus Falls, Minnesota (4)

Findlay, Ohio (7)
Flint, Michigan (5)
Florence, Alabama (2)
Flushing, New York (3)
Fond du Lac, Wisconsin (6)
Fort Collins, Colorado (2)
Fort Dodge, Iowa (8)
Fort Lauderdale, Florida (4)
Fort Myers, Florida (4)
Fort Scott, Kansas (4)
Fort Smith, Arkansas (2)
Fort Wayne, Indiana (12)
Fort Worth, Texas (8)
Frankfurt-am-Main, Germany (1)
Freeport, Illinois (4)
Freeport, New York (2)
Fremont, Nebraska (1)
Fresno, California (2)
Friedrichshafen, Germany (1)
Gainesville, Florida (7)
Galesburg, Illinois (11)
Galveston, Texas (4)
Garden City, Kansas (2)
Garden City, New York (1)
Gary, Indiana (1)
Gaylord, Minnesota (2)
Glen Ellyn, Illinois (2)
Glencoe, Minnesota (1)
Glens Falls, New York (1)
Goshen, Indiana (2)
Grambling, Louisiana (2)
Grand Forks, North Dakota (24)
Grand Island, Nebraska (4)
Grand Junction, Colorado (4)
Grand Rapids, Michigan (9)
Grand Rapids, Minnesota (3)
Grandview, Washington (1)
Great Bend, Kansas (1)
Great Falls, Montana (7)
Great Neck, New York (1)
Greeley, Colorado (3)
Green Bay, Wisconsin (7)

Greencastle, Indiana (2)
Greensboro, North Carolina (17)
Greenvale, New York (5)
Greenville, North Carolina (1)
Greenville, South Carolina (1)
Greenwich, Connecticut (1)
Grinnell, Iowa (8)
Guthrie, Oklahoma (2)
Hamilton, Canada (10)
Hamilton, New York (1)
Hammond, Indiana (1)
Hannibal, Missouri (1)
Hanover, New Hampshire (4)
Harlingen, Texas (2)
Harrisburg, Pennsylvania (3)
Hartford, Connecticut (4)
Hastings, Nebraska (6)
Hattiesburg, Mississippi (1)
Havana, Cuba (6)
Hays, Kansas (3)
Hazleton, Pennsylvania (1)
Helena, Montana (4)
Hershey, Pennsylvania (1)
Hibbing, Minnesota (17)
Highland Park, Illinois (2)
Hinsdale, Illinois (2)
Hiroshima, Japan (1)
Holland, Michigan (1)
Hong Kong, Hong Kong (5)
Hot Springs, Arkansas (1)
Houghton, Michigan (2)
Houghton, New York (1)
Houston, Texas (12)
Hudson, Wisconsin (5)
Huntington, New York (1)
Huntington, West Virginia (4)
Huntsville, Alabama (1)
Huron, South Dakota (5)
Hutchinson, Kansas (8)
Hutchinson, Minnesota (3)
Ibaraki, Japan (1)
Indianapolis, Indianapolis (14)
International Falls, Minnesota (5)
Iowa City, Iowa (76)

Iowa Falls, Iowa (1)
Ironwood, Michigan (2)
Ishpeming, Michigan (2)
Istanbul, Turkey (3)
Ithaca, New York (9)
Jackson, Michigan (4)
Jackson, Mississippi (4)
Jacksonville, Florida (19)
Jacksonville, Illinois (4)
Jamestown, North Dakota (1)
Jamestown, New York (4)
Janesville, Wisconsin (4)
Jefferson City, Missouri (1)
Johnstown, Pennsylvania (1)
Joplin, Missouri (10)
Kalamazoo, Michigan (12)
Kankakee, Illinois (1)
Kansas City, Missouri (18)
Karachi, Pakistan (1)
Kearney, Nebraska (2)
Keokuk, Iowa (2)
Kewanee, Illinois (2)
Kilgore, Texas (1)
Kingston, Canada (4)
Kirksville, Missouri (12)
Knoxville, Tennessee (3)
Kohler, Wisconsin (3)
Kutztown, Pennsylvania (1)
La Crosse, Wisconsin (44)
La Porte, Indiana (4)
Ladysmith, Wisconsin (1)
Lafayette, Indiana (16)
Lafayette, Louisiana (2)
Lake Charles, Louisana (1)
Lakeland, Florida (1)
Lancaster, Pennsylvania (3)
Lancaster, Wisconsin (2)
Lansing, Michigan (6)
Laramie, Wyoming (3)
Laredo, Texas (1)
Las Vegas, Nevada (1)
Laurel, Mississippi (2)
Lawrence, Kansas (26)
Le Mars, Iowa (1)

Le Sueur, Minnesota (1)
Leavenworth, Kansas (4)
Leeds, England (1)
Lenox, Massachusetts
   (Tanglewood) (1)
Lethbridge, Canada (3)
Levittown, New York (1)
Lewisburg, Pennsylvania (4)
Lewiston, Idaho (3)
Lexington, Kentucky (6)
Lima, Ohio (4)
Lincoln, Nebraska (14)
Litchfield, Minnesota (2)
Little Falls, Minnesota (1)
Little Rock, Arkansas (8)
Ljubljana, Yugoslavia (1)
Lockport, New York (1)
Locust Valley, New York (1)
Logan, Utah (3)
Logansport, Indiana (2)
London, England (1)
Long Beach, California (2)
Lorain, Ohio (1)
Los Angeles, California (8)
Louisville, Kentucky (17)
Lynchburg, Virginia (3)
Macomb, Illinois (3)
Macon, Georgia (7)
Madison, South Dakota (1)
Madison, Wisconsin (86)
Madrid, Spain (1)
Malverne, New York (1)
Manhattan, Kansas (10)
Manitowoc, Wisconsin (1)
Mankato, Minnesota (26)
Mannheim, Germany (1)
Mansfield, Ohio (3)
Marietta, Ohio (2)
Marquette, Michigan (1)
Marshall, Minnesota (5)
Marshalltown, Iowa (3)
Maryville, Missouri (4)
Mason City, Iowa (9)
Mattoon, Illinois (1)

McAllen, Texas (1)
McPherson, Kansas (2)
Medford, Oregon (3)
Melbourne, Australia (2)
Melbourne, Florida (2)
Memphis, Tennessee (19)
Menomonie, Wisconsin (1)
Merrick, New York (1)
Mexico City, Mexico (4)
Miami Beach, Florida (5)
Miami, Florida (17)
Michigan City, Indiana (2)
Middletown, New York (3)
Midland, Michigan (4)
Midland, Texas (2)
Milaca, Minnesota (1)
Miles City, Montana (1)
Milford, Connecticut (1)
Milwaukee, Wisconsin (24)
Minot, North Dakota (15)
Missoula, Montana (8)
Mitchell, South Dakota (10)
Mobile, Alabama (7)
Modesto, California (1)
Moline, Illinois (3)
Monmouth, Illinois (3)
Monmouth, Oregon (1)
Monroe, Louisiana (1)
Montclair, New Jersey (1)
Montevallo, Alabama (1)
Montevideo, Minnesota (3)
Montgomery, Alabama (14)
Montgomery, Minnesota (1)
Monticello, Minnesota (1)
Montreal, Canada (5)
Moorhead, Minnesota (50)
Moose Jaw, Canada (1)
Morioka, Japan (1)
Morris, Minnesota (4)
Moscow, Idaho (1)
Mount Clemens, Michigan (2)
Mount Pleasant, Michigan (4)
Mount Vernon, Iowa (1)
Mountain Lake, Minnesota (2)

Muncie, Indiana (2)
Muskegon, Michigan (1)
Muskogee, Oklahoma (3)
Nacogdoches, Texas (1)
Nagoya, Japan (1)
Naples, Florida (2)
Nashua, New Hampshire (1)
Nashville, Tennessee (19)
Neenah, Wisconsin (1)
New Bedford, Massachusetts (2)
New Brunswick, New Jersey (5)
New Castle, Pennsylvania (3)
New Haven, Connecticut (1)
New Hyde Park, New York (1)
New London, Connecticut (6)
New Orleans, Lousiana (57)
New Ulm, Minnesota (7)
New York, New York-
   Carnegie Hall (43)
New York, New York-Other (7)
Newark, Delaware (2)
Newark, Ohio (1)
Newton, Kansas (2)
Niagara Falls, New York (1)
Norfolk, Virginia (2)
Norman, Oklahoma (1)
Northfield, Minnesota (57)
Norwalk, Connecticut (2)
Nottingham, England (1)
Oak Lawn, Illinois (1)
Oakland, California (2)
Oberlin, Ohio (3)
Oceanside, California (1)
Ogden, Utah (6)
Oil City, Pennsylvania (1)
Oklahoma City, Oklahoma (3)
Olean, New York (1)
Omaha, Nebraska (17)
Oneonta, New York (1)
Orange City, Iowa (1)
Orlando, Florida (7)
Orono, Maine (1)
Oshkosh, Wisconsin (10)
Oskaloosa, Iowa (6)

Oswego, New York (3)
Ottawa, Canada (6)
Ottawa, Illinois (1)
Ottumwa, Iowa (6)
Overland Park, Kansas (1)
Owatonna, Minnesota (5)
Oxford, Mississippi (3)
Oxford, Ohio (1)
Paducah, Kentucky (1)
Palm Beach, Florida (7)
Palm Desert, California (3)
Paris, France (1)
Park Forest, Illinois (2)
Park Ridge, Illinois (1)
Pasadena, California (2)
Pendleton, Oregon (2)
Pensacola, Florida (3)
Peoria, Illinois (10)
Philadelphia, Pennsylvania (2)
Phoenix, Arizona (2)
Pierre, Soutn Dakota (2)
Pipestone, Minnesota (1)
Piqua, Ohio (1)
Pittsburg, Kansas (7)
Pittsburgh, Pennsylvania (35)
Pittsfield, Massachusetts (3)
Plainfield, New Jersey (1)
Platteville, Wisconsin (2)
Plymouth, Massachusetts (1)
Pontiac, Michigan (1)
Port Arthur, Texas (1)
Port Huron, Michigan (1)
Portland, Maine (4)
Portland, Oregon (5)
Pratt, Kansas (1)
Princeton, New Jersey (1)
Providence, Rhode Island (3)
Provo, Utah (7)
Pueblo, Colorado (3)
Pullman, Washington (5)
Quebec, Canada (4)
Quincy, Illinois (5)
Racine, Wisconsin (5)
Raleigh, North Carolina (4)

Rantoul, Illinois (1)
Rapid City, South Dakota (3)
Reading, England (1)
Red Bank, New Jersey (3)
Red Wing, Minnesota (4)
Redlands, California (1)
Redwood Falls, Minnesota (2)
Regina, Canada (12)
Reno, Nevada (2)
Rice Park, Minnesota (2)
Richmond, Indiana (1)
Ripon, Wisconsin (7)
River Falls, Wisconsin (6)
Riverside, California (1)
Roanoke, Virginia (1)
Rochester, Michigan (3)
Rochester, Minnesota (102)
Rochester, New York (2)
Rock Hill, South Carolina (5)
Rock Island, Illinois (3)
Rockford, Illinois (12)
Rome, New York (3)
Ruston, Louisiana (4)
Rye, New York (1)
Sacramento, California (1)
Saginaw, Michigan (9)
Saint Cloud, Minnesota (35)
Saint Joseph, Michigan (1)
Saint Joseph, Minnesota (135)
Saint Joseph, Missouri (23)
Saint Louis, Missouri (10)
Saint Peter, Minnesota (3)
Saint Petersburg, Florida (6)
Salem, Oregon (1)
Salina, Kansas (3)
Salonika, Greece (1)
Salt Lake City, Utah (6)
San Antonio, Texas (4)
San Diego, California (2)
San Francisco, California (8)
San Juan, Puerto Rico (3)
San Marcos, Texas (1)
San Mateo, California (1)
Santa Ana, California (1)

Santa Barbara, California (4)
Sarasota, Florida (10)
Saskatoon, Canada (14)
Savannah, Georgia (6)
Schenectady, New York (3)
Scranton, Pennsylvania (2)
Seattle, Washington (7)
Sedalia, Missouri (4)
Selma, Alabama (3)
Sewanee, Tennessee (1)
Sharon, Pennsylvania (1)
Sheboygan, Wisconsin (4)
Sherman, Texas (1)
Shorewood, Wisconsin (1)
Shreveport, Louisiana (2)
Sioux City, Iowa (15)
Sioux Falls, South Dakota (20)
Skokie, Illinois (2)
South Bend, Indiana (10)
Spartanburg, South Carolina (4)
Spokane, Washington (6)
Springfield, Illinois (8)
Springfield, Massachusetts (2)
Springfield, Missouri (6)
Springfield, Ohio (7)
Stamford, Connecticut (3)
Staples, Minnesota (3)
Sterling, Kansas (1)
Stevens Point, Wisconsin (8)
Stillwater, Minnesota (3)
Stockton, California (1)
Stony Brook, New York (1)
Storm Lake, Iowa (1)
Storrs, Connecticut (4)
Streator, Illinois (3)
Stuttgart, Germany (2)
Superior, Wisconsin (1)
Sydney, Australia (2)
Syracuse, New York (6)
Tacoma, Washington (3)
Tallahassee, Florida (9)
Tampa, Florida (3)
Teheran, Iran (2)
Tempe, Arizona (2)

Temple, Texas (1)
Terrace, Minnesota (3)
Terre Haute, Indiana (7)
Thief River Falls, Minnesota (2)
Tokuyama, Japan (1)
Tokyo, Japan (2)
Toledo, Ohio (39)
Topeka, Kansas (10)
Toronto, Canada (7)
Torrance, California (1)
Tottori, Japan (1)
Towson, Maryland (1)
Trenton, New Jersey (1)
Troy, New York (3)
Tucson, Arizona (3)
Tulsa, Oklahoma (11)
Tuscaloosa, Alabama (4)
Tuskegee, Alabama (2)
University Park, Pennsylvania (3)
Urbana, Illinois (23)
Utica, New York (3)
Valdosta, Georgia (1)
Valley City, North Dakota (6)
Valparaiso, Indiana (6)
Vancouver, Canada (5)
Venice, California (1)
Vermillion, South Dakota (10)
Vero Beach, Florida (1)
Vicksburg, Mississippi (2)
Victoria, Canada (1)
Vienna, Austria (3)
Virginia, Minnesota (3)
Waco, Texas (1)
Wadena, Minnesota (3)
Wahpeton, North Dakota (1)
Walla Walla, Washington (1)
Walnut Creek, California (1)
Warren, Ohio (1)
Warrensburg, Missouri (3)
Washington, District of
   Columbia (11)
Waterloo, Iowa (3)
Watertown, South Dakota (1)
Watertown, Wisconsin (1)

Waukegan, Illinois (2)
Waukesha, Wisconsin (1)
Waukon, Iowa (1)
Wausau, Wisconsin (6)
Wauwatosa, Wisconsin (4)
Waverly, Iowa (2)
Webster City, Iowa (3)
West Chester, Pennsylvania (4)
West Palm Beach, Florida (3)
West Point, New York (3)
Wheaton, Illinois (2)
Wheeling, West Virginia (3)
White Plains, New York (3)
Whitewater, Wisconsin (1)
Whittier, California (1)
Wichita Falls, Texas (1)
Wichita, Kansas (11)
Wilkes-Barre, Pennsylvania (1)
Williamsport, Pennsylvania (1)
Willmar, Minnesota (5)
Wilmette, Illinois (3)
Wilmington, Delaware (5)
Windom, Minnesota (2)
Winfield, Kansas (6)
Winnetka, Illinois (1)
Winnipeg, Canada (93)
Winona, Minnesota (27)
Winston-Salem,
   North Carolina (8)
Worcester, Massachusetts (3)
Worthington, Minnestoa (4)
Yaizu, Japan (1)
Yakima, Washington (4)
Yankton, South Dakota (4)
York, Pennsylvania (4)
Youngstown, Ohio (4)
Ypsilanti, Michigan (2)
Zagreb, Yugoslavia (1)
Zanesville, Ohio (3)

———

Board Chairs

Presidents of the Board

Frederick Fayram (1903-05)

Elbert L. Carpenter (1905–1945)

Sumner T. McKnight (1945-48)

Loring M. Staples (1948-50)

Stanley Hawks (1950-53)

Kenneth N. Dayton (1953-55)

Philip W. Pillsbury (1955-58)

Charles S. Bellows (1958-61)

John H. Myers (1961-64)

Judson Bemis (1964-68)

Paul Christopherson (1968-71)

Board Chairs

(the name was switched from "President" to "Chair")

John S. Pillsbury, Jr. (1971-74)

John W. Windhorst, Sr. (1974-76)

George T. Pennock (1976-78)

Stephen R. Pflaum (1978-80)

Luella G. Goldberg (1980-83)

Dale R. Olseth (1983-85)

George H. Dixon (1985-87)

N. Bud Grossman (1987-90)

Nicky B. Carpenter (1990-95)

Michael E. Shannon (1995-98)

Thomas M. Crosby, Jr. (1998-2000)

Douglas W. Leatherdale (2000-ongoing)

2002 Minnesota Orchestral Association

Officers

Douglas W. Leatherdale, *Chairman of the Board*

Thomas M. Crosby, Jr., *Immediate Past Chairman*

Eugene C. Sit, *Vice Chairman*

David J. Hyslop, *President*

Andrew Czajkowski, *Vice President*

Stephen R. Demeritt, *Vice President*

N. Bud Grossman, *Vice President*

M. Joann Jundt, *Vice President*

Douglas A. Kelley, *Vice President*

Ronald E. Lund, *Vice President*

Douglas A. Scovanner, *Vice President*

Stephen M. Baker, *Vice President of Marketing*

E. Benton Gill, *Vice President and Chief Operating Officer*

Mary Ellen Kuhi, *Vice President and Director of Development*

Robert R. Neu, *Vice President and General Manager*

Nancy E. Lindahl, *Treasurer*

Deborah L. Hopp, *Secretary*

Board of Directors

Life Directors

Nicky B. Carpenter*

Luella G. Goldberg

N. Bud Grossman*+

M. Joseph Lapensky

Betty Myers

Rosalynd Pflaum

John S. Pillsbury, Jr.

Honorary Directors

Randy Kelly

Paul Ostrow

R. T. Rybak

Jesse Ventura

Directors

Ronald L. Abrams

Peter Armenio

Douglas M. Baker, Jr.

Karen Baker*

Karl J. Breyer

Jeffrey S. Brown

Wayne H. Brunetti

Barbara Burwell*+

William J. Cadogan

Jon R. Campbell

Mari Carlson

Nicky B. Carpenter*

Carolyn W. Cleveland

David D. Cousins

Thomas M. Crosby, Jr.*+

Kathy Cunningham*

Andrew Czajkowski*+

Stephen R. Demeritt*+

David Docter+

Jonathan F. Eisele

Joel A. Elftmann

Rolf Engh*

Carole Erickson+

Richard M. Fink

Luella G. Goldberg

Lynda Burke Grady

Paul D. Grangaard*

Jane P. Gregerson

N. Bud Grossman*+

Beth Ann Halvorson

Van Zandt Hawn*

Shadra J. Hogan

Deborah L. Hopp*+

Hella Mears Hueg

David J. Hyslop*+

Frank J. Indihar

David L. Jahnke

Barbara M. Johnson

M. Joann Jundt*+

D. William Kaufman

Douglas A. Kelley*+

Jolie Klapmeier+

M. Joseph Lapensky

2002-2003 Volunteer Leadership

Douglas W. Leatherdale*+

Judith A. Lebedoff*

Stephen Lieberman

Nancy E. Lindahl*+

Ronald E. Lund*+

Warren E. Mack

Harvey B. Mackay

Roberta Mann-Benson

Jan McDaniel

Mary Grotting Mithun

Joan A. Mondale

Susan M. Morrison

Alice D. Mortenson

Betty Myers

Lynn A. Nagorske

Marilyn C. Nelson

Bruce J. Nicholson

Dale R. Olseth

Chris Oshikata

Rosalynd Pflaum

John S. Pillsbury, Jr.

Susan Platou*

Rebecca C. Pohlad*

Anne Pierce Rogers

JoEllen Saylor+

Mary H. Schrock*

Judi Schuman

Douglas A. Scovanner*+

Robert L. Senkler*

Peter W. Sipkins

Eugene C. Sit*+

Douglas M. Steenland

Ronald L. Turner

Scott B. Ullem

James S. Wafler*

Maxine Houghton Wallin

Hiroshi Yamashita

Howard M. Zack

Emeritus Director

Kenneth N. Dayton

———

* Member of Executive
  Committee
+ Ex-Officio Director

WAMSO
Minnesota Orchestra Volunteer Association

Barbara Burwell, *President*

Jo Ellen Saylor, *President-elect*

Kari Rominski, *Secretary*

Terry Benson, *Treasurer*

Cynthia Sutter, *Director At Large*

Karen Himle, *Director At Large*

Joan Manolis, *Director of Development*

Erika Zetty, *Director of Development*

Irene Suddard, *Director of Education*

Shirley Taradash, *Director of Education*

Ann Pifer, *Director of Marketing/Communications*

Kiki Rosatti, *Director of Marketing/Communications*

Dorothy Halverson, *Director of Membership*

Addie Ingebrand, *Director of Membership*

Jan Michaletz, *Director of Volunteer Resources*

Karen Walkowski, *Executive Director*

Janet Ryan, *Office Coordinator*

———

YPSCA
Young People's Symphony Concert Association

David Docter, *President*

Dave Colwell, *President-elect*

Bonnie McLellan, *Secretary*

Liz Nordling, *Treasurer*

Katie Berg, *Vice President, Concerts*

Judy Ranheim and Bonnie Gainsley, *Vice Presidents, Competition*

Linda Smith, *Vice President, School Programs*

Natalie Guyn, *Vice President, Publicity*

Cynthia Tambornino, *Member-at-large*

Marilyn Miller, *Chair, Membership*

Sharon Hayenga, *Chair, Hospitality*

Jim Bartsch, *Ex officio*

———

2002-2003 Minnesota Orchestra Staff Roster

David J. Hyslop, *President*

John Swanson, *Executive Assistant to the President*

E. Benton Gill, *Vice President and Chief Operating Officer*

Sharon Huikko, *Administrative Coordinator*

Robert R. Neu, *Vice President and General Manager*

Kristina Arkis, *Operations Coordinator*

Jim Bartsch, *Director of Educational Activities*

Scott Chamberlain, *Events & Facilities Assistant*

Beth Cowart, *Artistic Planning Associate/ OMS Project Leader*

Michael Dalke, *Stage Door Receptionist*

Dustin Dimmick, *Facility Engineer*

Timothy Eickholt, *Stage Manager*

Mark Gagnon, *Building Services Supervisor*

Myron Gannon, *Maintenance*

Mark Georgesen, *Events Manager*

Paul Gunther, *Principal Librarian*

Julie Haight-Curran, *Orchestra Personnel Manager*

Beth Kellar-Long, *Orchestra Operations Manager*

Dan Kupfer, *Facilities Manager*

Heather Larson, *Orchestra Personnel Assistant*

Ken Lorence, *Maintenance*

Dave McKoskey, *Assistant Stage Manager*

Reid McLean, *Director of Presentations*

Jill Mount, *Assistant Principal Librarian*

Michael Pelton, *Executive Assistant to the Music Director*

Mary Rascop-Peterson, *Training & Personnel Supervisor*

Gail Reich, *Assistant Stage Manager*

Matthew Ritter, *Associate Orchestra Personnel Manager*

Eric Sjostrom, *Associate Principal Librarian*

Kari Sonnichsen, *Artistic Administrator*

John Swanson, *Executive Assistant to the Vice President & General Manager*

Kerry Teel, *Rental Administrator*

Terry Tilley, *Audio Engineer*

Mele Willis, *Manager of Outreach & Educational Partnerships*

Mary Ellen Kuhi, *Vice President and Director of Development*

David Banham, *Gift Accountant/Information Services Coordinator*

Michael Black, *Manager of Development Operations/Corporate Donor Benefits*

Deborah Brown, *Director of Planned and Major Gifts, and Centennial Projects*

Mary Carroll, *Manager, Guaranty Fund and Director of Major Corporate and Foundation Giving*

Elaine Cowles Fogdall, *Manager of Special Events & Donor Relations*

Lisa Forrette, *Development Associate*

Katy Gaynor, *Director of Individual Gifts and Major Projects*

Heather Heger, *Receptionist, Administrative Assistant*

Stacy Johnson, *Development Assistant*

Dawn Loven, *Associate Director of Individual Gifts*

Sean McGinity, *TeleFund Manager*

Penny Newstrom, *Executive Assistant*

Thomas O'Brien, *Director of Major Grants and Special Assignments*

Anne Pinney, *Director of Special Events and Projects*

Sara Scheevel, *Centennial Gifts and Symphony Ball Coordinator*

Dawn Stafki, *Development Assistant*

Debbie Westerland, *Director of Research Services*

Gwen Pappas, *Director of Public Affairs*

Sandi Brown, *Public Affairs Coordinator*

Sandra Hyslop, *Publications Editor*

Mary Ann Feldman, *Historian/Special Projects*

Stephen M. Baker, *Vice President of Marketing*

Annette Balkenende, *Financial Coordinator*

Jennifer Bingham-May, *Ticket Services Manager*

Sarah Bober, *Performance Supervisor*

Yvette Bray, *Group Sales Coordinator*

Patrick Brueske, *Customer Service Specialist*

Nina Heebink, *Marketing Product Manager*

Jen Jackson, *Marketing Product Manager*

Chris Johnson, *Group Sales Coordinator*

Harvey Kimball, II, *Customer Service Specialist*

Garnette Mattison, *Patron Services Manager*

Michael Meyer, *Assistant Product Manager*

Bradley Momsen, *Director of Ticket Services*

Cassandra Nordstrom, *Subscription Manager*

Dan Rech, *Marketing Database Manager*

Darla Rehorst, *Graphic Designer*

Daryn Skrove, *Customer Service Specialist/ Ticket Donations*

Sara Specht, *Marketing and Creative Assistant*

Breanna Tivy, *Marketing Assistant*

Jason Triemert, *Performance Supervisor*

Dan Walls, *Creative Manager*

Chrystal Williams, *Customer Service Specialist*

Holly Duevel, *Director of Finance*

Wayne Brandtner, *Staff Accountant*

Jerry Gunderson, *Payroll Administrator*

Bill Mask, *Assistant Finance Manager*

Cheryll Walker, *Staff Accountant*

Gean Halstead, *Director of Information Technology*

Jason Wagner, *Data Administrator*

Grant Armstrong, *Systems Administrator*

David Banham, *Data Coordinator*

Jan Johnson Hoglund, *Director of Human Resources*

Angela Haughton, *Mail Clerk/Stage Door Receptionist*

Tassa Nelson, *Human Resource Generalist*

Roster of full-time staff, as of August 31, 2002

Minnesota Orchestra at One Hundred

Thanks and Acknowledgements

The family of Mrs. DeWalt Ankeny, Sr.

The family of Mrs. Theodora Lang

Bolger Concept to Print

CRC Marketing Solutions

Minneapolis Public Library, Special Collections, Art and Music Department

Minnesota Orchestra Centennial Board Committee, Nicky B. Carpenter, chair

St. Paul Pioneer Press

Star Tribune

University of Minnesota Performing Arts Archives

This project is made possible in part by a grant provided by the Minnesota State Arts Board, through an appropriation by the Minnesota State Legislature and a grant from the National Endowment for the Arts.

The Minnesota Orchestra expresses profound thanks to the photographers whose work appears on these pages. Without them, the book would not have been possible.

Editorial and Production Staff

EXECUTIVE EDITOR, Gwendolyn Pappas

EDITOR, Sandra Hyslop

DESIGNER, Kathleen Timmerman

PHOTOGRAPHY EDITOR, Karl Reichert

EDITORIAL ASSISTANT, Brooke Fermin

HISTORIAN, Mary Ann Feldman

ARCHIVIST, Leslie Czechowski

ADDITIONAL RESEARCH AND ASSISTANCE BY:

Bruce Becker

Sandi Brown

Paul Gunther

Marie Harvat

Suzanne Sentyrz Klapmeier, Skyway Publications

Kirsi Ritosalmi-Kisner

Debbie Westerland

Image Credits

Don Berg Studios: 3 (Skrowaczewski)
Stephanie Berger: 49 right
Peter Berglund: 20 top, 69 top, 139
Nancy Bundt: 83 bottom
Stephen Chenette: 41 top
Cosmo-Sileo Co.: 33
Courtesy of Judy Dayton: 71 bottom
DeBellis Studios: 159 fifth down
Erica New York: 14 top
Mary Ann Feldman: 75, 140 bottom right
Samuel Flor: 35 left
Greg Helgeson: 21, 22, 23, 61 top left, 63, 70 top, 84, 85, 86, 87 top left,
    87 bottom left, 89, 91, 92, 106 right, 109, 111, 126 bottom right,
    127 top right, 129, 142, 164
Mel Jacobsen: 65 right, 168
Robert V. Kasowan: 77
Mark Luinenburg: 144, 145
Ann Marsden: 3 (Oue)
Wayne R. Martin: 68 lower
Sandy May: vii
Minnesota Orchestra Collection, University of Minnesota Performing Arts
    Archives: 2, 3 (Dorati, Marriner, de Waart) 4, 5, 8, 9, 11, 16, 17, 26, 27, 28,
    29, 31, 32, 35 right, 36, 37, 39, 41 bottom, 42, 44, 45, 46, 47, 48, 54 top,
    58, 59, 60, 61 bottom, 64, 66, 67, 69 bottom, 70 bottom, 71 top, 72 bottom
    left and right, 74, 80, 81, 82, 83 top, 87 right, 88, 90, 93, 95, 97, 98, 99,
    103, 104, 105, 108, 113, 115 (Krasner, Druian, Saslav, Foli), 116, 117, 119,
    121, 122, 125, 126 left, 127 left, 128, 131, 132, 134, 135, 136, 137, 140 left
    and top right, 141, 143 top, 149, 151, 152, 153, 155, 157, 159 top four
    and bottom, 160, 161 top two and bottom three, 162, 163, 165, 166, 167, 169
Mike Myers: 154
Marc Norberg: 20 bottom, 170
Norton & Peel Commercial Photography: 7, 30
Jonette Novak: 106 left
Courtesy of Kitty Pillsbury: 68 top
Courtesy of Helen Rice and Arnold Walker: 133
Philip Ricketts: 19
Tim Rummelhoff: iv, 110, 126 top right, 143 right
William Schrickel: 24, 25, 50, 54 bottom, 55, 56, 107, 176
Ken Scott: 115 third down
Andre L. Speyer: 15
Star Tribune: 38, 40, 51 (photographer Jeff Wheeler), 52 (Jeff Wheeler), 65 left,
    72 top left, 73, 123, 127 bottom right, 138, 150, 156, 158
Steiner/EMI Ltd.: 161 third down
Art Stokes: 115 (Fleezanis)
St. Paul Pioneer Press: 102 (all)
Wallert-Socit: 49 left